For Carolina and Ian Batey
with love

BALI DAZE

FREEFALL OFF THE TOURIST TRAIL

CAT WHEELER

TOKAY
PRESS

Bali Daze
A Tokay Press Book

ISBN: 978-152-03794-7-0

First published in Indonesia by Tokay Press as Dragons in the Bath in January and September 2009, then as Bali Daze in 2011

Front cover design and line drawings by Michael Ng (Mindflyer, Singapore)
Page layout and back cover by Bayugraphic (Denpasar)

Back cover photo by Neal Harrison

BALI DAZE

Writing a book is a very solitary enterprise, but bringing this one to life has been a community effort. With love and very special thanks to Carolina and Ian Batey for their huge hearts. Thanks to Diana Darling for moral support and editing the manuscript. Thanks to Chris Samson of the Bali Advertiser, where these stories were first published, for giving me such a very long editorial rope all these years. Thanks to the many readers whose positive feedback has been so supportive. Deep thanks to my dear friend Jenny Bigio, whose vision and inspiration kept my nose to the grindstone and to Kathy, Donna, Janet, Patricia and the many other friends who kept encouraging and bullying me to write a book. I humbly offer you the fourth edition.

INDEX

Stepping off the Cliff 1

Scriptless in Bali 4

Passion & Tragedy in the Duck Pond 8

The Concept of Abundance 12

The Paradox of the Bali Starling 15

Projects, Bali Style 18

Coming Home 23

Nocturne 27

Pit Bulls Don't Eat Tofu 30

Three Thousand, Two Hundred and Seven Smiles 34

A Day Out of Time 38

Hard Times 42

Lessons by the Pond 45

On The Road Again 49

Blessed 52

A Dog Too Far 55

Ethical Villas 58

Gamelan Nights 65

Being Ibu 72

Kasey and the River People 75

Two Naked Men in a Ditch 79

The Sound of Silence 83

The Septic Tank Chronicles 86

Roots 90

Doberman Lite 93

Rescued Smiles 97

Pretty Bird 101

Electric Adventures 104

Reptilian Revelations 109

The Cult of Canine.. 113

Coffee Break at the Warung 117

Snake Oil... 121

Walking on the White Side... 124

The World According to Wayan 127

It's About Time 131

Hazels' Begonia 135

Cuisine Unseen 138

Puppy Love 141

The View From a Small Town 144

Snakes Alive 147

Chop Wood, Carry Water 153

To Dye For 156

Communication Breakdwon 162

A Sense of Humus 165

Bringing Home the Bacon 168

Pigs in Love 174

Fishnapped 177

Accidental Jungle.. 181

A Bowl of Honest Rice 184

Feeding Frenzy 192

Home Leave 195

Out of the Dust... 199

No Parking 204

Dancers on the Wind 208

High Finance.. 211

Mother Goose.. 214

Three Dog Night 217

A Car With Character 220

Monsoon 224

On Tonight's Menu.. 227

Bali's Secret Recipes... 230

Magic in my House.. 233

Amorous Amphibians.. 236

Balance of Nature 240

Upacara 243

Rat Race... 247

Respect... 251

Dragons in the Bath 254

Fine Feathers.. 257

The Battle of the Compost 260

And Then There Were Two.. 264

Zapped 268

Postcard from the Edge... 271

Animal Days 274

Vision Quest... 278

Lions and Tigers and Bears... 282

Stepping off the Cliff

The decision to leave Singapore after ten years was pretty much thrust upon me by circumstances. The Asian monetary crisis had driven my client base to less costly cities and my contracts were drying up. I'd had a wonderful decade writing about Southeast Asia's boom, based in her most efficient city, traveling widely and interviewing a range of fascinating subjects from Cabinet Ministers to rice farmers. By the year 2000 the party was over, but the last thing I wanted to do was return to Canada. Asia was in my blood and under my skin.

But where to go from here? I tried to make sensible decisions about relocating to Bangkok or Kuala Lumpur, but a softly stubborn little voice inside kept murmuring the same word over and over.

Ubud.

It made absolutely no sense to even think of moving to Ubud, an artisan's village in the hills of Bali. The immigration bureaucracy was said to be a nightmare, I didn't speak the language and how on earth could I make a living in rural Indonesia?

But the subtle siren song would not stop. It was true that I'd loved the little mountain village (now a busy town) since my first visit in 1969. Its stunning scenery, unique Balinese Hindu culture, tropical gardens and friendly people became an addiction. After a second visit in 1993, I found myself returning to Ubud at every opportunity. But to live there full time? At that time even email access was difficult. The two people I knew there were out of circulation and it was hard to get information. I had no idea about the visa situation, the cost of living or work opportunities. Moving to Ubud would be the most impractical move I could possibly make.

I stepped off the cliff in November 2000 and moved to Ubud.

People were right about the immigration bureaucracy. The rules shifted like quicksand underfoot and my paperwork took months longer than anticipated. So did almost everything else. This was quite a shock after Singapore, where my request for a dedicated fax line in my home was met with indignation by the Singapore Telecom clerk. "We can't do it today," she snapped, "You have to call before ten for same-day service. The earliest we can connect it is tomorrow at noon." Compare this with Indonesia, where the application for a phone line to my house is still languishing in the Ubud telephone office after eight years. It took three days for my sea shipment to travel from Singapore to Surabaya, the nearest international port in Indonesia to Bali, and four months to clear Customs and arrive at my house. Living here is a lesson in patience.

The first year was full of interesting discoveries and adjustments. I rented a cottage outside town and eighteen months later built a house. I began to write a column in the local English language paper, the *Bali Advertiser*, because it gave me an excuse to call up perfect strangers and ask them about their projects. The column is supposed to be about the environment but I'm kindly allowed to interpret that widely as my immediate personal environment, which includes my dogs, garden, staff and any other straws I can clutch at as my bi-weekly deadline closes in.

Living here, I find myself increasingly drawn to the environmental and human problems that are not always in focus to visitors. I use the column to bring attention to the island's challenges with waste management, poverty, food security and to the many angels and philanthropists who are helping to find solutions.

I live close to the ground here, which can mean tree frogs in my shoes, scorpions in the cupboards and lizards in the bath. The first year, I tucked my mosquito net tightly under the mattress every night before I went to sleep to keep out the night life. The second year, I didn't bother with the net half the time. A few years ago I sent it to the laundry and it never came back; I didn't replace it.

Ubud is unique in many ways, one of which is its high expat population of accomplished single women. Generally speaking, I've never met a group of happier, more positive and grateful people anywhere. Like me, most live on a pension or small fixed income that would deliver a pretty depressing lifestyle in our own countries. In Ubud we can rent a modest cottage with a garden, hire a housekeeper, take some form of transportation (a number of game ladies over 70 can be seen zooming around town on the backs of motorcycles) and hang out at the local restaurants. It gives us a lot of pleasure to know that almost every rupiah we spend goes to support someone in the local economy. And my simple lifestyle gives me the time and space to do community work and help raise money for grassroots projects. There are downsides, of course. But we've learned to be comfortable with calculated risks because we love living here and are not fearful by temperament.

Living in a small, aware community I'm privileged to have access to what Barbara Kingsolver calls 'food with integrity'— chemical-free, fresh, and grown just a few miles away. Our air is relatively unpolluted here, and there are still rice fields close enough to town for early morning walks. Life is good.

So here I am living happily ever after with my dogs and parrots, a few metres from the jungle and about a centimeter from heaven.

Scriptless in Bali

When I first established myself in Bali, I lived in an isolated cottage in the rice fields and slept on a lumpy mattress on the floor under a ragged textile. The pantry held three plastic plates, two glasses and a couple of spoons. There was a two-burner hot plate, a kettle and one aluminum pot, all kindly left behind by the former tenants. No lampshades. No curtains. There were insects in every corner, snakes in the garden and rats in the ceiling.

It wasn't supposed to be like this. I had to keep reminding myself that I'd paid quite a lot of money to move to Bali. I'd planned to be well settled in by now—four months after my arrival—but Bali, I was beginning to learn, was no respecter of plans.

Somewhere on a dock in the distant port of Surabaya was a nine cubic metre box with my name on it, containing six Persian carpets, my kitchen, library, office and various other necessities of life.

"Ibu, bed is where?" enquired my sweet housekeeper Wayan Manis. "In Surabaya."

"Sold," she nodded sagely, sweeping dead bugs off the patio. She was convinced that my shipment had found its way to some street market. After a few months, so was I.

Whether the box was still waiting to clear Customs or my linen was being picked over by Javanese housewives at the local flea market made little difference. Right now I was living a very simple life. Spoiled after ten years in remorselessly efficient Singapore, I was marking time until my life in Bali would officially begin with the arrival of my personal effects. This was the unofficial bit that I hadn't bargained for.

I'd been in my house about a week. It rained constantly. The roof leaked. I had no security doors in my bedroom. Both ponds needed cleaning. I wanted to rent a car, but the man was away at a ceremony in his village. (I soon learned that the word upacara (ceremony) meant that staff and other workers could be absent for periods of time lasting from a day to six weeks, sometimes at a few minutes' notice.) I couldn't figure out how to hook up my email, and it was much more than a comfortable walk to the nearest internet café. The new kitchen was sitting in five centimetres of water. I kept asking for things to be done and nothing kept happening, although there were plenty of smiles and nods. By Monday I was despondent. Had I made a terrible mistake, moving here?

Ten years later, I realize that this is typical of life in Bali. Energy gets blocked, and nothing happens. Then suddenly the log jam clears and everything surges ahead again...

On Tuesday morning my house began to buzz with activity. The sun came out and the standing water in the garden started to trickle into the rice field beside the house. The garden looked quite attractive. Pak, the farmer from the rice fields next door, appeared with a sturdy-looking bamboo ladder and disappeared into the space between the woven bamboo ceiling and the tile roof. Wayan Manis handed him up new tiles and shouted the location of the leaks to him, and he handed broken tiles back down to her. I remembered the mammal that thumped and banged in the ceiling at night and hoped it was small and timid. Pak seemed quite unconcerned about meeting wildlife; not surprising since he spent most of his life barefoot in a rice field.

Then Madé, the handyman I'd entrusted with home improvements, arrived in a battered pick-up truck and with great drama unloaded the wrought iron security door for my bedroom. It had been made in an attractive spider-web design that looked too pretty to be effective. They carried it into the bedroom and there was a moment of embarrassed silence when it proved to be hilariously short for the opening. I remembered Madé's furrowed brow as he had ostentatiously measured the door frame several times. I tried to see the humour as they banged away installing this frail grille, drilling holes in the floor and screwing it to the door frame. The door didn't look as though it would keep out a determined five year old. Once it was up, Madé demonstrated how it would neither open nor close. He seemed surprised when I politely indicated that I required it to do both before I would pay for it. After another hour of noisy manipulation it would open and close, but there was about 30 centimetres of open space above it through which almost anything between a python and Jack the Ripper in size could easily climb. The whole security door adventure had taken about three weeks from the time the opening was measured.

Meanwhile Ibu, Pak's wife, climbed into one of the murky fish ponds with a two-litre child's plastic bucket and began to throw water over the bank onto the terrace below. It took me a moment to understand that she intended to empty the large pond in this manner. It was going to be a long day.

Madé came out and sat on the concrete bench—I had not yet located someone who could make cushions. He was a dainty young man with long, wavy hair, an earring and meticulously manicured hands. Lighting a cigarette, he checked his hand phone for messages and then permitted himself to be drawn into a conversation about leasing his car. He pleasantly agreed to the price I proposed and went off to change the oil. As he went out the gate, another pick-up truck rattled up and braked in a spray of gravel. A heavily-tattooed youth in a Sting T-shirt got out and strutted up the path with a heavy gas cylinder on his shoulder. Finally, I would be able to make a cup of tea in the empty little kitchen.

Wayan Manis enjoyed all this activity after a week of watching me mope around the empty house with a tape measure around my neck. There was hardly any housework to do because everything was in my shipment ("Sold") and she was getting bored. Balinese dislike silence and solitude, and she was happy with all the banging and crashing and to-ing and fro-ing. She made coffee for Pak, tidied my pathetic bed, monitored the pond work and rearranged the two glasses in the kitchen.

There was no point buying things I already had, provided they ever arrived. Ubud was proving to be a rather unique little town in terms of what was available. There was not a tin opener to be had at that time, or mosquito netting or a mattress. However, it was possible to buy balsamic vinegar, bagels, a Merry Widow corset in three colours and the latest model of hand phone. In 2000, Ubud's stores reflected the needs of tourists and Bali Hindu ceremonies. A new householder in search of a frying pan was out of luck. By the time I managed to locate one in the nearby town of Gianyar, I felt enormously lucky. Then began the search for sheets.

It was just the beginning.

Passion & Tragedy in
the Duck Pond

Even resolutely cheerful people get a bit grumpy when it rains and rains and rains. Especially when the roof leaks and all the Persian carpets start to smell strongly of old camels. Even the dogs smell like old camels. Your clothes and sheets are always a little damp and jungles of mildew spring up in all kinds of surprising places.

For my first rainy season in Bali, I lived in a house in the rice fields. I quickly learned that this location offered a unique perspective on rising damp and more than the usual allotment of snakes and rats. Of course the roof leaked. I tried to be cheerful about all this but the challenge was too great. After three days of leaks and grumpiness I decided that since the universe had handed me a lemon, I might as well make lemonade. Ducks liked water, so I would have ducks.

Little did I realize I was inviting a soap opera of lust, attempted rape, homosexuality, polygamy and infanticide into my quiet life.

The next morning found me at the public market at six thirty. "Too late," Madé said gloomily as we vied for a parking spot. At this slothful hour, all the good ducks had already been taken and there were no ducklings left. "That's okay. Many babies die, you get depress," consoled Madé. "Bigger better." We had our choice of adolescents which were being peddled out of big round wicker baskets from the backs of pick-up trucks. The smell was… interesting.

Every time we paused to assess a flock, the ducks would stampede to the opposite side of their basket and gabble in alarm. I began to get a sense of the intellects that would be sharing my space. After deliberation I chose three ducks and a drake. Cash changed hands and my new companions were tied together in pairs by the feet. I sat in the back seat of the car while the ducks muttered on the floor in front, which had been heavily lined with newspaper. I soon saw why.

I learned that the only thing dumber than a duck was four ducks. Short-term memory in these creatures can be measured in eye blinks. They have serious co-dependency issues. They are impossible to house train. That said, they do possess a certain demented charm. The flock spent its mornings in expeditions around the garden, stopping periodically for conversations that sometimes became so heated I would leap from my office chair in alarm, certain that they had flushed a cobra. But they would just be standing there debating some fine point of duck philosophy at full volume while liberally decorating the path. Of course they spent a lot of time sailing elegantly around their pond, after tearing up all the pond plants and turning the water an unusual shade of green.

Randy the misnamed drake was singularly clueless, even for a duck. He swam, wandered, ate and slept with three attractive lady ducks for months before his hormones kicked in. As the female ducks matured they began to display hopefully in front of him, bobbing their heads and murmuring seducktively. Randy observed these tactics blankly, but the roosters from the next field got the message and would sometimes fly over the fence and try to mount a duck. This variety of duck only breeds under water, so the demonstration was not very enlightening to either gender. Randy and the ducks were unalarmed but puzzled, and the roosters were not having much fun either. About this time, the female ducks began to take an unusual interest in each other. Wayan Manis didn't know the word for 'lesbian' and it wasn't in the dictionary we relied on to communicate, but she never failed to call my attention to this activity with an embarrassed giggle.

Then one morning she found an egg in the garden. We admired its subtle blue colour. Wayan polished off the muck with a tea towel I hoped she wasn't planning to use on my coffee mug later. We decided that Wayan should have it for lunch; we were both too fed up with duck muck to entertain immediate thoughts of expanding the flock.

As this discussion was going on, there was a sudden commotion in the duck pond. All the ducks were bobbing their heads vigorously like clockwork toys as they swam in tight formation. Suddenly, one disappeared under the drake, which quite submerged her in his unpracticed passion. He held her head under water with his beak and there was a lot of splashing as he had his way with her. "Together!" exclaimed Wayan with a grin. Randy had finally figured it out. The next morning and each morning after that, there were eggs all over the garden.

As the weeks went by the ducks became increasingly bold. Equating my appearance with food, they began to seek me out when they got hungry. This seemed endearing at first. They followed me around the garden, and I would wake from an afternoon nap on the patio to find four pairs of beady eyes regarding me obsessively from a few feet away. Then one afternoon I was at the keyboard when I heard a "Quack" much closer than usual. A duck stood in the middle of the Persian carpet in the front room, very pleased with herself, while the rest of the flock hovered at the front door gabbling in admiration. This was going too far; I immediately had an enclosure built around their pond. It was very low and they could have easily flown over it, but they never did get their tiny thinking boxes around this concept.

Then the ducks went broody. They began to lay their eggs together in the same spot instead of all over the place, and practically sat on top of each other to keep them warm. By the time I left for a month's trip they were sitting grimly on nine eggs and I was confidently promising ducklings to all my friends. I should have known better. My house sitter found one newly hatched duckling trampled to death by its parents, and the next hatchling was promptly eaten by a snake. The ducks then rolled the remaining eggs into the pond as if to declare their experiment with parenthood over.

But a few weeks later, a glint appeared in Randy's obsidian eye. He was soon ducking his harem in the pond, one after the other. By this time the jettisoned eggs from the previous adventure were beginning to rot in the pond and explode like noxious little bombs, directly under the unglazed window of my office. A Balinese friend regarded this mayhem thoughtfully, and told me that this particular kind of duck was actually so stupid it couldn't breed by itself. The eggs had to be incubated in a box or under a cooperative chicken, since the ducks themselves couldn't seem to get their heads or tails around the situation. This was the first time I'd heard of any animal that had lost the ability to procreate without human intervention. (Later I would add dachshunds to the short list of creatures requiring technical assistance in this activity.)

I'd like to report that this story had a happy ending. But I was moving into a new house soon, and the new house required a Balinese ceremony that required the sacrifice of two ducks. Wayan Manis pointed out that since I already had several quite useless ducks...

The duck project ended in a very Balinese fashion, with succulent morsels decorating the offerings and a much quieter pond. The survivors went home with Wayan to augment her little flock, and I have been duckless ever since.

The Concept of Abundance

When you're a Bali street dog, you take nothing for granted.
So when my house sitter lured a bony nomad off the main road into my compound, the creature came with a certain curiosity, accepted a light meal, then wandered away again. When I returned a few days later, Caroline brought her down from the road to introduce us. "This is Ibu, your new dog," she explained.

Ibu and I examined each other dubiously. We both felt that Caroline was rushing us into a relationship for which neither of us was quite ready. I was looking for a dog, but this one? Ibu ate a few dog biscuits—I don't think she liked them much, she was just being polite—then followed Caroline back up to the road when she left. I came to recognize her over the next few days, trotting along Jalan Raya Andong, nosing a discarded food wrapper here and being bullied by a scrappy mongrel there. She seemed to have a busy life.

A week later, Caroline returned with Ibu in tow. "This is your dog," she repeated firmly. I have learned over the years that if someone feels that strongly about something I had better pay attention, so I looked at Ibu more carefully. She wasn't mangy or pregnant and had no festering open sores; those were advantages. Still, she was an unprepossessing creature. Her skinny frame was covered in a thin brown and white spotted coat that badly needed dusting. Her hip bones jutted out like an extra set of ears. Ibu's body language indicated that she had never been anywhere near Top Dog, but she was friendly and gentle. She sat on the garden path regarding us timidly and when we didn't chase her off, she lay down and went to sleep.

She gradually worked her unassuming way across the patio as we had our tea, ending up at our feet. Soon a warm tongue was exploring my toes. A few minutes later we saw that she had quietly made a nest on a cushion on the floor. My first instinct was to shoo her off, then I thought, "The cushion cover will wash. She's probably never been this comfortable in her life."

Ibu hardly left her nest for the next 36 hours. I had to persuade her to get up for meals, which in itself was a revelation. She was evidently not used to finding food in the same place twice, certainly not in a stylish purple bowl all the way from the Hero Supermarket in Denpasar. She ate daintily and went straight back to bed. Twice she walked slowly and sadly to the gate and sat there as if expecting to be asked to leave. Each time I welcomed her back to the patio with biscuits and kind words. Then she would creep onto the cushion and curl up in a dusty, bony knot with her paws over her eyes.

Several times a day I left the computer to speak to her quietly and try to imagine what was going on in her mind. She'd probably lived all her life on the busy, noisy street without a permanent place to sleep or knowing where her next meal would come from.

Now she slept undisturbed on a clean, soft bed. She was offered food without asking for it. The street noise was distant here, overlaid by the sound of water running into the ponds.

I watched her affectionately as she slept, seeing a loyal, sweet-natured companion, a guardian of my compound. When she was used to me, I would give her a bath. A red collar. Shots. Nice smelly bones from the roast pig stall. Meanwhile I let her slumber on, imagining that she was dreaming through the transition of becoming Someone's Dog at last.

Then, damned if she didn't up and leave me. A day and a half after Ibu lay down for that long sleep she rose, stretched, walked to the gate and demanded to be let out. I explained that she didn't have to go but she insisted that I open the gate. Then she loped up the driveway toward Jalan Raya Andong without a backward glance.

For several days I expected her to return. I walked up to the road, found her on the piece of exposed sidewalk she called home and tried to lure her back. She smiled and the bony brown tail wagged in recognition, but she showed no interest in coming with me. Why had she abandoned comfort, food and safety to return to life on the street? It took me a few days to realize that while I was 'saving' this little street dog, thinking that she would be grateful and happy to be looked after, she had probably found life with me very boring indeed. Her days were a circus of whizzing motorcycle wheels, the roar of container trucks, diesel smoke, pungent smells, shouting workmen, wandering tourists, little carts selling noodles and the complex warp and weft of social life as a Bali street dog. It was humbling to realize that she wasn't about to trade all this for regular meals in my quiet garden.

But a relationship had been established. Every few days I'd see her on her patch of sidewalk as I drove by. I'd call, "Ibu!" And she'd leap up and canter down the driveway behind the car. I worried that she'd miss me when I moved, but now I realize she wasn't just dropping in for a meal. She felt sorry for me because I lived all alone in this quiet compound without the smells and noise and constant activity of the street.

This small friendship taught me that abundance is all a matter of perspective. Long after I left that house I remembered Ibu dancing in the dust outside my gate, consoling me with a damp nose before returning to her more interesting life.

The Paradox of the Bali Starling

Once common in Bali's highlands, the distinctive Bali Starling is now highly endangered. Only about 140 can be found in the wild in two locations in Bali, almost all captive-bred or first-generation wild. The Bali Starling should be as common as the pigeon in Bali. The glossy little blue and white bird breeds freely in captivity, even thriving in outdoor aviaries in the English winter. In captivity, a single breeding pair can parent up to 25 birds a year. In more natural conditions, a pair of birds produces between one and four eggs every three months with a survival rate of about ten chicks a year. They begin breeding at about the age of two and continue reproducing for ten years. That's a lot of birds.

So the rarity of the Bali starling in its own territory is a paradox. The cost of these birds is higher inside Indonesia than anywhere else, and breeding permits here are very difficult to obtain. This has the result of keeping the price of the birds artificially high.

Why is the Bali Starling still so scarce that almost nobody has ever seen one? Unfortunately, the little bird is a lot more valuable as a rarity than it would be if it was allowed to reproduce with its customary enthusiasm. And there are vested interests in keeping it that way. It's extremely difficult to obtain a captive breeding license; in Bali, there are only three. Illegal trade in Bali Starlings is rampant, with each bird fetching up to

$1000 on the black market. In Java there are several commercial breeders of the Bali Starling, in Bali there is only one. Captive breeding programs at Bali Barat National Park and the Begawan Foundation have experienced robberies of their Bali Starlings. Poaching in the National Park is common.

In 1999 Drh Bayu Wirayudha, a Balinese veterinarian specializing in birds, helped start a captive breeding program with the Begawan Foundation. After several months of paperwork, two breeding pairs of Bali Starlings were imported to the island. From these four birds, and with exchanges of birds to increase the breeding stock, many generations were hatched. Bayu, who had successfully bred Bali Starlings at the Bali Bird Park since 1993, built up the collection. He began to look for a safe place in which the birds could eventually be released back into the wild. Although he located several areas that would be ideal, he was unable to get official approval.

In 2004, Bayu approached the communities on Nusa Penida with the concept of making the entire island a bird sanctuary for Bali. Over time, 41 traditional villages agreed to support the program. Reforestation, conservation education and other support activities began in the villages. In 2006, the Begawan Foundation moved all its Bali starlings to Nusa Penida. Since then about 65 starlings have been released. The adult birds have paired, nested and begun breeding in the island's coconut plantations. At the time of writing (November 2010), there are about 100 Bali Starlings breeding in the wild on the island. The Begawan Foundation now maintains its captive breeding program in Mambal and the Bali Starling project on Nusa Penida is managed by the Friends of the National Parks Foundation.

Bayu has high hopes that the program will succeed. Through his approach to all the villages individually Bayu, in his role of founder of the Bird Sanctuary, has concluded a traditional agreement known as awig-awig with all 35 villages to declare Nusa Penida a sanctuary for birds. Awig-awig is a religious commitment to protect the birds, which are individually dedicated to the local temples before release. Highly trained local staff monitors the birds and continues local education programs. The survival rate is very high and not a single bird has been poached. Tourists are already beginning to visit Nusa Penida to see the Bali Starlings, the beginning of an eco-tourism that could bring badly needed income to the island.

In April 2007, President Yudhoyono of Indonesia visited Nusa Penida and personally opened the cages to release 12 young Bali Starlings. He thanked Bayu for his work conserving the species—the first official support the initiative has ever received.

"Many donors don't like to see birds in cages, even for captive breeding purposes," says Bayu. "We urgently need to build up the stock on Nusa Penida, so we welcome donations of Bali Starlings or the funds with which to buy them. We also need donations for our reforestation program, seeds and scholarships for poor local children." Learn more about the Bali Starling project at www.fnpf.org

Projects, Bali Style

Moving from efficient Singapore to laid-back Bali is somewhat like coming to another planet. I've decided that there's a certain chaotic fascination in getting things done here. This attitude usually keeps me sane, if not sweet-tempered, in the face of the most astonishing misunderstandings.

It took me a couple of years to begin to comprehend the nuances of how things worked. When I first moved to Bali, I contracted a house and garden at the end of a lane off the main road. An unlovely barbed wire fence, strung from a series of concrete posts, was my sole barrier against the world. There was a steep ravine to one side of the house, and the busy road 50 meters away. My fence had collapsed in places and could easily have been broached at any time by an enterprising child with a pair of strong scissors. I was not very happy there alone at night.

With the coming of Karma, a Kintamani puppy, I decided that we both needed a fence. He would have the run of the garden instead of living at the end of a long chain to prevent him wandering up to the road and being hit by a car. And I wanted the psychological barrier that six feet of bamboo would provide. Madé Car assured me that he could get good bamboo near his village, so I embarked on my first building project.

Madé knew of a workman who could make a good fence, and one afternoon brought him back from the village for a meeting. His name was Wayan, (every third Balinese is named Wayan), and he was accompanied by an unnamed giggling youth with a wall eye. We sat around the big table on the patio and Madé served as middleman and interpreter. I already had a good idea of the cost of materials and knew what the daily wage was. I'd measured the perimeter of the property and estimated the number of metres of bamboo required.

Only after Wayan had toured the garden, taken part in a long general chat about the house, consumed a glass of coffee and smoked two clove cigarettes did he feel it was appropriate to get down to business. How long did he estimate the fence would take to build? About a month, he stated gravely. A month? With two men working on it full time? Why so long? Because, he indicated with a sweep of his arm, the garden was very big. The fence would be at least 200 metres in length.

I very gently informed him that I had measured the perimeter and the fence would, in fact, be about 65 metres long. Aha, he said without blinking. In that case the fence would take about 16 days. Of course, he and his friend would both be paid a premium on the going daily rate and provided with two meals and a place to sleep and wash.

Wayan Manis, who had been eavesdropping shamelessly while sweeping the same step for twenty minutes, furrowed her brow in a way that clearly informed me that this was not appropriate. The men suggested hanging a few sarongs in the carport for privacy and setting up housekeeping there. Of course they would have to use the house for washing and the toilet. Wayan Manis' body language indicated that she would not be happy with this arrangement. Nor was I.

I thanked them most kindly for their time as Madé brought the car around to drive them back to the village. As the black Katana lumbered up the lane I sat back and gazed blankly out over the rice fields with the calculator in my hands. Pak, the neighbouring rice farmer, was squatting in a corner of a field, hammering a wooden box into shape. Wayan Manis swiped at a cobweb with a bundle of twigs, her face expressionless.

"Wayan," I ventured, "Could Pak make the fence?"

Her expression changed instantly. "Pak can make," she assured me with a wide smile. The next morning Madé confirmed this. We called Pak in for a meeting. We went over the same territory again, with Wayan Manis taking a place at the negotiating table. At one point Madé turned to me and said, "We should be friendly. Sometimes Pak fix the roof. Sometimes you ask Pak to cut the grass. So…" I got the message; don't negotiate too hard. I needed Pak for future work around the house. It turned out he was happy with the going rate and required neither meals nor housing. The deal was struck. I left a wad of rupiah with Madé and departed on a six-week business trip.

Email communication with my house sitter informed me that the fencing project was not proceeding particularly smoothly. Madé had not ordered enough bamboo. He'd had to bribe the truck drivers to bring it from the mountains late at night because it was illegal to cut bamboo without a license (now he tells me) and Pak was not working every day. I read the periodic updates from cyber cafés in Manila, Bangkok and Singapore and congratulated myself on being absent during all this drama. In fact, when I returned, the fence was fine, just what I'd wanted.

Emboldened, I decided to undertake another project. When I first took the house, I had quickly (by Balinese standards) added a two-bythree metre nook to the patio. This would be my kitchen; I envisioned myself contentedly chopping and stirring while enjoying the ravishing view, with my guests sipping arak cocktails at the dining table on the patio a few feet away.

The addition had stood empty for two months. Now it was time to build the prep table/storage unit for the kitchen. This piece of furniture, lovingly designed over many weeks, was to be nearly three metres long and a metre high, with enough drawers and cupboards to store my dinner service for 16, Cuisineart and other exotic kitchen accessories I'd been crazy enough to bring to rural Indonesia.

The household negotiating team convened once more. Pak and Madé muttered in Balinese over the calculator, explained to me about the different kinds of wood that could be used and their cost, and named a figure that made me groan. This was on a Wednesday afternoon. We agreed that Pak and Madé would go and buy the wood on Monday, and construction would begin immediately. Pak sauntered off to his fields.

On Friday morning at eight o'clock, Wayan arrived on the back of a motorcycle. This was unusual enough but her driver, a handsome lad in jeans, followed her into the yard, settled comfortably on the top step of the patio and lit a cigarette. Wayan went about her morning routine and I returned to my computer, somewhat puzzled. I peeked out a few times but the man showed no signs of going away. Finally I asked Wayan, "Who is that?"

"My brother," she explained. Oh. She continued to wash dishes. "Why is he here?" I finally enquired.

"Talk to Madé Driver." Oh. I returned to my office. Evidently a meeting had been set up for some reason. All would no doubt be made clear when Madé arrived.

But it wasn't. Wayan's brother chatted briefly to Madé, then roared away on his motorcycle. When Madé and I had left on our round of errands, I asked, "What did he want?"

Madé looked puzzled. "He was talking about making the kitchen cupboard."

"But Pak is doing that." "Yes, he is."

"And Wayan knows that." "Yes."

We drove in silence for a while, digesting this. "So why did he want to talk to you?" I pressed.

"I don't understand."

At least I wasn't the only one out of the loop. Only later did Madé discover that a relative of Pak's had died the night before, and Pak would be required to work on the cremation ceremony for two weeks. Wayan, who lived in a different village, had somehow got wind of this. Knowing that I was eager for my kitchen project to proceed, she'd asked her brother, a woodworker, to step into the breach. But she hadn't thought it necessary to mention this to either me or to Madé.

The prep table was made, on time and within budget. Then I had a bookcase and a duck enclosure made. Dizzy with success, I went on to build a house. Having learned by then to make my expectations crystal clear and having the luck to find a wonderful contractor, the project went quickly and smoothly.

I've learned that an apparent lack of structure in the project planning stages does not necessarily mean that chaos will follow, although it's certainly an option. My Singaporean friends, who like everything cut and dried and signed and sealed, can't stand this. I find, now, that I rather enjoy it.

Coming Home

My friends shook their heads when I told them I was going to build a house in Ubud. They said I would lose three quarters of my mind and all of my sense of humour. They muttered about shoddy workmanship, exceeded quotations and hopelessly lost timelines. Several reminded me that the construction of their house in Paradise ran years over schedule and massively over budget. So it was with some trepidation that I signed the quotation and shook hands with the contractor.

I'd never had a house before and couldn't afford an architect. Long evenings with paper, pencil and a very large eraser eventually produced the outline of what seemed to me a workable house. On March 15, 2002 we pegged out the footprint of the house with little white strings. Then 14 men moved onto the land, built a bamboo shack to sleep in and started building my house.

They moved the earth with shovels and filled in the foundation with crushed limestone carried in little black buckets. Singing and smoking, they mixed cement and laid bricks day after day. One bucket of cement and one brick at a time, the walls of my home began to rise. Unnervingly soon I was being asked where the doors and windows should be.

I'd forgotten to specify the height of the walls and the foreman decided that 3.6 meters would be a good height. So I have very high walls and excellent air circulation. I didn't make it to the site for several days at one point and found a wall where no wall should be—they were working from an old drawing. But no one was the least put out when I asked them to knock it down. They laughed, and knocked it down, and by that afternoon the new wall was nicely finished. After that I went every day. Pyramids of sand and stacks of bricks morphed into walls and floors. One of the workers spent his days making pretty edges in cement to frame the brick walls, every detail perfect. They worked with the simplest tools and without electricity. I never saw a spirit level but the walls were even and straight, guided by bits of string with chunks of broken brick at the end. Then a load of timber arrived and with it, the first and only power tools—a saw, planer and drill—along with a small generator to run them. A roof specialist with merry dark eyes took charge of this important component and the work crew grew to 20. Drifts of fragrant camphorwood sawdust appeared under the planer. A massive timber roof frame was assembled on the ground and magically raised between one evening and the next morning with two bits of cloth tied to the highest point, red and white to represent the Indonesian flag.

Now the shell of the house teemed with workers—the walls inside and out, the roof, the windows, the floor. One man squatted at the edge of the roof, effortlessly catching roof tiles flung to him from below and fitting them in neat rows over the struts. Muddy ducks from next door marched in and out of the house in formation and muttered in the corner where my office would be.

I visited every day to measure walls and walk the land and marvel that I was building a house in a language I could hardly speak. Yet we seemed to comprehend each other very well, the house and the workers and I. It's very simple here. You lay a foundation, put up walls, drop a roof over it all and hang some doors. Even I could understand it. If there are building codes, I never encountered them.

The foreman, Pak Manto, was competent and unflappable. Most of the workmen had never left Lombok or Java and were surprised to find themselves at the mercy of a foreign woman with bizarre building ideas and an obsession with litter. Already astonished by the concepts of a glass block shower wall and terra cotta sinks (not usual, they pointed out), they also had to deal with my daily appeal that they pick up their litter and bag it for collection. I already had a reputation as a bit of a fanatic in this regard. Eyes would roll and jokes in dialect would be made. It took several weeks, but eventually the site began to look cleaner. One day a large white cloth flag appeared on the sand heap, hand lettered in Indonesian to read, "It is forbidden to throw rubbish here! Penalty death!" A black collection bag full of garbage stood tidily beneath it. Only later did I discover that they had been burying the rubbish so I wouldn't see it. When I started the garden I dug up bags and bags of it and still occasionally unearth an old sweets packet from that era.

Friends dropped by often to commiserate and stayed to be astonished. The walls were so straight! The finishing was so tidy! And most remarkable, it was all happening so fast! A German friend who had volunteered to design my kitchen with her CAD program arrived one day with a tape measure and a diagram accurate to one centimetre, and was speechless to find everything exactly where it should be. Pak Manto smiled smugly. He was a pro, all right.

When he began to lay the first floor tiles, the house suddenly began to take on a new energy. It was no longer just a structure of bricks and concrete. It felt alive, organic. I could imagine it with furniture in it, with friends in the kitchen and flowers growing around the windows. After the walls had all received their third coat of paint, the electricians arrived and began to hack deep channels in the brick. Why hadn't the placement of the wiring been considered when the walls were going up? I couldn't help wondering aloud. Everyone looked at me as if I was mad, and I was sent off to buy lampshades and light bulbs.

The next day the head electrician showed me the quality of the wiring he was using and where my house had been earthed. The water workman placed bamboo stakes along the water lines so I wouldn't cut into them when I was digging the garden. They were nice men.

My house ceremony was on the day of a full moon. Auspiciously, it poured with rain and the ritual bamboo exploded like gunfire, frightening any malign spirits off the land forever. But I'd never felt anything negative here. The house faces a tranquil bamboo forest across the river and the land is full of light. The topsoil is rich and dark and many metres deep. My sister, who homesteads in British Columbia, wrote the other day, "Having stewardship of your own land is like having your own small country." It's a good feeling.

I'd known the face of every man who worked on this building that would be my home. I'd watched the walls grow, seen the ribbons of wood peel out from the planer, smelled the sawdust. I knew how the septic tank was made and where the water pipes were laid. This house would have no secrets from me.

Three and a half months after we staked out the foundations with string, I slept at home.

Nocturne

After several weeks in sanitized urban Canada, where even a tiny spider on the wall is cause for alarm, I returned to my cottage at the edge of the jungle in Ubud with relief. What an adaptable species we are, I thought sleepily as jet lag propelled me towards the bed and I nodded to the big tokay who lives behind a picture in my bedroom. The concept of lizards in the bedroom would be outrageous in Vancouver. In the 25th floor apartment my 90 year old parents had recently rented (after fleeing the comfortable assisted living facility they'd settled in after selling the family home last year) there was not so much as an ant to be seen. I slept in the small white cube of a bedroom far above the ground, dreaming of my lush garden at home and its many creatures.

As always after a trip, I was very glad to be back in Bali. I prepared for bed and the dogs bounced into the bedroom to flop down in their usual posts. Outside, the parrots grumbled softly. A few metres away the jungle welcomed me back with rustles and squeaks and sighs. There was a huge splash in the pond, as if a small whale was sounding among the water hyacinths. I went to sleep with a smile.

Hours later when the night was darkest, all the dogs started to bark at once. Upon investigation, they'd been disturbed by a couple of glossy rats chasing one another along the top of the bathroom wall. I reminded myself to talk to the staff again about the merits of acquiring a small python. They were still quite resistant. ("If I saw it, I would have to scream and run," explained Wayan Manis.)

Back in bed and reaching again for sleep, I recalled some of the other nocturnal visitors I'd encountered over the years. Once as I was reading in bed I noticed all the dogs staring onto one corner of the room. I squinted to see what they were looking at, and a long, snake-like shadow rose against the wall. After locking the dogs in the office, I returned with a broom. There had never been a snake in the house before and I was hoping the intruder would prove to be something else. Indeed, it revealed itself a moment later. Rolling out of the corner on a moving frill of legs was a large, blue-tinged centipede.

Gentle reader, do your utmost to avoid being bitten by a centipede. There is something quite horrid in their venom that not only causes a large, painful swelling, but the twin entry points of the wound turns the flesh to jelly for a few days. (By the way, there only three creatures on Bali that leave two fang marks when they bite: the snake, the centipede and the spider.)

Centipedes move with astonishing speed; there was not a moment to be lost. I grabbed a big book, dropped it on the intruder and jumped up and down on it a few times. Centipede legs flew out in all directions. When I was quite sure it was flat, I scraped the remains into a glass jar and carefully washed the floor. The next morning when I showed the jar to my staff, the vestiges of the mangled centipede were still moving. "These are very hard to kill," said Nyoman, taking it into the garden and carefully chopping it into small pieces.

A whole new cast of characters takes the stage after dark here in Ubud. We are all used to the lovelorn vocalizations toads and frogs, but my friend Susan reports that every few months she is kept awake by the lovesick koi in her pond, which thrash and splash in an excess of amorous ardour that can go on for days. Then they lay eggs which produce baby koi, which they then consume.

My patio has been the arena of many nocturnal adventures. A few days ago I came onto the patio in the morning to find a large splat of half-digested wild figs on the floor, evidence that a fruit bat had been hanging out there. The next morning there was another splat in the very same place, which thoughtfully avoided the dining table and the cushions. I became intrigued. Judging by the volume of evidence, either the bat had been very large or it had brought several of its friends back to party. That night I caught the visitor in the act. It was quite a small black bat, hanging by one foot from the ceiling while liberally decorating the tile below. Wayan said that bats were seldom alone, and probably a group of ten or so would gather here later to sociably digest their figs together. Not wanting my dining room to become Fruit Bat Central I turned off the light, asked the bats to leave, and they never came back.

The dogs killed a civet in front of me on the steps one night, where it had unwisely followed a juicy bug. Once I was woken by strange noises, and went out to find Kipper the pit bull in enthusiastic sexual congress with Kalypso on the dining table. I had to dispatch a green pit viper which Daisy had dragged in from the garden at three o'clock one morning. Another time I found two big tokays on the table locked in a death battle which had, by the look of the carnage, been going on all night.

I used to tell my family and friends about the wildlife that shared my space, but they were always so horrified that I eventually stopped. How could I live like that? they wondered. Why didn't I seal up my windows and install air conditioning so glacial that no self-respecting reptile would take up residence in my bedroom?

Well, I could. But what fun would that be?

Pit Bulls Don't Eat Tofu

The Bali dog can be a hell-hound when encountered on a dark street at night, but is a remarkably gentle and intelligent pet when well-treated. Bali dogs are said to be the Australian dingo's closest surviving relation. Isolated from other canines until the last century, there are still a few purebred Bali dogs in the mountains. Most of the others have had some kind of romantic encounter with a Western breed, creating some pretty bizarre specimens. Kipper was one of these, manifesting a strong throwback to some mysterious pit bull ancestor.

He came to me as a rotund, nearly hairless teenage pup with a wrinkled brow, huge paws and a voracious appetite for absolutely everything: shoes, books, candles, newspapers—nothing was safe. This enthusiasm extended to everything he found in his food bowl.

He quickly grew into his paws and became a massive, chesty chap with a cheerful disposition. New to dog-owning and painfully aware of Indonesia's poverty, I decided to try and raise a meatless dog. Tinned dog food was out of the question; I couldn't justify feeding more protein to my dog in a day than many Indonesian children consumed in a month. Besides, at that time there was no where to recycle the tins. Kipper got plenty of protein raiding the duck enclosure, sometimes consuming all the new eggs before I got up in the morning. (He always seemed astonished that I knew what he'd been doing, having forgotten the trail of eggshells on the path.) His rice was cooked with vegetables, garlic, a few commercial dog crunchies, tofu or tempe and a scrambled egg. He wolfed this down happily and grew glossy and bright-eyed, exercising his mighty jaws on pig knuckle bones, chew toys and the toes of the occasional tolerant visitor.

But dogs are social animals and I was away a lot. Even when I worked at home I was in my office and out of sight of the patio door. (Kipper was banned from the house after a gustatory encounter with a Persian carpet.) He pined whenever he couldn't see me, and my neighbour reported that he cried for hours when left alone. I began to find my role of Alpha Dog stressful. Consulting my canine psychology books, I decided to expand the pack.

Paolo was looking for a new home for one of his dogs, and Kalypso arrived soon afterward to balance the pack dynamic and keep Kipper company. She was slender and delicate with long, black hair and a seductive fox-like tail. Kipper was instantly besotted with her, following her everywhere and gazing adoringly at her for hours on end. Reserved by nature, Kalypso resisted his overtures to play bouncy pit bull games. Almost overnight Kipper became a Dog of Dignity. For months he had kept all his toys and other treasures in the folds of the tattered blanket where he slept. Now he shyly laid them before her one by one—his squeaking dolly, his rawhide chew, his rubber ring and even his eviscerated purple teletubby. It was very touching. Within hours I was congratulating myself that the new relationship had done wonders for his social skills.

But there was trouble brewing in the kitchen. I'd taken special pains with their first meal together, serving it warm with nicely scrambled duck eggs mixed in with the rice. Kipper began to snuffle happily into his dinner, then glanced over at his adored one who was regarding her bowl with polite disdain.

Kipper: "What's wrong?"

Kalypso: "At my last home, we had chicken livers in the rice."

Kipper: "What's chicken? What's liver?"

Kalypso: "It is succulent, smelly, tasty meat, the natural food of dogs. What's this disgusting white stuff? And these dreary little brown crunchy things?"

Kipper: "Dunno. We always have them." Kalypso: "I can't eat this rubbish."

She wandered off a few steps and lay on the cool tile, forepaws elegantly crossed, back to the despised offering. Unhappily, Kipper looked from his bowl to Kalypso and over to me. He nosed into his food, picked out a chunk of tofu and laid it carefully on the floor beside his bowl, then another and another, giving me what my grandmother would call an old-fashioned look each time. He finished his rice and eggs and vegetables with less appetite than I had ever seen and departed, leaving a pile of rejected tofu beside his bowl. I am not making this up.

The second day I put down the bowls; it was tempe today. Kipper looked hopefully at his dinner and then checked Kalypso's response. She gave hers one sniff and recoiled.

Kipper: "You haven't eaten since you got here." Kalypso: "I'm not hungry."

Me: "Kipper, dogs are starving outside our gate. Eat your dinner."

Kipper: "I guess I'm not very hungry either." Me: "Kalypso, you are a bloody princess." Kalypso: "Yes. I am."

The hunger strike went on for a week. I took this very personally, being a good cook who seeks the fine balance between flavour and nutrition whether preparing food for people or creatures. I made a strong stock from the bones of spit-roasted pork and cooked the rice and vegetables in that. I napped warm rice with fat skimmed from a smoked duck. I fried the tempe until crisp. Neither dog would eat. I started to take the disdained meals out to the starving old dog on the main road. She wouldn't eat tofu either. Kipper even stopped eating the crunchies that were his late-night snack. Kalypso didn't approve of crunchies.

Finally Wayan Manis intervened. "Ibu, they want to eat meat. Let me bring some chicken heads from my village. Very cheap." I knew I was beaten. Kalypso had only been with us a week but already I thought I could see the shadow of ribs under her coat.

Wayan brought a large bag of the disgusting items the next morning. The dogs gave her their full attention while the little heads bubbled in the stock pot, beaks pointing straight up. I couldn't bear to watch as she cracked the skulls and mixed it all up with the rice and vegetables. I resolved never to run out of dog food over the weekend.

That night the dogs danced around me as I spooned their bowls full, averting my eyes from what must have been tiny brains. Kipper whined anxiously as Kalypso sniffed, paused and began to nibble daintily at her meal. He dove into his dinner with all his previous enthusiasm. They licked their bowls clean, tails wagging gently, then exchanged a long look. Okay, I'd been manipulated. But I don't eat tofu, either.

Three Thousand, Two Hundred and Seven Smiles

There is a village in Indonesia so isolated that until 1998 there had been almost no contact with the outside world. Few of its people had ever seen a westerner or an Indonesian flag. No one spoke Indonesian and most of the children suffered from iodine deficiency and malnutrition. But this community is not in the interior of Papua or some remote island. The 72-square-kilometre village of Ban with its 19 hamlets spans the arid wasteland between the peaks of Mount Agung and Mount Abang in Bali's Karangasem regency.

Until about 2000, no one knew how many people lived in the upper reaches of Ban, or how they survived. They subsisted on corn and cassava, the only crops that would grow in the parched earth. If they needed anything else and had the cash to buy it, the market was a five hour walk down a vertical mountain trail. There were a few primary schools at the lower end of the village closer to the road, but the teachers rarely came and the buildings fell into disrepair. Illiteracy was almost universal in the highest hamlets, where about 1,500 families lived in single-room homes with bamboo walls and dirt floors.

The situation has improved dramatically since then. Ban's 3,000 families are the focus of the East Bali Poverty Project (EBPP), an integrated and holistic program that was started in 1998 by Founder/Chairman David Booth. Today, a dedicated staff of over 90 young Indonesians, mostly from the lower hamlets of Ban, runs a variety of sustainable programs from the EBPP centre at the base of the mountain. The comprehensive centre for sustainable development, research and training includes offices, a humming network of computers, a library, and a permaculture-type community learning centre with a composting worm farm, organic vegetable patch and a small herd of dairy goats. Teams responsible for programs in children's education, health improvement, nutrition, appropriate technology, safe water resource development, organic farming and erosion control with vetiver grass fan out through the remote villages every day. They drive dirt bikes up impossibly steep and narrow tracks to gather data, deliver training, teach children and build schools. The most distant hamlet is a daunting 14 kilometres from the centre and 1150 metres above sea level.

It's the very end of the dry season as we lurch up an unpaved track on the slopes of Mount Abang through clouds of pungent dust. Today's mission is to follow a mobile dental clinic which is visiting one of the hamlets. The fully equipped clinic, which has its own generator, was at that time lent to the project twice a week by the Bali International Women's Association (BIWA). Dr Panji Triadnya, a Master of Health Sciences who lectures in dentistry at University Mahasaraswati, leads a group of 15 final-year dentistry students who have volunteered to treat the school children today. Dr Panji started working with the project as a volunteer in 2001. "When I first started treating the people here, not one had ever seen a toothbrush," he recalls. "The rate of gingivitis (gum disease) was over ninety percent due to malnutrition and a complete absence of dental hygiene. Now the figure is about half that." Dr Panji's ambitious goal is to deliver top dental services to all the forgotten people of the remote community. "This is my hobby," he claims modestly.

Between June and August that year he single-handedly assessed over 2,000 children below the age of 12, making his grueling rounds on the back of a dirt bike. Only two kids, from hamlets closest to the road, had ever seen a dentist before. Now each child is being checked and treated through the mobile clinic.

Today the clinic parks near a school and the dental students give each class a simple presentation on oral hygiene and basic nutrition. Crowded five to a bench, the kids are riveted. Proper brushing technique is demonstrated, and dusty forefingers obediently probe 39 mouths.Then the dentists don gloves and start calling up the kids by name. Each has his or her teeth examined and cleaned, a chart filled out and those who need fillings or rotten baby teeth extracted line up outside the mobile clinic. Inside the spotless clinic, one child lies back in the dental chair and another four perch on a row of chairs waiting their turn, all agog at the chill of the air conditioning.

Ten minutes up the mountain, another group of dentists have arrived in the back of a truck at an even more remote hamlet. Here, the school built by the EBPP is so new that the doors are just being fitted into the classrooms. The kids line up happily for their check-ups. Those who need anaesthetic are driven down to the clinic, others have their baby teeth extracted on the spot and go back to their classes with wads of cotton in their mouths. Not one of them sheds a tear or shows any apprehension. These kids are tough—they have to be. Until the EBPP came, only the strongest survived.

Some of the lower hamlets have newly staffed and repaired government schools; more remote areas are served by schools built by EBPP.The children at the latter attend three times a week and are given milk and a nutritious meal. "Now they're growing so fast they need new school uniforms every few months. It's great," beams David, who was awarded an

MBE for his work. Each of the five EBPP schools has its own organic garden. Here the children learn to grow 20 kinds of vegetables for their school meals, making their own compost from cow manure and worm castings and stabilizing the steep slopes with vetiver grass.

These gardens are the core of a sustainable food security program for the future.

The children love school and are eager to learn, sometimes achieving literacy in a single day. Most now speak Indonesian. Six students graduated from EBPP's junior high school in Bunga hamlet this year, a real victory considering the almost universal illiteracy rate of just a few years ago. They recently started senior high school, still sponsored by EBPP.

At day's end, we crash back down the dusty mountain track to the EBPP centre, followed by the mobile clinic. Another two hundred children have been treated today. As the dental program reaches further up the mountain, the dentists will access the more remote hamlets on the back of dirt bikes, sending the kids who need more complex treatment down to the mobile clinic the same way. Transportation becomes even more problematical during the rainy season.

Bringing dental care to these hamlets is indeed a bold and challenging initiative. But thanks to the East Bali Poverty Project, thousands of smiles will be lighting up Bali's poorest community over the next few years.

A Day Out of Time

T'was the night before Nyepi, and ghosts were walking the land. Nyepi, the Balinese new Year, is a holy day of silence and retreat that almost always falls during the spring equinox. Everyone on the island, including tourists, is confined to their house, compound or hotel. On this day no food is cooked, no lights lit, no work done; Balinese are supposed to spend the day in meditation and prayer, although I am reliably informed that many pass the time furtively watching television.

For 30 hours the island is completely still—even the airport is closed—so that any visiting demons will think Bali is deserted and leave it alone for another year.

The night before Nyepi, however, is raucous in the towns. Young men parade the streets with huge ogoh-ogoh, demonic effigies of monsters they've taken weeks to build. Sweating, excited teams of men carry them on massive bamboo rafts, spinning them in the crossroads to confound the demons they have evoked. It's a night of high energy, when legions of ghosts lurk in the shadows.

I was coming back from Jo's house in the mountains about nine o'clock, driven by a strong but irrational desire to be home well before the midnight curfew. As I left her village, a row of pacalang (village police) with blazing torches marched by the roadside, the flames lighting their apprehensive young faces. It was not a night to be abroad.

The deep, fern-lined ravines that had seemed romantic only hours before now appeared sinister. My seatbelt, which had always been perfectly reliable, kept coming undone. The headlights dimmed for no reason. I crept along in low gear, barely able to see the road and feeling unaccountably edgy. There didn't seem to be any other traffic in the world.

I turned a corner and suddenly there was a motorbike close in front of me. Relieved, I followed it down the steep, twisting road, across the bridges and up the other side of the final gorge. In first gear, I negotiated the precipitous S-bends behind the reassuring red tail light. The bike was uncannily silent on that steep hill. Then we were on a flat, straight stretch—and the red tail light in front of me disappeared into thin air. I was close behind it, there was no place it could possibly have turned off. I remembered that my car windows had been open, and the engine of my own car had been the only sound.

I could feel the hair on my arms stand straight up as I drove as fast as I dared toward the road to Ubud. This, too, was deserted except for isolated clumps of people. Then I came upon a procession, banging cymbals. A pacalang directed me up a dark little lane off the main road, and I tried to think of this as a grand adventure as I crept along its deserted length. Imagination can be very helpful when writing advertising copy or designing baubles, but is not exactly an asset on a dark night haunted by demons and dreams. There seemed to be an unusual number of dogs about and small tables of offerings outside the compound gates. Little wildfires flared in the distance.

I am a rational, pragmatic person, but I badly wanted to be home. By the time I drove into Ubud I was on the edge of the driver's seat and cursing every innocent who had inadvertently gotten between me and my house. I parked, leapt out of the car and barred the garden gate as if the hounds of hell were after me. My Nyepi had begun.

Most of the expats who live here love Nyepi. It's a magical day out of time—the first long night, the uncannily quiet day and then the night again. For me, it's a time to renew a pledge of stewardship and harmony with the house and land and all the creatures, seen and unseen, that share it with me. A day of retreat. Imagine if every country had an enforced day of silence and introspection not just once a year but, say, once a month.

All the senses become more acute when not bombarded by the assaults of the ordinary day. They seem to become stripped back, overly sensitive. The sounds of Nyepi are subtle, many-layered and all the more mysterious because they are the unheard warp and weft of our daily life, suddenly brought into sharp aural focus. I'm always astonished at the number and types of birds I hear on waking, the small-voiced ones whose calls are lost in ambient noise. A chicken clucks softly in the next village; I can hear it. A small child calls out across the river, quickly hushed. Then the crickets fire up, a background curtain of noise I never focus on as a rule but today it has the volume of a bulldozer. There was a small sighing sound every few minutes like a sad old man… I finally tracked it to the automatic water pump. It had probably been making this little noise for months, but I hadn't heard it.

Tokays scampered in the rafters and the dogs decided that there might be a rat under the refrigerator. The parrot screeched for papaya. It seemed deafening.

The darkness of Nyepi night is always extraordinarily dense, moonless, nearly starless. Every night creature on the undercliff was out, chattering, muttering under its breath, crashing around. I had to restrain Daisy from checking it all out. A dachshund is bred to chase and kill things, and the principals of peaceful coexistence are slow to penetrate that silky head. But on Nyepi night I kept her in. As the demons looked down, they mustn't glimpse a small, long dog with a pearl collar nosing through the undergrowth. Too tempting by half. Kalypso had no such aspirations. At the first sign of darkness she curled up beside my bed and dug in for the night.

I'd just returned to Bali from a trip, and Wayan had taken advantage of my absence to wash all the Persian carpets. Unfortunately they hadn't had a chance to dry completely and the whole house smelled like a bus full of wet Englishmen. In the morning I festooned the lawn with carpets, following the sun around all day. I learned what parts of the garden are in sun, which is shadow, when. I'd never taken the time to observe this before.

Cooking food and using tools is forbidden on Nyepi. I had a fruit salad instead of fresh juice, and later there was smoked chicken and salad, savoured slowly as I watched Daisy try to catch fish from the edge of the pond. My neighbour, Pak Mangku the priest, was out in his temple as I wandered through the garden. We exchanged smiles, put fingers to our lips. Shhhh. We were conspirators to preserve the holy silence of the day.

I confess that I sometimes read during Nyepi, or draw, or answer email, but it's hard to concentrate. It's very hard to do nothing all day, but I try. I have lengthy, unnecessary naps. I try to teach the parrot to say things. There's so much nothing to do that there's no time to do all of it.

Monday dawned. I woke to the buzz of motorcycles across the river. I got up, tied on my sarong and unbarred the gate to the world again. The ghosts had walked away. For another year, Bali would be safe from demons.

Hard Times

I've crunched the numbers and think Nyoman's great-grandmother must be about 100 years old. Family lore claims she is 130, but there may have been a few decades of slippage in the accounting department. My own grandmothers were over 90 when they fell off the perch, and I can understand the temptation to exaggerate.

Dadong still has a good appetite although she constantly apologizes for eating when she can no longer work for the family. She gets around the compound with a little help and is still able to do simple tasks. One eye is sightless now and the other often out of focus, but she is amazingly alert. One afternoon when Wayan was sick I came into the compound with some fruit. There was no one around but ancient, halfblind Dadong, propped up in the bale. Instantly she figured out who I was and what I wanted, and jerked a crooked thumb to the room where Wayan was resting. There are no flies on Dadong.

Life was hard for Dadong. She married young and bore seven children, and they were often hungry. Nyoman was driving me to Lovina once and mentioned casually that Dadong and her husband had walked all the way from Ubud to Gilimanuk on Bali's west coast looking for work. What an incredible journey that must have been, over the cold mountains and along the dry north coast.

Her husband died when the children were still small. Dadong became desperate. Depressed and unable to feed her children, she tried to hang herself in the bale banjar one night. But her unskillful knot slipped and she fell unhurt to the floor. She lay there awhile, disappointed, then decided that God had decided she should live. So she dusted herself off and went home.

At some point there had been a little plot of rice land near the Singakerta police station that belonged to her husband. After he died, a rich man came and told her to sign a piece of paper, and took the land. "People were a bit stupid in those days," Wayan says sadly. "They didn't understand."

Wayan is only 35 but her own story is hard to listen to. Her father became chronically ill when she was about five, and for the next 15 years she had to find the money to pay her school fees, forage for food for the family and hunt for healing herbs in the forest and fields. The family lived on sweet potatoes and weeds from the fields, with a handful of rice shared between them. There was never any meat. By the age of seven, Wayan was working side by side with her mother washing clothes for the neighbours and weaving lontar baskets. Her baskets were popular and sold quickly, but all the money went for medicine for her father. By this time there were two small brothers to feed as well.

She was rarely in bed before midnight and up early to attend school each morning. Exhausted and malnourished, she found it hard to learn to read. While the other children played, she asked the teacher to help her with her work. The other kids mocked her because she was always too busy to play… too busy keeping herself and her family alive. She has a picture of herself taken by tourists, a skinny kid sleeping on a mat on the ground under a rough coconut frond roof.

Although her father had several brothers that lived nearby, none of them ever visited or offered to help. Neither did the neighbours, although they helped themselves to the coconuts from the family's trees.

When she was twelve, Wayan started carrying stones from the river for a local contractor to pay her school fees. Before school every morning and without breakfast, she would climb the steep river bank carrying heavy rocks. Often she fell and hurt herself. After school she would go back and work until dark. At the end of two months the contractor sold his stock of stones. But when Wayan asked for money to pay her school fees, he brushed her aside. She was never paid.

Her father owned some rice fields but was too weak to work them, and there was no water for irrigation in those days because the other farmers didn't share it fairly. At one point, the banjar took the land when the family couldn't pay for ceremonies or support the temple. By working day and night they were able to get it back.

A few years later, both parents became sick. Her mother cracked under the stress of constant poverty. Tears run down Wayan's brown cheeks, and mine too, as she told how her mother picked up a big knife one afternoon and threatened to stab her. "She was a little bit crazy," she recalls. "I prayed and prayed, and the knife dropped, and Ibu slept for ten days." It was a terrible time. No one came to help.

The story has a happy ending. She met Nyoman when she was 23, and he started to drop around and fix up the family compound. Three years later they married and she moved to his family compound nearby. She's loved and respected by his family, and she and Dadong are very close. The skinny little girl is a curvy woman now who loves to cook.

Tempered by hard times, Wayan is a cheerful and compassionate spirit. She's quick to share everything from money to clothing with others. "Food is more delicious when you share it," she smiles. She should know.

Lessons by the Pond

Never underestimate the power of a small body of water to teach mindfulness and break bad habits. For the ten years I lived in Singapore, I was a champion multi-tasker. It wasn't unusual to have half a dozen projects spinning in the air at the same time while zooming around Southeast Asia and managing a large house and endless houseguests without a housekeeper. I moved in a flurry of efficiency as I cooked, solved problems and met clients. I forgot how to do just one thing at once, mindfully.

When I moved to Bali, my first pond taught me to mono-task. Instead of drinking my tea while doing my email, scheduling my day, making juice and brushing the dog, I learned just to enjoy my morning tea by the pond. This simple exercise took months to learn and I still don't always make it to the bottom of the mug without being distracted. But now I know it's possible just to do one thing at a time. Just be, with my tea and the pond.

No one who has a pond could possibly require a television. A pond offers constant drama without advertising. Life is endlessly being born, eaten, eating something else, blooming, or making sticky love under a leaf. A lily unfolds to the sun, dragonflies the colour of jewels hover in the heat. A frog lays her eggs on a lily leaf, and they float like black pearls among the blossoms. Basking snakes eye tadpoles with calculated interest. Delicate lizards cling to plant stems. Toads and fish splash and flash between the lotuses and at night bats torpedo down for resting insects.

I was hooked on ponds. How could I continue to hone my monotasking skills without one? So as soon as my new house was ready to sleep in and the books and spices were unpacked, we started digging a big hole in the ground in front of the patio.

Advice began to pour immediately. The pond should be oval, it should be square. It should be lined with cement; no, it should have a plastic liner. The cement should be three or five or ten centimetres thick, poured in one or two layers with iron bars or finishing nails or chicken wire or staples for strength. Or not. The corners should or need not be reinforced. The cement should dry for one or four days or a week, kept damp or soaked daily with a hose, or not. It should be finished with water-proof paint or an expensive plastic barrier or nothing at all. No wonder the damned project took so long.

Nyoman thought it was all a load of nonsense. A Balinese pond, he announced, was a hole in the ground with a layer of concrete. Period. Upon gentle interrogation he allowed that yes, Balinese ponds did leak and were hard to clean. Rolling his eyes discreetly, he accompanied me on my mission for the Perfect Pond. Together we quested for information through the back alleys of Denpasar and the thinking boxes of longsuffering engineers and architects.

It took a long time just to dig the hole. I'd drawn a modest rectangle at first but people kept making what seemed like sensible suggestions and in the end it was quite a bit larger than first planned. We used the excavated dirt to make the garden bigger, reclaiming a couple of meters of the precipitous slope that fell away to a river far below. That project necessitated retaining walls; we consumed huge amounts of cement.

As soon as the first layer of cement was laid in the pond, the dogs leaped in to leave their mark. The next morning we found a couple of frogs under the wet sacks. "Looking for a house for later," observed Wayan as she released them. A pair of Javanese kingfishers flashed past, monitoring the work and biding their time until the hole in the ground was stocked with succulent fish. Already the nascent pond was attracting life.

One day, removing the plywood siding from the damp walls of the pond, Nyoman shouted, "Binatang!"our code word for wildlife. Clinging to the wall was a black scorpion the size of my hand, a perfect museum specimen. My staff wanted to burn it alive, which seemed excessively brutal. We caught it in the biggest glass jar in the house and I took it to a restaurant where I was meeting a friend for dinner that night, hoping to glean some information on its life and habits. This being Ubud, people would wander by, casually pick up the jar, say "Big scorpion," and carry on with their conversations. No one offered to give it a good home. It began to look quite depressed and eventually Maite and I liberated it in the jungle behind her garden.

It took Nyoman about four months to finish the pond. Dig the hole, measure, pour the cement, bend the metal rods, pour more cement, lay the edging, apply the plaster, paint on the waterproofing, absorb a huge amount of information about building ponds...it was very much his project. One day I came home to find NYOMAN carved in bold letters along the brickwork. The artist had signed his work.

The next day we filled it with rainwater and bought lotus plants and water lilies. I joined Nyoman in the half-filled pond, placing bricks and pots and arranging leaves to float in the clear water. We agreed that the water would not be so clean for long. "Soon there will be fish shit," said Wayan pragmatically.

For a pond must have fish. It seemed impersonal to just buy them when friends were offering stock from their own ponds. I spent a hilarious Sunday morning trying to catch fingerlings from Wendyl's pond. Graceful swoops of the net proved fruitless, and soon we were dragging the bottom and bringing up muck, dead leaves, sticks and the occasional infant carp. As I walked up the path with my pathetic catch a neighbour in the complex called out that she had too many fish in her bathroom pond. A very messy five minutes later I had a grand daddy carp in a bucket and a dress that was wet to the waist. The new members of the family were tipped triumphantly into the pond and the next day Nyoman installed the pump.

Then we all sat quietly for a long time looking at our pond in the slanting light of the late afternoon. A dragonfly arrived, circled and landed on a leaf. The fish flashed among the plants. From nowhere a frog appeared and pensively crouched on the edge. A kingfisher landed on a high branch and eyed the water with satisfaction. In a single day the pond had come alive.

I start the day now sitting on the patio step with a dog on each side and a mug of tea in my hand, busily mono-tasking. It's not an easy skill to acquire, but yes, it can be learned.

On The Road Again

Ubud is a small town with narrow roads which are often choked with vehicles. There's no public transport apart from the ubiquitous bemos, rickety old vans that ferry around school children and market ladies. Taxis have not penetrated the town as yet. Some of the bolder visitors rent motor scooters or bicycles; others drive cars. Many, however, are at the mercy of the local transport mafia.

"Trrransporrrt?" is the eternal, maddening chorus as one negotiates the dangerous sidewalks of Monkey Forest Road. "Trrransporrrt?" chirp idle groups of young men hanging out at street corners or sitting in rows in the shade. Anyone who has a motorcycle, car or van or knows someone who does is in the transport business. It's something to do in a town with few jobs.

The rolling Rs are reminiscent of my Glaswegian-born grandmother but the resemblance ends there. The Ubud boys sport dreadlocks, blond streaks, tattoos, body piercing and funky T shirts. They chain-smoke Marlboros and strum guitars. They are ubiquitous—except when you actually need to be driven somewhere. Then they magically melt away. This phenomenon becomes evident around dark, when their priorities shift to getting home for dinner, attending a temple ceremony or seducing a sunburned Australian lass. Just when you need a lift to a remote restaurant or to bypass the hell hounds on the way to your hotel, there is not a set of wheels for hire in town.

I came to Bali with the firm intention of not driving. During my ten years in Singapore I had managed to avoid getting behind the wheel at all, abetted by cheap taxis and a good public transport system. When I visited Ubud, I knew I could get just about anywhere for a dollar. But gradually, as I morphed from a tourist to a resident, I began to understand local economics. That five-minute ride cost the equivalent of half a day's wage for a salaried driver, or about what a pembantu (housekeeper) made in a day. My house at that time was a mile from the centre of Ubud—not a comfortable walk hauling groceries in the heat past packs of unsocialized dogs. After a week of social and gustatory isolation I finally gave in and leased a battered jeep-like Katana. I arranged for a driver three days a week, and the rest of the time the car gathered dust in the parking lot next to my house.

The arrangement worked well for a couple of weeks. Komang spoke good English, knew how to photocopy, mail letters, deliver things to friends and buy groceries. He was personable, reliable, fixed the car and kept meticulous accounts. Of course it was too good to last. Just as I was getting smug, Komang came down with typhoid and disappeared to his village, never to reappear.

I could avoid the issue no longer. It had been a decade since I'd last driven a car, and I couldn't have chosen a more challenging arena in which to re-enter the fray. It felt odd to be in the driver's seat again. I turned the key and the engine started. Instinctively my feet found clutch, brake and gas pedal and my hand located the gears. I was off.

Very slowly I inched up the rough driveway and turned onto the main road. It was only two lanes wide but there was plenty of action. Handcarts selling noodles, bicycle vendors, school children, stray dogs with alarming cases of mange, big piles of sand, stacks of bamboo and holes big enough to swallow a wheelbarrow. And that wasn't even counting the traffic. I tiptoed along in second gear as far as the supermarket. Actually, it hadn't been too bad.

I persevered in the days that followed, learning to deal with motorcycles peeling off in all directions, including those headed directly toward me in my own lane. Some drivers wore helmets to avoid fines, but it was considered effete to actually fasten the chin strap. Drivers chatted animatedly to their passengers over their shoulders. Young men in full temple gear steered their motorbikes with one hand while smoking and checking the messages on their hand phones with the other.

It was worse at night. For some reason, many motorcyclists considered it undesirable to use headlights, and cyclists never had them at all. Oncoming traffic remained a mystery until it was within a few metres. Was that single light coming up fast a motorcycle, or a truck with one headlight burned out? Was the pair of lights speeding along two motorbikes or a truck? Perhaps that darker shadow ahead of me was an unlit motorbike driven by a father in full ceremonial dress clutching a baby with his spare hand while his wife rode side-saddle behind him with a tall tower of offerings on her head. Or was it a dog or an unmarked pile of boulders on the road? There was never a dull moment.

Gradually I became braver. The day I executed a U-turn in the middle of Jalan Hanoman in heavy traffic was a breakthrough— tourist buses, trucks and motorbikes all waited patiently while I completed this manoeuvre. I realized then that anarchy was actually expected. Things were easier after that. Now I charge around town in second and even third gear, executing sharp three-point turns and reversing stylishly down narrow lanes. I have been known to drive as far as Sanur.

Now the same transport guys who used to nag me every day have become old cronies. When I'm stuck in a traffic jam in town, a familiar face will sometimes appear at my window. "Mau ka mana (where are you going), Ibu Kat?" inquires a dreadlocked, tattooed Balinese, who then proceeds to complain about the traffic.

Blessed

I had the flu.

Normally that wouldn't raise more than a sympathetic eyebrow, but these were not normal times. It was 2003. With SARS paralyzing Singapore and Hong Kong, there was a tendency to take what may be an ordinary bug pretty seriously.

It started the night before Nyepi. This was the one night of the year when everyone in Ubud turns out in the football field to socialize, admire the huge effigies of monsters called ogoh ogoh and drink in the pure Balinese energy of the celebration. Usually I love it, but this year I felt overwhelmed. The crowds and darkness, the rafts of roaring men and huge lurching demons made me dizzy. I went home early.

This was my second Nyepi in my new house. It was very quiet in my street, everyone was at the crossroads. Trailed by the puzzled dogs, I paced around my dark garden banging on a saucepan to drive away any bad spirits. It was purely symbolic; there were no demons here. I sat on the daybed in the patio and counted my many blessings.

But I was still dizzy. I went to bed and fell into a strange embrace of aching bones, aching skin, heat and chill, bizarre and busy dreams.

Nyepi passed like a hallucination. I managed to feed the animals and slept again. Another night passed. I woke to see Wayan Manis' concerned face at the door.

"I'm sick," I explained. "Flu."

Wayan has a television in her compound (I have none) and was perfectly cognizant of the implications. "It might be SARS."

Well, it could be. I'd recently returned from Singapore, where I'd stayed with a friend just off the plane from Hanoi. And I really felt quite ill.

But I'd staggered out of bed to check the internet, and my research indicated that it was pretty much guesswork whether one had SARS or not. There was no test and no treatment for it yet. They seemed to be deciding on the basis of where you'd been and how quickly you fell ill. The mortality rate was under five percent in most places, and confined to people who'd had close exposure to the very ill or who were elderly. It didn't appear to be virulently contagious. Lots of people who'd been exposed to sick people hadn't developed SARS at all. Most of those who got sick eventually got better.

There was no sense getting into a flap about it. If I had SARS the most sensible thing was to quarantine myself and rest. I wasn't all that sick, given that I could still check my email. I conveyed all this to Wayan, with the suggestion that she wipe down everything I touched with bleach just in case. She gave me to understand that she thought this was a load of nonsense.

From the bedroom window I watched her go into the garden and return with a basket of roots and leaves. There were sounds of chopping and pounding in the kitchen and the blender whirred. Then began a regular procession of cups, glasses and bowls of Balinese traditional medicines, lovingly prepared with herbs from my own garden.

First was the jamu, a tangy concoction of juiced turmeric root, honey and lime juice. Turmeric has been scientifically proven to be such a potent natural antiseptic and antibiotic that one American pharmaceutical company tried to patent it. I began to consume it in quantity. Next came a traditional boreh. Wayan pronounced me hot and produced a small blunt root. "Kencur," she announced. "Very expensive." Luckily we had it growing wild in the yard. She pounded it in the mortar with raw red rice, red onions and a little water, then plastered my face, chest, throat and legs with it. The boreh felt cold going on, then began to burn intensely as it dried. Only when it was completely dry and flaking off was I allowed to shower. Oddly, I did feel better after that.

The bubur she made for me was dynamite in a bowl. The thick soup was brewed from chicken, red rice, vegetables, the leaves of a variety of cinnamon tree which I didn't even know I had in the garden and lashings of garlic, ginger and chilies. By the time I finished the first bowl my sinuses were completely clear and stayed that way for hours. After the coughing started she made up an odd green drink from the leaves of the areca palm, which seemed to relax my chest.

Days passed as I drifted in and out of deep, strange sleeps, rubbed joints that ached abominably and sneezed my way through a box of tissues a day. Every time I woke up there was a bowl of steaming soup or a glass of jamu by my bed. Friends kept phoning to ask if they could bring me anything but it was a full time job just keeping up with the herbs.

In moments of lucidity I contrasted all this with the kind of care I might receive as a suspected SARS case hospitalized in Singapore or Hong Kong. There would be needles, IV drips, masks on every face. A cold room without a view, fluorescent lights. No freshly made jamu, no messy boreh. No herbs plucked from the garden to make medicines and soups just for me. No birdsong at my unglazed window. No prayers, no holy water. No dogs under the bed....

A week has passed. I have a pesky cough and don't have much energy but the worst is over. Perhaps it was SARS, perhaps it was a less exotic bug. Anyway, I feel better now. And I feel blessed.

A Dog Too Far

I never had a dog until I came to Bali. Now I would never be without one again. Or two. Or three…

The latest was Chloe, a little Bali mongrel who was abandoned on the street. Some people in Bali find female puppies inconvenient because they get pregnant later, and are therefore expendable. The lucky ones are drowned outright, the others starve to death slowly or are hit by cars. A kind foreigner saved this one from a watery death and took her to veterinarian Madé Restiati in Canggu, who gained major karma points by caring for her until a home could be found. Mine.

I never planned to have four dogs. Even I know that's a handful. My staff had recently lost a puppy and they were looking for a replacement—male of course. I had persuaded them to make a home for this one on condition I paid for neutering it. However, I'd misunderstood the message about this foundling and thought she was an adult dog. When we arrived at the clinic one hot Saturday afternoon a small pack of dogs raced to meet us. Which was the adoptee? When Wayan Manis and

Nyoman saw that it was the tiny, nervous puppy with the huge ears—a female and not even pretty—they rolled their eyes and indicated that they would hold out for a Kintamani with a bushy tail, thanks all the same. Male, yes.

What to do? The kennel maids had made a pet of the puppy, and she snuggled contentedly into my lap. She was small, edgy and insecure. We'd come a long, hot way from Ubud (I have become very parochial). She seemed to sense I was vacillating and a rough little tongue darted out and painted my arm tentatively.

What the hell. I had a big fenced garden, staff, three dogs already, a book on canine psychology... there was plenty of food and love for this little scrap. I bought her a cheerful yellow collar, she was given her first injection and we made our way back up the mountain.

The pack dynamic shifted as soon as I carried Chloe through the gate. Kasey was wild about her from the beginning—finally, a playmate even younger than he was. This must have been heaven after Kalypso's cool, slightly depressing dignity. Chloe instantly became his personal pet to be chased, chewed, bullied and bounced on. Kalypso was disgusted. She'd barely gotten used to the nuisance of Kasey, and now here was another damned puppy. Crossing her white gloves primly, she turned her back, laid down on the cool tile and ignored the newcomer. Daisy the dachshund didn't care either way.

Chloe was a real Bali dog—passionately affectionate, completely omnivorous and very vocal. She was compact and wiry, with huge ears over a bony face, looking rather like a science experiment that went wrong somewhere between a kangaroo and a sheep.

Dogs are mercilessly hierarchical. Chloe was, of course, the lowest dog on the totem pole here (smallest, newest, youngest, most submissive) which she constantly demonstrated in usual doggy conduct. She approached all of us with a deferential crab-like sideways walk, tail tucked firmly under her belly, and lay down to expose her undercarriage at the least sign of attention. When one of the bigger dogs casually knocked her down she put on the full Drama Queen act, screaming as if she was being slowly disemboweled. With me, alas, respect was demonstrated by 'submissive urination', a documented behavior which was intended to gladden my heart by assuring me that I was Mega Alpha Plus Top Dog.

Kipper used to do this and occasionally Kalypso too, but just a few drops and usually when being scolded. Chloe saved up the whole bladderful until she saw me for the first time in the morning or when I came through the gate during the day. Then she squatted subserviently and let rip. I quickly learned to dash outside and greet the dogs on the lawn at dawn, but she got around that by deferring the honour until I could really appreciate it, usually when some time had passed and I'd gone back inside.

Sometimes this accolade would be delivered on the Persian carpet and I responded with the approved noisy scolding and instant removal to outdoors recommended by the dog training books. I tried to explain to her that it was not appropriate, but she plainly felt it would be beneath my status to offer me a dry greeting. I'd hoped the other dogs would assist with her training but Kalypso just looked deeply offended at the sight of the puddle and Kasey, being a guy, didn't notice until he stepped in it.

After a month with us Chloe had doubled in size. Her confidence had about doubled, too. Sometimes she went off down the river bank all alone, following her nose happily, knowing that there was a safe place to come back to. She was the best guard dog of the lot, her little hackles rising furiously at every visitor long after Daisy, Kalypso and Kasey had made friends with the intruder.

They all hang out together obsessively to make sure that none of them is getting more of my attention than the other. That means four dogs under my office chair, four dogs around my feet at the dining table, four dogs closely underfoot wherever I go in the garden and at least one dog resting its head on my knee when I'm on the loo. It's a bit much, really. I love them all, but I may have gone a dog too far.

Ethical Villas

Bali is a real estate hot spot for the villa culture these days. Land prices are shooting up like bamboo and real estate agents are rubbing their hands together so hard they could start a fire.

How good is all this for Bali? Many of the developments are cookiecutter, off-the-shelf plans without much Balinese character. They run the full range of environmentally sustainable design to who-gives-a-damn extravagance. We assume that environmental safeguards are in place, as they are in our home countries, when we build our dream homes. But sadly, that's not the case. Everyone who builds or buys a house in Bali needs to take responsibility for the social and environmental impacts it will cause. Unfortunately, many people buy or build villas without considering the increasingly rare resources they are thoughtlessly consuming. And a marble-floored palace in the rice field with five air-conditioned bedrooms gives a mixed message to the farmer next door who is struggling to feed his family.

On the other hand, there are ethical designers and builders in Bali who are creating beautiful, sustainable homes which have a minimal impact on the environment.

Anyone who harbours a fantasy about building a house in Bali is encouraged to ponder the following issues:

No agricultural land will be lost when I build/buy my villa.

Is your dream villa beautifully located in the middle of rice fields? That means you've directly contributed to the rapid decrease of Bali's precious and limited agricultural land bank. About 1,000 hectares a year of rice land is lost to development here each year. Yes, there's a law that says you can't do this. No, it's not enforced. The ethical choice is to build on the land at river edges that the Balinese don't use for farming, and which will also safeguard your view. Because if you've chosen to live in the rice fields, in the next few years you can count on someone building their dream home right in front of you.

I will be sensitive to the water issues in my neighbourhood.

Water is the biggest issue in Bali today. There simply isn't enough, and what remains is increasingly polluted. The four crater lakes that provide household water to most of Bali are now also being tapped by developers and desperate farmers; water levels have dropping alarmingly in three of them.

Water tables in the cities are also dropping, because so much of the land is now covered with buildings and roads that rainwater can no longer permeate the ground. Instead, it runs into drains and rivers and then into the sea.

All wells lower the ground water table. If you drill a deep well that taps the same water supply as your neighbours who have shallower wells, they may lose their water supply. A big problem in the coastal areas is that if the fresh water wells take out more than rainfall returns to the ground, then the heavier salt water from the sea will intrude inland and rise into the existing wells. The cancellation of irrigation water brought in from the mountain subaks (rice field irrigation systems) is another problem. "Much of Seminyak has been blocked off in the last few years due to building," notes engineer Nick Lee. "The irrigation water was helping to keep the fresh water table up and hold back the saltwater intrusion. I fully expect our wells in Seminyak to become saline in the next few years."

The water situation on the Bukit is unique. The whole peninsula is formed of very porous limestone starting near the surface and going down to sea level. Nick, who helped conduct a ground water investigation there in the 1980s, found the fresh water table was very far down. "There's only a shallow layer of fresh water (rain water that filters through the limestone) on top of saline water, which will quickly be exhausted if uncontrolled development is allowed," he stated. And guess what?

Australia has a great system of capturing and storing rainwater in underground cisterns; it would make sense to adopt it here; we get plenty of rain in most areas but it is not captured. And desalinization plants the size of domestic refrigerators are now available—a sustainable choice for coastal developments.

My septic tank will have a floor and run through a wastewater garden.

Sewage is a subject not often discussed in the villa set, but it's a growing problem in Bali. Many builders skimp on the important issue of the septic tank, making it too small and/or allowing polluted water to enter the water table. Your septic tank should flow into a simple, inexpensive waste water garden. If you're building on the beach, make sure you know where your effluent is going.

I will not use chemical fertilizers and pesticides in my garden.

All the chemicals you use in your house and garden will eventually leach into the surrounding water table (ending up in your well if you have one) and/or enter the rivers and irrigation systems used by Balinese for bathing.

Dangerous chemicals banned in the west are often sold here, including DDT.

I will recycle as much of my solid waste as possible.

Even the most distracted visitor can't help but notice that Bali has overwhelming solid waste management issues. There are systems in place in the most populated parts of Bali to recycle plastic, paper, glass and metal. The informal bicycle scavengers seen all over Bali provide a valuable service; arrange to leave your recyclables outside the gate for them to take away. EcoBali Recycling (telephone 844-6602)) collects recyclables weekly and delivers hotel and school programs in waste management. Organics can be composted. It's not perfect, but it's the best we have for now.

I will use minimal or recycled wood in my villa.

Wood is one of the hottest political issues in Indonesia today. The country's rapidly disappearing forests are being plundered for this increasingly valuable resource, and trees in national parks and other protected areas are routinely harvested as well. There is practically no legal hardwood left in the country. Kudos to those who are creative enough to use recycled hardwood or treated bamboo, or minimize the amount of wood used in building.

I will be sensitive to the amount of electricity I consume and incorporate solar/alternative power where possible.

Bali is already facing serious power problems. Most of its electricity is imported from Java, which itself is experiencing shortages, and is derived from coal or diesel. The typical Balinese compound, which is these days often home to large extended families, is wired for between 400 and

800 watts of electricity. Villas are often routinely wired for up to 55,000 watts. How would you feel if your kids didn't have enough light to study at night, while the villa down the road is burning tens of thousands of watts to run its air conditioning, garden lights and water features?

I will support sustainable projects in my community.

When a foreigner builds a villa in Bali, the local community seldom benefits. The owner of the land you 'bought' usually runs through the windfall in a year. Locals may or may not be used in the actual building of the villa (Javanese being so much more cost-effective and not having to constantly stop work for ceremonies). If you rent out your villa, the money usually goes overseas. I know of foreigners who make a point of repairing village schools which they then sponsor local children to attend (visit www.ykip.com), subsidize older or handicapped kids in job training (j-mantjika@yahoo.com), sponsor recycling programs (ecobali@yahoo.com), teach English (info@starfishubud.com) and bring craft production or other work to their communities.

So please give a thought to how you can benefit your new community.

The way many of these properties are being sold these days is anything but ethical. I picked up a glossy real estate magazine the other week which featured dozens of pictures of land for sale. Most of the photos were of productive rice fields. And almost all the ads stated that the land was freehold.

There are two serious issues here... the legalities of land ownership and Bali's rapidly diminishing agricultural land bank.

First, let's look at this loaded word freehold. There's no such thing as freehold title as we know it in the west for foreigners in Indonesia. Notary Ibu Rainy Hendriany informed me that under no circumstances can foreigners own property under Hak Milik (Freehold) title in Indonesia.

According to Ibu Rainy, many of these land and villa sales involve the use of 'name-givers' or 'nominees' whereby the freehold land certificate is in the name of the Indonesian nominee instead of the foreign buyer. This is an arrangement that carries risks which will vary according to the full documentation involved and has the potential to create some very unhappy scenarios.

"As the value of property in Bali increases toward international levels and if young Balinese find that they can no longer afford land on their own island, it is possible that legal disputes will become much more widespread than has been the case to date," said Ibu Rainy. "As a general rule, it is not advisable for foreigners to enter into legal disputes in Indonesian courts."

(This is a masterful understatement. It will be a snowy Nyepi indeed when a foreigner wins a land dispute on Bali.)

Then there's the interesting issue of due diligence, which is very complicated in Bali due to the custom of multiple children inheriting land under customary law, usually without a will or any kind of documentation.

Ibu Rainy continues, "In advising clients I often ask if, in their own country, they would entrust the ownership of their house or apartment to someone they did not know and, if not, why would they do so in a country they don't know? I've been amazed by how easily normally rational people—who would be very careful about buying a used car in their own country—can commit to a substantial real estate transaction in Bali without having a true understanding of the facts." Quite.

My own experience after two decades of living and working in Southeast Asia is that a contract is just about as good as your relationship with your Asian partner or landlord.

So foreigners cannot own a piece of Paradise, period. Nor should we. The Balinese benefit very little from losing their land. Middlemen pressure farmers into selling their land, then they resell it to foreigners at a huge profit. Most land deals leave only a few of those big bucks in Bali; the bulk of the money goes to Jakarta or overseas. According to an editorial in the Bali Post back in February 2005, about 85% of the substantial amount of money invested in the island's tourism industry is in the control of non-Balinese investors.

High real estate prices are very tempting to Bali's poor farmers. But what could be sadder than a farmer selling the family's rice fields because his son wants to buy a car or motorcycle? The vehicles will be history within a few years, the money will be long spent and the land gone forever. Spiraling land costs are also creating new social problems. Consider the anger and resentment generated at a local level when huge amounts of money change hands in poor communities. The Balinese don't even benefit much from increased employment opportunities. Labourers from Java and Lombok are cheaper during the construction phase. Once completed, most villas employ just a few staff and some villa complexes actually hire maids from Java.

And consider this. Every year, Bali's agricultural land bank is reduced by up to 1,000 hectares—lost to strip malls, tourism projects and villas, mostly owned by non-Balinese and with profits going offshore. Common sense suggests that it's a bad idea to take farmland out of production on a small, agriculture-based island in a country where food security is an urgent matter. Let me rephrase that. It's not just a bad idea. It's insane.

Then we have the issue of aesthetics. No one sets out with the intention of turning a beautiful vista of rice fields into a suburb, but has anyone seen Penestanan lately? And just what is a villa, actually?

Let's not be so pretentious, please. Most so-called 'villas' are very ordinary houses or townhouses of generic design, many shoddily built, and with electrical wiring that will literally make your hair stand on end. And do they have to be so ugly?

Bali is beautiful, magical—and finite. Every year more of that beauty and magic—the reason you came here in the first place—is buried under concrete. If you must build, please do so on the Bukit, where there is little agricultural land, or on the beaches, riversides and other land that the Balinese don't use. And don't expect to own an asset to hand down to your children. "This villa situation is like a trailer park," mused a visiting friend who is very savvy about real estate. "You might own the trailer, but you just rent the pad."

Gamelan Nights

Love it or hate it, nothing is as evocative of Bali as the gamelan. And there is nothing so maddening, humbling and entertaining as learning to play in one.

My musical career began and abruptly ended many decades ago, when our Grade Five class was studying the recorder. I couldn't learn to read music and memorized the first two bars of the 'The Old French Song' by playing it so often that my poor father bricked my instrument into the basement wall one night when I was in bed. He still talks about it. I quit piano lessons after the first week because I couldn't make the connection between the squiggles on the score and what my hands were supposed to be doing. The sight of a piano keyboard still makes me apprehensive.

But the gamelan seemed less structured, somehow. The players at performances seemed to spend a lot of time drinking tea, smoking cigarettes and cheerfully telling each other lies. So I decided to join the Ubud women's gamelan group at the end of 2002. I'd done my homework—nearly all the instruments were percussion and none of them had more than 10 keys. Small boys could do it. How hard could this be? Well, harder then I thought.

We were 25 women, about half from Bali and Java and the rest from North and South America, Europe and the Middle East. Our ages spanned half a century. Pak Gus and Pak Madé had been engaged to teach us, which they did by simply playing the same music over and over many times a night. We sat staring glazedly at them as we hammered away, trying to interpret the apparently random shrugs, scowls and twitches which they used to direct us.

To the Western mind, which expects to learn new subjects intellectually, this was maddening. There were no diagrams, explanations, demonstrations or written music. The few women who had a clue what they were doing just played doggedly on, and the rest of us struggled to follow. Eventually, numbered labels were stuck to the bronze keys and some of us started to scribble scores in the vein of 141414125224. This helped quite a lot. So did the beer which was consumed in quantity by the foreigners during each practice.

A gamelan has several types of instruments. Most of them have between four and ten bronze keys and play the melody, harmony and background bongs. They are played by hitting the keys with a little hammer, then pinching off the sound as you go on to the next key. This can get quite complicated when the tempo increases.

A placid grandmother sits between two big gongs and whacks them at intervals. Then there is the fiendishly difficult reyong, a series of graduated fixed gongs which are played bonkbonkbonk or bonkbonk bonkbonk or bonk bonk bonkbonk depending on the melody and the players' state of confusion. The reyong players, my Wayan Manis among them, wear permanent expressions of intense concentration and bewilderment. Finally there are two big drums and a tjeng-tjeng, a carved wooden turtle with 6 upturned cymbals fastened on its back, upon which another 2 cymbals are played.

All these sections play different tunes and tempos at the same time. When played well, they knit together into a harmonious, complex tapestry of sound. When played by us for the first three months, the result was a discordant cacophony that made our teachers wince.

By the time I joined the gamelan, the group had already been together for a couple of months. The only instruments still free were the flute and the tjeng-tjeng. A flute is very much like a recorder, so I sat on the floor to acquaint myself with the turtle. It seemed straightforward enough, and I would be merrily clashing away until Pak Gus started sending me huge black scowls. I had never had any instruction and had no idea what I was doing wrong. Too loud? Not loud enough? Wrong wrist action? But I was left to puzzle it over as he went on to shake three fingers at the reyong or roar "Dah dah DAH DAH!" at the baffled drummers.

I began to enjoy my four hours a week in the crystal cave of harmonics. During the breaks while the teachers smoked, the women showed each other where the music went up and down and how to tell when to stop. I learned when to make crisp little sounds on the tjeng-tjeng and when to really give it the works.

Ours was a very public education, being held at the Pondok Pekak Library in plain sight of bemused tourists and curious Balinese. Laurie's two year old son would caper about trouserless during our practice, occasionally grabbing a pair of drumsticks to show us how it should be done, and politely applauding us at the end of each set.

He was our only fan. We were hopelessly bad. All through December we practiced madly for our first gig, booked at the big temple in Pengosekan for mid-January. Every night more Balinese men appeared to encourage us and help with the tricky bits. We clonked and clashed and bonged determinedly through our two party pieces as the expression on Pak Gus' face grew ever bleaker.

Then one night we got it. Like magic, the music finally entered our energy fields, which is the only way I can describe it, and became part of us. Our hands flew instinctively through the complex rhythms; we grinned and shouted and played on and on. Pak Gus smiled for the first time. The band of watching Balinese men clapped, which they had never done before. At last we were ready for Prime Time.

On the appointed evening we donned, with varying degrees of grace, our uniforms of bright turquoise kebaya and sarong. To those unfamiliar with pakaian adat, or Balinese traditional dress, many Western women find it uncomfortable in the tropical heat. A balcony bra and broad elastic waist cincher form the infrastructure, over which is pulled the tube top, a 'new tradition' reaching from under the arms to the hips. Then the sarong is knotted tightly on, the lace blouse buttoned up and the sash tied. It is all very tight and very hot. I decided to minimize the agony by forgoing the bra on the assumption that the newfangled tube top would hold the fort, so to speak.

Just after dark, we climbed the temple steps for our premier performance. Twenty-five turquoise bottoms perched on tiny wooden stools and 50 nervous hands picked up our hammers, sticks and cymbals in unison under Pak Gus' watchful eye. The drummers tapped our cue, and we began to play.

We played well, and we played for much longer than usual as a modest audience of friends, relatives and Balinese watched us politely. Playing the gamelan can be quite energetic during the fast parts and requires both hands, constantly. Halfway through the second piece, my tube top drifted from its moorings. Suzan's nose began to run. Beth got a bug in her kebaya. Like true professionals we soldiered on with bland smiles, concealing our misadventures from the spectators whose eyes, fortunately, were beginning to glaze over...

Flushed with victory, we returned to our next practice session to find ourselves at the bottom of the learning curve once more. Pak Gus launched us on our third piece of music, without diagrams, explanations, demonstrations or written music.

But we were figuring it out much faster now. After a year of banging the wrong keys, missing cues and watching our teacher sadly put his head in his hands at the end of practice, our women's gamelan group was finally getting it. We were actually pretty good. Things became easier once we foreigners stopped trying to learn the music intellectually. There is no conscious, cerebral path to playing the gamelan. You just practice and practice until the music becomes part of your cell structure, a component of your energy field. It has nothing to do with your brain. Maybe that's why we Westerners, most of whom had never done anything musical, enjoyed it so much.

Now that we were performing professionally (ahem), we donned our uniform of sarong and lace kebaya about once a month. We foreigners become quite expert at dressing ourselves, although our Balinese colleagues generally gave us a few tweaks before we piled into borrowed vans and headed off into the unknown.

I don't know who organized our performances. We played in little family temples, in huge, awesomely decorated ones, in the mountains and in a factory courtyard. We played at the local police station and were booked for a wedding. It was all enormous fun, and generated a warm feeling of community between the women that transcended religion and ethnicity.

At one ceremony in a village that shall remain unnamed, we filed demurely onto the stage in our tight kebayas and took our places. Immediately we were aware of a very adjacent pigsty, complete with flies and interesting smells; in fact it seemed to be located directly behind the woven bamboo wall to the rear of the makeshift stage. The assembled throng stared at us expectantly. At that time, older Balinese were astonished to find Western women playing the gamelan. As I lifted the cymbals of the tjeng tjeng, I noticed that my sarong was already dotted with flies. The drummer tapped our cue and we began to play.

Legions of small, determined flies instantly gathered around us. Soon we were vigorously shaking our heads to get them out of our ears and noses (it seemed strategic to keep our mouths firmly closed). They strolled across our foreheads and tap-danced along the backs of our hands as we played. For some reason they were particularly attracted to the harmonics of the tjeng-tjeng and landed on it as if drawn by an irresistible force. Inevitably some were caught in the flying cymbals, and a little pile of bodies began to collect in the upturned cymbals attached to my instrument, bouncing with each clash. It was quite mesmerizing.

I was trying hard to behave myself but the torment of all those tiny feet was impossible to ignore. Every woman in the gamelan was twitching wildly and shaking her head to dislodge the flies, since it was impossible to remove our hands from our instruments. Our audience watched impassively. Apparently all the flies were on the stage with us.

We took a brief break after the first set to compare casualties. I helped Iluh remove a bug from her eye; Wayan Manis had one in her ear. Several of us had numerous visitors in our cleavages which were difficult to remove unobtrusively. Then during the second set, a large cockroach made its way determinedly across the stage heading directly for me. A bystander tried to head it off, but it veered quickly under my instrument, only to abandon its position after a particularly energetic riff. Our teacher smacked it to oblivion with a packet of clove cigarettes, and it joined a growing number of dead and dying flies on the frayed red carpet around us. I think we played pretty well, considering the distractions.

The performance ended with the usual snack, traditionally offered to performers to refresh them after their exertions. These cardboard boxes invariably contained a piece of fruit, a mound of cold rice and half a hard boiled egg, some noodles with vegetables, a splash of incendiary sambal (hot sauce) and some kind of meat. On lucky nights it was a savoury morsel of fried chicken. That night it was little glands on a stick.

Playing in the gamelan gave me a new identity in my own neighbourhood. Once the big temple near my house had a major ceremony. Clad in full temple dress, I inched my battered car through a seething crowd of worshippers to the end of the jammed lane, where I was ordered to turn back. Then a neighbour recognized me and asked where I was going. I told him I was playing gamelan at a ceremony in Gianyar. Broad smiles appeared, and a path was made for me through the crush of people and vehicles. I notice that more men nod and smile at me now when I pass them at the temple.

That particular gig took us well beyond Gianyar to a village whose name I never learned. We were shown to a very small stage inside the temple itself and crammed ourselves onto tiny stools or minute patches of carpet. With the first two bars it became agonizingly clear that the gamelan was tragically out of tune. We clashed on through our party pieces while toothless old men stared at us unblinkingly. Then a squadron of lovely children, dressed for the dance, filed in to pray. When they filed out again our whole audience followed them. Philosophically we played our last piece to an empty house, and were rewarded with an unusually savoury snack.

As I drove home that night through the moonlit rice fields with my little car full of joking Balinese, I realized that playing the gamelan is not just about making music together. It's about sharing the experience, sharing food, taking bugs out of each other's eyes, making sure one another's sashes are on straight. Being a community within a community as we make music for the gods.

Being Ibu

I didn't even know what an Ibu was, until I became one pretty much overnight. Ibu means Mother, and is the honorific used for any mature women in Indonesia. Being Ibu was rife with delights and responsibilities. As Ibu, I was the boss of my household. Having full time staff was both terrific (I hated housework) and daunting in terms of cultural chasms. Wayan Manis was competent, helpful and had a great sense of humour. It wasn't long before I was casting spells to ensure that she would stay with me forever. Fortunately she felt the same about me.

Learning to manage the woman who was now managing my house was a delicate dance in the early days. I didn't speak much Indonesian. She didn't speak much English. I was constantly seeking the balance about what needed monitoring and what didn't. Reluctant to be a micromanager (it was not my nature anyway), I was constantly hearing stories about staff cooking the housekeeping books. Wayan kept meticulous records about the housekeeping money I gave her, but I didn't like to check them in case she felt I thought she was being dishonest. When

I finally did get around to it, I found that she had indeed been cooking the books. She'd been making up the housekeeping with her own money each month because I wasn't giving her enough. We got that straightened out, and I checked the book regularly after that. But it was years before she would tell me when she was running low on housekeeping money.

The second year I was in Bali, I built a house. After that Nyoman, Wayan's husband, came to work full time as a gardener, driver and handyman. This was indeed heaven, but doubled the responsibility of ensuring that everyone knew what they were supposed to be doing, and doing it the way I wanted it done—often two very different things. Fortunately, both Wayan and Nyoman are sweet-natured, competent and honest, so I'm happy to be a hands-off Ibu. After ten years of living in Bali, I'm profoundly grateful for my luck in having them in my life. Through them, I've learned so much about Bali, the Balinese and myself.

We've morphed into a kind of family now. I look forward to seeing their cheerful faces in the morning, but they respect my space. When they come to work and sit down at the table instead getting straight to their tasks, I know a meeting has been called. Sometimes this is for input on household decisions, or requesting a soft loan for a motorbike or an advance for an upcoming ceremony. I make cameo appearances at family weddings, funerals and children's dance performances in their village. They come in on their day off if I'm sick, and have been known to drive the 15 minutes from their village at 10 o'clock at night to open my front gate when I'd locked myself out, laughing merrily.

Every year before I depart on my trip to Canada, Wayan makes a special offering and we all pray in front of the temple in the garden for my safe return. Wayan sprinkles holy water over me from my grandmother's silver-plated milk jug. This seems normal to me now.

Being Ibu doesn't necessarily mean I'm consulted on all the decisions, however. I'll be asked what colour to paint the garden shed, but not on the placement of a picture on the wall. It's important to make sure Nyoman's job list is long enough, because he's so industrious he'll find himself something to do that may never have occurred to me, like digging a new pond in the front garden when I'm out for lunch. When they thought there were too many green pit vipers in the garden, I was gently informed that they weren't happy about my unglazed windows, and stapled mosquito netting over every window in the house. This didn't seem to be optional, and I'm now quite glad they did. I'm right on the edge of the jungle and there's a lot of wildlife out there.

Being Ibu means I must be rich because I built a house in Bali, hire them to look after me and have a computer, all with no visible means of support. It's entirely outside their ken how this can be possible when I have never been married. Having no children is also very odd, tragic even. So why am I so happy?

Kasey and the River People

When I started to build a house on this little piece of Bali, my contractor stood at the edge of the precipitous riverbank and said, "It's a long way down." It was impossible to see the river through the jungle and I could only hear it, faintly, after a heavy rain. When they began to build the house, the workers needed to drop thirty metres of pipe down the cliff face to reach the water.

Wayan Manis has told me about the ghostly River People who live in the deep river gorges. The Balinese sometimes see them when they go to bathe, and strike up conversations with what seems to be a perfectly ordinary person... until he shimmers into smoke and disappears. The River People are generally friendly and sociable, but have been known to become angry when people throw rubbish down the riverbanks. Then they will drag the polluter down, sometimes to his death.

According to Wayan, the River People live parallel lives to the Balinese. They wear the same clothes, bathe in the river and keep chickens and dogs. Sometimes they visit nearby compounds where certain people can see them. They're not fearsome, says Wayan, but she would rather not see one herself. You never know.

Oblivious to our unseen neighbours, the dogs happily occupied themselves in the garden chasing chickens and digging up rare vegetables, but never ventured down the riverbank. Then in the middle of September, Kasey began to visit the River People. Never one to miss a meal, he failed to turn up with the others at dinner time one night. After dark he bounced excitedly into my office, his short legs thick with mud that could only have come from the river. As I scrubbed him clean, I warned him of the dangers of the undercliff. But Kasey was a young dog of considerable character, charm and willfulness. Very much like a teenage boy, in fact. He brushed my advice aside with a flick of his silky ears.

A few evenings later, he disappeared down the riverbank just before dark. Between his excited yelps I could hear the furious shriek of a musang, a mongoose-like creature that lived in the undercliff. Kasey loved a chase and had evidently followed his prey down the bank. When it was time for bed the other dogs filed into the house and settled on their cushions around the bedroom wall, but Kasey's remained empty. I could hear him making unhappy noises in the distance.

It was beginning to rain a little as I set out for the end of the garden with a torch. The cliff edge was treacherous with fallen bamboo leaves and I couldn't approach too closely. Even in daylight it's impossible to see very far down, and the futile torch beam revealed only shadows of denser shadows. There was nothing to be done but go to bed and organize a search party in the morning. I slept fitfully, though, disturbed by dreams of broken legs and snake bite and the long drop to the river. Kasey cried all night.

For five months Kasey had lived in that garden and had never shown any interest in the steep riverbank. It was as if the River People had enchanted him, luring him away from safety like unseen Pied Pipers to the dangerous phantom world of the undercliff.

At first light I was back at the cliff top. I could hear Kasey's plaintive yelps far below. He sounded frightened. Pacing the edge of the bank, I called down to him, which only made him cry harder.

I phoned my trusty staff.

"Kasey has been down in the river all night," I reported, not knowing the word for cliff.

"Aduh! Did he fall?" "Maybe. He can't get back."

"Just wait, Ibu, we're coming."

They roared up on their motorcycle 20 minutes later. Nyoman donned his Wellington boots and cast about the edge for a suitable point of descent from a neighbour's yard. Wayan Manis made her special Missing Dog offering, then hung over the cliff edge clinging to a bamboo and calling out at intervals. Suddenly there was an answering shout from the river and a rapid exchange of Balinese. A bather had spotted fifteen kilograms of wet, traumatized dog on a small outcrop high above the river.

I don't know how Nyoman reached him. It was quite awhile before he staggered back into our garden with Kasey collapsed around his neck. While Wayan revived Nyoman with a cup of tea, I ministered to the dog. He wasn't physically hurt, but very wet, shocked and dirty. He slumbered close to me all day, whimpering a little with bad dreams and only moving when I did.

He was a smart guy, so I figured he'd learned his lesson. But the next day I heard all four dogs baying down a different part of the bank. This time we could see the vegetation waving at the very edge of the thirty-metre drop to the river.

Nyoman and I went down after them. It was horribly steep and there was very little to hang on to. Tapioca stems snapped off in my hand as I skidded down to land on one narrow ledge after another, then inch along them clinging to whatever vegetation was there. Finally I made my way to where I could see the dogs, scrambling and leaping perilously close to the edge.

They were on the hunt, and they flushed their prey as I watched. A young monitor lizard lumbered toward me in a panic through the brush. At first I thought it hadn't seen me, then realized it had nowhere else to flee but right across my feet, which it did, followed by four baying dogs who paid no attention to me whatever. It was as if they were bewitched. They didn't return home for hours, then dropped down to sleep as if drugged.

The next morning was a radiant Sunday. I was working in the garden when Daisy went down the bank again after some unseen creature with Kasey in hot pursuit. Almost immediately I heard the unmistakable sound of his heavy form crashing through the undergrowth at the cliff edge. I knew at once that he had gone over. Except for Daisy's excited barking, there was ominous silence.

It was like déjà vu to watch Nyoman stagger into the garden again under Kasey's weight—but this time the dear golden head swung loosely from a broken neck.

We buried him in the garden, under flowering shrubs and climbing roses. Nyoman dug a deep grave while Wayan made offerings and I sat weeping on the grass.

"He's gone to the River People," Wayan comforted me later as she brought a cup of tea. "He was special. They wanted him."

But he hasn't really left. I can still see him sprawled on the patio gazing out over the jungle with his intelligent brown eyes, or under my desk with his head pillowed on his paws. I sense him near my bed at night in his usual place. Wayan reports dreams of seeing us together in the garden. Perhaps he did visit the River People when he lived with me. And now that he's gone to them, he comes back to keep me company.

He was a fine dog. He still is.

Two Naked Men in a Ditch

Although I've lived in Asia for many years, I never had the chance to study rural plumbing until coming to live in Ubud. Opportunities are numerous now, as so much ablution is public.

In rural Bali, where many people don't have bathrooms, it's a popular custom to use the rivers and irrigation ditches to bathe and wash clothes. Public nudity is unacceptable, but everyone maintains the polite fiction that people are technically invisible when bathing in the open. In villages where the ditch doubles as the bath house, men will sometimes bathe on one side of the road and women on the other. Usually young women will keep their underwear on, but often the old ladies will strip right down. It's not uncommon to be driving along a country lane as a naked man casually emerges from a ditch or under a bridge, wrapping on a sarong.

I was coming home from a friend's house one evening, just after dark. Using my torch, I picked my way carefully along the concrete path beside a big ditch that irrigated the rice fields nearby. I was just a few feet from my car when I realized that two naked men were sitting in the ditch right beside the door on the driver's side, casually chatting and smoking.

This was a dilemma. Not knowing the protocol for closely approaching two naked men in a ditch, I opted for discretion. I politely alerted them to my presence, switched off my torch and averted my eyes while fumbling to unlock the door in the dark, balanced precariously on the bank. They sat very still, busily being invisible. I got into the car and drove a short distance with the lights out to preserve their privacy. In my rear view mirror I saw their shadows climb slowly out onto the grass and reach for their clothes.

Two days later I was visiting someone up in another neighbourhood. There was a row of residences between the road and the rice fields, with an irrigation ditch running between them. As I turned the corner, there sat a naked man in the ditch. It was high noon, and he sat there soaping himself with great dignity as people passed, stepping around his shampoo bottle on the sidewalk. No one looked at him and he looked at no one.

I mentioned this to Annette who lived nearby. "I've seen all kinds of things in that ditch," she told me. "When they slaughter a pig, they wash the intestines there. People bathe in it, wash their plates and toss their litter." It was also a favourite haunt of an old lady who was, to be polite, losing the plot. She roamed the neighbourhood filching bags of rubbish that people had left out for collection, then she'd head for the ditch, remove all her clothing and climb in with her treasures. Annette told me she would spend the morning sorting through the rubbish, washing and organizing it meticulously according to category. All the chicken bones went into one pile, the empty noodle packets in another... then she would carefully put everything into plastic bags and take it all home.

Pak Mangku, from whom I contracted the land for my house, had no bathroom. His modest compound had a loo of sorts, but the only running water came from a standpipe in the courtyard. Because the town pumped water only a few times a week and he had no storage tank, his household often had no water at all. During the months I was building my house, he'd stroll down the lane past the construction site each evening with his soap and toothbrush in a little plastic pot, on his way to the river to bathe. This involved a dangerous climb down steep, slippery stone steps, and Pak Mangku was no spring chicken.

I built a water tower at the border of our properties, with a large tank and a network of pipes and valves to ensure that both our residences would have plenty of water. I looked forward to the day that Pak Mangku didn't have to walk all the way to the river for his daily bath. Having handed him a large whack of cash for a 20 year land contract, I expected that he'd take advantage of his new free, constant water supply to construct a bathroom.

But it didn't happen. Eventually a very small cistern appeared in the middle of the courtyard, but that was all. Pak Mangku still walked cheerfully to the river every evening with his soap and toothbrush. I asked Wayan Manis why this was, and she looked surprised. "His friends are there; it's more fun to bathe with other people," she explained. She preferred it herself. I'd missed the point.

In warm climates and cultures that are deeply social, the public water supply has been a traditional meeting place. The pragmatic Balinese take this a step further by taking off their clothes and jumping in. I thought about the congenial groups of women I'd watched bathing and washing their clothes in roadside ditches, splashing the children and screaming with laughter over a bawdy joke. Bathing together is a chance to meet, to hang out and gossip. Yet Balinese women consider the bikini top and tiny pair of shorts that some western women wear around Ubud unacceptably immodest.

The chilly climate of northern Europe, where our own culture evolved, discouraged roadside ablutions. So did the early Christian disapproval of nudity. As a result, we still close ourselves into a small room to bathe alone. Ironically, the northern Europeans are now more comfortable with nudity than North Americans, who can be quite prim. While enjoying a massage at a local spa, I've sometimes heard a male voice in the next cubicle raised in some distress when requested to remove his knickers. Yet this same man will wander shirtless through the shops and into restaurants, which the Balinese find rather improper.

They really must think us very odd.

The Sound of Silence

Robin sat bolt upright in bed in the dark. "Doesn't the damned noise ever stop?" she wailed.

I woke from a sound sleep and gazed across the room at her in puzzlement. We were staying in a comfortable guesthouse on the estate of Thai friends north of Chiang Mai. The secluded property had been landscaped into a huge park and we were the only guests. "What noise?" I asked.

The overhead light went on with a snap. My sister gestured indignantly. "All that noise! It hasn't stopped since we went to bed."

I came into focus. The dogs were barking down by the pond. A couple of testosterone-driven roosters were facing off on the patio downstairs. A radio blared in the staff quarters across the grounds. The night watchmen were gossiping by the gate. In the distance a loudspeaker tolled the merits of the local political candidate. The usual orchestra of lizards, bats and other night creatures patched the holes in the fabric of background noise. I hadn't heard any of it.

Robin lives on a remote homestead in British Columbia where the sound of a single cricket in the night is enough to wake her. She, like so many others, come to the Asian countryside with the romantic expectation that it would be quiet and peaceful. Big mistake. After two decades of living and traveling in Southeast Asia, I think it must be the noisiest region on earth. You quickly learn to tune it out or you keep traveling till you get to somewhere really quiet, like the Australian outback.

Unlike the dour north European stock from which so many of us spring, the Asian in general is neither quiet nor solitary by nature. In Bali, no one lives alone if they can avoid it. And being with others means conversation, laughter, cockfights, cooking, radios and the other noisy adhesives of Asian society. Noise is reassuring.

Bali is not quiet, as any traveler here soon learns. There's a trick to letting the chaos knit itself into a complex curtain of white noise that you can push aside at will. In my town of Ubud there is traffic noise, the honking of horns and, increasingly, the roar of outsized tour buses. The ubiquitous motorcycles tear up the air day and night. A tapestry of bells, gamelan and chanting weaves its way through the intermittent baying of dogs. Wherever water gathers, there is soon a quorum of noisy frogs. Roosters play a special role in the daily cacophony. I stopped hearing them long ago, but some of my houseguests never learn to tune them out.

Graeme lives in the rice fields above Campuan in a compound guarded by a local dog he rescued from starvation and abuse. Petal demonstrates her gratitude by barking at intruders, as one expects a responsible dog to do. One day the furious face of a new neighbour appeared at the gate. She had come to Bali to write a book, she announced, and couldn't work for the noise of his barking dog and the landlord's roosters. Oh dear. It's either going to be a very short book or it will have to be written in a diving bell off Ulu Watu.

The background noise is so constant that only during the silence of Nyepi, Bali's annual day of stillness, can you hear creatures whose subtle sounds are usually lost to us. If you sit very quietly in the garden on Nyepi you'll hear the grass move as a skink slinks through it, the whisper of dragonfly wings near your hair, the drone of a giant bee hovering in the vines. You can hear what is really going on at ground level. Without traffic and the sound of human voices, the volume of birdsong seems amazingly loud.

The same travelers who complain about noise in Bali put considerable energy into tracking down the perfect guesthouse way out in the rice fields, far from the disturbance of traffic and other tourists. Then they turn on their iPods and add their own dimension to the curtain of background noise from the cows, chickens and ducks.

To me, Ubud is a haven of peace compared to Denpasar. But even the decibels of Denpasar seem reasonable compared to those of Singapore. This is a city where you can get into trouble for tossing a tissue on the sidewalk; that is recognized as pollution. But your high-rise neighbour downstairs may jackhammer the tile from his floors with complete impunity until the fillings are shaken out of your teeth, as long as he stops at five pm sharp. The concept of noise pollution is in its infancy. It's not unusual to flee an apartment made hellish by jackhammers a few feet away only to find the same thing going on in the street, with pile drivers banging into the ground in the next block. Roosters and temple bells seem very acceptable in comparison.

Robin continued to complain about the noise in Thailand for the two weeks we were there. Finally we made our way south by rail from Chiang Mai. About midnight the train paused by a tiny station, its unlit platform deserted. Behind the station a radio played from a parked car, keeping the lonely night at bay in its halo of sound for the slumbering driver. Robin glared at me accusingly. "It's company for him;" I apologized. Maybe I've been in Asia too long...

She still doesn't understand why, when I stay at her house in British Columbia, I can't sleep for the dense silence of the forest.

The Septic Tank Chronicles

I led a very sheltered life before I moved to Bali. I knew what a septic tank was in theory but had never had closer acquaintance with one other than making regular donations. Moving into a badly built and maintained cottage was a crash course in plumbing, electrical wiring and leaky roofs. My first introduction to the septic tank was the realization that there was something very wrong with it. Following my nose to the wall behind the bathroom, it was immediately clear even to a novice like myself that the damn thing was overflowing. My landlord summoned a truck with a long hose that pumped out the tank the same day. This was another revelation. I hadn't really focused on the fact that there was a whole subculture around building and emptying septic tanks. And where was the truck going to discharge its pungent cargo? Was there a sludge subculture in Bali as well?

When it came time to build my house, I'd done some research. I knew I wanted a wastewater garden that would purify the overflow from the septic tank. My contractor was a civil engineer and believed in doing things right. Two men measured out and began to excavate a huge hole behind the bathroom wall. A truck full of steel rods, sand and cement unloaded nearby. The two men dug deeper and deeper, and another shoveled the piles of dirt into a wheelbarrow and trundled it away. A crowd of neighbours gathered as the excavators disappeared into the hole that was now deeper than they were tall. They had never seen anything like it. Later Wayan Manis reported that they couldn't decide whether it was a swimming pool or a fish pond, but thought I had placed it in a pretty eccentric location.

When the hole was nearly three meters long, one and a half meters wide and two meters deep, the workmen lined it with reinforced concrete and separated it into chambers. The neighbours returned for another look, really puzzled now. Septic tanks in Ubud are a fairly new concept, and this one had three rooms and a floor.

It takes a very long time for a single woman to fill a large septic tank, no matter how regular her habits. I was under some pressure to do so, because until it was full enough to overflow I wouldn't be able to plant the wastewater garden. I gave a lot of dinner parties and encouraged visitors to drink plenty of beer and tea. The staff toilet also fed into the septic tank, but because Nyoman and Wayan Manis didn't start work until mid-morning, I suspected they were making their major donations at home. At that time I did not have the language skills to renegotiate this arrangement.

Some months later, Nyoman reported that the wastewater garden was ready to plant. We filled it with lilies and giant yams and bananas and papyrus and it soon became a vibrant green jungle. All went well for several years. The bacteria in the septic water was consumed by the plants and colonies of organisms that lived on the gravel. There was no overflow, no smell, no problems at all. Ecowarriors from around the world came to admire it.

But a few years later I suspected that there was trouble in Paradise. Alerted by a certain aroma behind the bathroom wall I prowled around wondering what could possibly have gone wrong with my big, strong septic tank that was built to last a hundred years. Then the plants in the wastewater garden started to look peaked and eventually died. Nyoman dug around a little and reported that it was dry as far down as he could push his stick. We wrestled open the port hole over the final chamber of the septic tank and saw that the level of the contents was well below the outlet pipe that led to the waste water garden.

This was a blow. Obviously there was a leak. How did one repair a septic tank? And how did one cope without a bathroom in the meantime? I pored over my old copy of the Humanure Handbook and wondered where to site a composting toilet in the garden while repairs were effected. Mercifully, it didn't come to that. The contractor returned to have a look, and pointed out that the weight of the huge rainwater tank on top of the septic tank had probably compromised the integrity of its walls or floor. It's important that a septic tank have integrity, it seems. Pak Priyo's solution was simple—build a new septic tank next to the old one. I put the Humanure handbook back on the shelf with some relief.

Two of the same workmen who had helped build my house five years before arrived at the gate and began to dig. Big piles of earth appeared around the garden as if monster gophers had invaded. The hole was not as big as the first one—Pak Priyo explained kindly that my household was not generating enough raw material to justify the larger size. I tried not to feel inadequate.

But 1.5 meters is a very deep hole. One night as I was sitting over dinner with a friend I heard a puzzled yelp from behind the house. Daisy's vocalizations are expressive, and I didn't like the muffled sound of this one. Grabbing a torch, we picked our way through the mud and piles of earth to shine the beam into the hole. Sure enough, Daisy's big brown eyes stared up at us from far below.

It was a long drop for a miniature dachshund, but Daisy has as many lives as six cats. She's survived an encounter with a green pit viper, three falls into the pond and many heroic leaps from the ironing board.

When Rehane eventually hauled her out of the pit, her only injury was found to be to her dignity.

The contractor designed this new septic tank to sit slightly below ground level so that it can be covered with soil and grass. I'm grateful for this refinement. It allows me to discreetly conceal the fact that I have not just one huge septic tank, but two (one with integrity). I'd like to think the chronicle is over, but a friend came by recently for a look and asked thoughtfully, "Don't they explode if there isn't a vent?"

There isn't a vent...

Roots

My grandmothers were both adventurous women, traveling far from their birthplaces to put down roots in distant lands. Hazel left New Brunswick on the east coast of Canada to cross the continent as a young woman early in the twentieth century. I have a picture of her standing in a logging camp on the coast of British Columbia in her long skirts, with giant fir trees towering around her. She found her husband in this wild land, and although they sometimes lived in cities they were happiest with plenty of space around them.

When I was young they had a small farm where I spent every holiday (in retrospect this was not so much a treat for me as a reprieve for my exhausted parents). The farm was a little universe with its own meadow, forest, orchard, hen house, rabbit house, hay stacks and fields of fruit and vegetables. My grandfather worked his acreage alone and we grandchildren were outside almost every waking minute. I fed rabbits, fetched eggs, picked raspberries, shucked corn and helped preserve berries, tomatoes and beans. There were two stoves in the big kitchen—an old cast iron wood-burning stove and a new electric one. Hazel preferred the wood stove and only resorted to the newfangled one when the whole extended family came for dinner.

Except in summer, the fire in the wood stove never went out. On chilly mornings the big kitchen was always warm, and once in a while during Easter holidays I would wake to find a tiny newborn lamb in a box on the open oven door, keeping warm until my grandfather reunited it with its dam.

Hazel used a heavy black cast-iron skillet at almost every meal, cooking on that wood stove. I remember rabbit stew with baking powder biscuits on top, eggs straight from the henhouse, garden potatoes and onions fried in bacon fat. The skillet was an icon of every memory I carry of those savoury farm meals. When Hazel's cooking days were over I took the precious skillet home. And when I moved to Asia, it was the first thing I packed. Wayan uses it to make wonderful curries, and to roast her mother's fragrant organic coffee.

A few years before Hazel arrived in Vancouver Meg, my other grandmother, set sail from Scotland for the same destination with her new husband. They disembarked at Halifax in 1912, then took the train right across the country. I have a sepia photo of Meg standing with my grandfather dressed very much like Hazel in demure long skirts and a long sleeved blouse with high lace collar. Both my young grandmothers look very pleased with themselves in the photos, as if they were getting away with something—an expression I call 'living without adult supervision'.

The holidays I spent with Meg as a child were very different from life on the farm. She lived in an apartment in the city with thick curtains, carpets and lots of heavy carved furniture. We children were taken for daily walks in the park (twice a day if we were very restless) and served soft-boiled eggs in porcelain egg cups for afternoon tea, with toast soldiers and jam in a cut glass bowl. I remember delicate bone china cups and saucers and a fat embossed silver teapot on the sideboard that was part of a tea service presented to my grandfather in 1947 when he retired from the Canadian Legion.

Packing up after Meg's death, my mother brought home the sterling silver tea service. Besides the teapot there was an elegant coffee pot, a big sugar basin and curvy milk jug. They spent most of the next 30 years carefully swaddled in blue flannel drawstring bags at the back of the sideboard in the dining room. I think I saw that teapot used about five times (we used a brown china pot for every day), when my mother had a special tea party and pulled out all the bone china cake plates, cups and saucers. She would wash and dry the silver pot with great care afterwards, then tuck it back into its blue bag like the family treasure it was.

A few years ago the sterling silver tea service made the long journey to Bali. My mother was clearing the decks and neither of my sisters wanted it. When I opened the blue drawstring bags for the first time at my Bali house, Wayan Manis gasped, "Like a rajah!" She was all for wrapping up the tea service and putting it away again, but I was determined that its time had come at last. It had spent most of the past 60 years in the dark, now it would gleam in the tropical sunshine. I bought a nice tray for it, and use that tea service almost every day. It never seems to need polishing. Another set of old sugar and milk pots in silver plate also made the trip from Canada, and these contain holy water for the daily offerings. They make a nice change from the empty jam jar that once performed this service.

I think my grandmothers would be pleased to see their things here; silver and iron, the precious metal and the practical. They'd appreciate this life of mine, living with my animals by the jungle. Like them, I've put down my roots far from my birthplace. And like them, I often wear the secret smile of someone who is living without adult supervision.

Doberman Lite

She's got the classic lean, mean muzzle, the long body and the distinctive black and tan markings. She has the heart of a lion and the will of an ox, taking no nonsense from anyone. She barks fiercely at strangers as they enter the yard and crashes boldly into the jungle, baying after the hapless creatures of the undercliff. And when there's a noise in the night, she growls most fearsomely deep in her throat.

"I am a huge, slavering Doberman Pincer," she announces, obsidian eyes gleaming dangerously.

"You are a miniature dachshund," I remind her.

Daisy knows this can't be true. She's a dog of considerable character, and isn't about to have her potential compromised by this kind of negative thinking.

Imagine your legs are just 8 cm long and your eyes are 15 cm from the ground. The average human is unimaginably taller than you are. I would certainly think a few times before engaging a monster this size, but Daisy is completely undaunted. "Let me out. Let me in. Lift me onto the chair. No, the other chair. I want to drive the car. Take me for a ride on the motorcycle. I'll have some of that toast, buttered, with a bit of marmalade. What's this nonsense about not feeding dogs from the table? My other person gives me anything I want, and I can sleep in her bed too."

Salena, another Ubud resident who travels a good deal, used to leave Daisy with me for months at a time. ("Is this a dog hotel?" asked Lily.) Daisy was used to sleeping with Salena, in the bed, with her head on the pillow. Call me unreasonable, but I'm not sharing my sleeping space with ticks and other interesting fauna; at my house, Daisy has her own pillow on the floor. She is bitter about this injustice, and often tries to scale the high carved bed when I'm asleep. I hear the determined scrabbling and sometimes catch a glimpse of flying ears. But I resist, imagining the tyrannical "I want up, I want down" demands that would make my nights hell if I ever surrendered.

So she finally established her private bedchamber behind the woven curtain under the bathroom sink where she made a comfortable nest in the towel pile. It can be disconcerting when a long nose emerges inquisitively from the curtains in the dark, especially after one glass of wine too many. Even Wayan, who isn't given to wine, screamed the first time she was goosed by Daisy while cleaning the bathroom.

There is a strict hierarchy in dogdom that dictates who is top canine and who sniffs whose bottom when. As matriarch, Kalypso is entitled to the deference of first sniff. But from the moment she arrived on her orientation visit, Daisy assumed top slot. She growled and barked at poor Kalypso, who was several times her size, as if she was under attack. Interestingly, Bali dogs don't seem to recognize Daisy as being the same species. Kalypso prowled around her politely, then backed away and peered at me in bemusement.

"Is it a dog?"

"Sort of. It's a dachshund." "She has no manners." "That's true."

"What does she think she is, a Doberman?" Honour ruffled, Kalypso knocked her down just to show her who was Alpha Bitch. Enraged, Daisy bounced up and chased poor Kalypso across the garden. Eventually they ironed things out. Daisy lets Kalypso knock her down now and then to assuage her pride, then nips her tail to keep her humble. Kalypso deals with this by pretending there are no dachshunds.

Then Daisy went into heat. She pined noisily for a lover, any lover. At that time I had four dogs but Kasey, the lone male, had been surgically removed from the competition. However a scabby local street dog had taken to broaching my garden walls from time to time just to prove that he could, and Daisy began to pursue him shamelessly. Long before I could hear his brass bell she would look alert, give herself a provocative little shake and scamper outdoors in anticipation. She flung her plump little body at him, embraced him with her forelegs and reached high to lick his neck in a shocking display of wantonness. As I raced across the yard to save her from a fate worse than death, she would be murmuring sweet nothings in his battle-torn ear. "Hey big guy, I'm a virgin. We could have a great time. I have this private little place in the towel cupboard. Let's go, quick!"

The visitor looked puzzled. Scabies: "Is this a dog?" Kalypso: "It's under debate."

Me: "Daisy, you little hussy, get in here this minute!"

Carrying the indignantly resisting little animal into my office, I fired off an email to Salena, who was touring the Himalayan foothills on an Enfield Bullet with only her own hormones to think about. "If you're not back in Bali for Daisy's next heat, I am going to mate her with a miniature poodle and start a race of Doodles", I threatened via hotmail. She doesn't believe I'd do it, but I'm a great believer in hybrid vigour. I think the willful dachshund character would benefit from the addition of tractable poodle blood, but the ears might look odd.

The sex drama passed, but then Daisy began to take an unwholesome interest in birds in general and Pak Mangku's chickens, which roamed my garden, in particular. One morning none of the dogs showed up for breakfast, a very unusual occurrence. I wandered around the garden in search of them, then followed a sinister trail of chicken feathers to the door of the staff bathroom. Little Daisy crouched in the corner behind a dead chicken twice her size, keeping the rest of the dogs at bay, the blood lust of her predatory ancestors burning in her eyes. She reluctantly allowed me to separate her from her prey and I closed the door on it.

"Daisy has killed one of Pak Mangku's chickens," I reported when the staff arrived. I feared that this might be a serious cultural misdemeanor, but they both brightened in gustatory anticipation.

"When, Ibu?"

"Just now..." but they were already gone, following the trail of feathers to a vision of succulent chicken curry.

Pak Mangku's family rarely visits, but that morning his son arrived unannounced at the kitchen door just as Nyoman was settling down to gut and pluck our ill-gotten lunch beside the rain ditch. I greeted Gusti as Nyoman rolled his eyes at me from a few metres behind him, bloody to the elbow. Inviting Gusti deeper into the porch, I engaged him in a long conversation about fruit trees as my staff busied themselves in the yard. When he turned to go, the carcass had been concealed under a cement sack and only a few random feathers remained in the grass. He never noticed a thing. The curry, however, was disappointing.

Daisy has now moved in permanently, and it's getting to be that time again. I've caught her practicing dachshund seduction in quiet corners. Soon the hormones will be raging and she'll be leading unsuitable suitors to her cosy nest in the towel cupboard. Tomorrow I'm going shopping for a poodle.

Rescued Smiles

There's a funky little shop in Ubud. tucked away on Jalan Sri Widari. Customers include Balinese, expats, tourists with dreadlocks, local children, cross-dressers, visiting diplomats and the occasional polite canine. The merchandise is eclectic, changing on a daily basis. There are no discounts and no returns, yet it does a thriving trade.

The Smile Shop was Ubud's (perhaps Bali 's) first thrift shop. The concept has proved wildly popular, drawing regular customers from as far away as Seminyak. Merchandise is gently used or new, and includes clothing, handicrafts, linen, toys and anything else generous donors leave on the doorstep.

The Smile Shop, opened in December 2006, is a project of the Smile Foundation (Yayasan Senyum Bali at www.senyumbali.com), which was founded to help poor Indonesians obtain surgery for facial deformities. Apart from rent, all the income from the Smile Shop goes to projects. Some is spent to meet the expenses of patients and their families who must travel to Denpasar for assessment and surgery, sometimes from other islands. Often the patient (usually a child) lives in a remote village and the family lacks the resources to even transport the patient and caregiver to Denpasar. Sometimes the deformity is so severe that they must travel to Australia for major surgery. The money raised by the Smile Foundation meets costs of transportation, accommodation, food and other needs for these patients. The Yayasan supports a residence (the Smile House) near the hospital in Denpasar where patients and their carers stay before and after surgery. The wages of the Smile House and office staff are all met from Smile Shop earnings. A beautiful new Smile House has recently been acquired and totally renovated for the needs of Smile by a kind and generous donor.

The shop, run by volunteers plus one local staff, is open every day except Monday. About eight five percent of shoppers are Balinese men, women and children looking for a bargain. The Foundation was hoping to raise US$10,000 in its first year, but due to the generosity of donors in Bali and the enthusiastic support of the store's customers, the Smile Shop earned over US$23,000 in the first year of operation and about the same in 2008. As one volunteer noted "Our Balinese customers get a kick out of being waited on by foreigners!"

Donations have included truckloads of new merchandise such as clothing, textiles and handicrafts from shops, boxes of used linen from the Bali Hotels Association and a mercifully endless stream of gently used clothing and household goods from mostly expat households.

Yayasan Senyum Bali was established in 2005 by Mary NorthmoreAziz to serve as a bridge between Sanglah Hospital, the regional public hospital, and the Australian Cranio-Facial Institute in Adelaide. This free-standing unit is one of just two or three in the world. The Institute is headed by Dr David J David, who has worked for almost 30 years in Southeast Asia. Dr David and his anaesthetist and nurse travel to Indonesia twice a year to hold clinics. Together with Dr Asmarajaya, a gifted and compassionate Balinese surgeon, they perform the life-changing surgeries and train local hospital staff in special procedures in Bali. The goal is to create centres of excellence for craniofacial surgery in Indonesia's public hospital system in Bali (which will also serve East Nusa Tenggara), Jakarta and Surabaya. In 2011, Mary was awarded an MBE for her work.

Surgery costs in Indonesia are met by funds from donors such as Rotary Clubs, Australian and British organizations and private donors. "We're trying to set up sustainable systems of health care delivery by training local doctors and nurses," explained Dr David on a recent visit. "We come and deliver trainings in Bali and also bring Indonesian doctors to Adelaide to learn new techniques." The Australian CranioFacial Unit in Adelaide offers this excellent program free of charge, so Yayasan Senyum only needs to find costs for the doctors' language training, local costs (passports, visas, etc) and air tickets.

Facial deformities, the most common of which are cleft lip and cleft palate, occur once in about every 600 live births in most countries. When relatives marry, the incidence is much higher and malnutrition may also play a role. I've seen photos of the more severe defects, where teeth grow out of the cheeks and the brain extrudes in a bubble over the nose. The World Health Organization recently included facial deformities among the world's top health issues.

A cleft lip is easy to repair, but anything more serious is a long term commitment. "Fixing faces involves much more than just a single surgery," says Dr David. "It takes about 18 years of multidisciplinary management involving specialists in craniofacial surgery, bone grafting, orthodontics, hearing defects, speech therapy and other support as the child grows." Yayasan Senyum monitors the children who will need further surgery.

Since 2005, the Smile Foundation has facilitated surgery for over 380 people of whom about forty percent come from Lombok. Of these, nearly 20 with severe deformities were sent to Adelaide for surgery and some will need to go more than once. Such complex surgeries (most for deformities which are rarely seen in Australia these days) cost about AU $250,000 each, and the South Australian government most generously provides ten such surgeries a year to Indonesians.

The Smile Foundation of Bali runs an outreach program to locate people in remote areas of Bali who need surgery. A young man was hired and trained at the Smile House. Using his home as a base, he makes day trips out to villages visiting public clinics, community leaders and midwives and talking to the local people before returning home each night. He found that by hanging out at the local warung chatting over coffee, he was able to overcome people's reluctance to admit that a family member had a problem. He's been locating three or four patients a week in this way. There are plans to hire more scouts in remote areas.

Personal appearance is important in all cultures, but perhaps a facial deformity causes the most acute personal suffering in a place like Bali, where physical beauty is so admired. I was working my shift at the Smile Shop one Sunday afternoon about two years ago, folding a pile of shirts, when a young Balinese girl came and stood beside me. "Hello, I am Ayu," she said shyly. "Hi, Ayu," I smiled. Gently turning me toward a poster on the wall, she pointed to a photograph of a girl with a deformed face, then at herself. "I am Ayu," she repeated more strongly. I barely recognized her. Standing beside me was a normal, pretty young woman with her life before her, only a small scar on her cheek to show where her jaw had been completely reconstructed. "I am Ayu," she whispered again, looking at that ruined face in the photograph. Then she gave me a radiant smile and walked away. My heart broke and was mended again in that moment.

It's just a funky little shop in Ubud (where Ayu now works full time) but it helps change lives, profoundly.

Pretty Bird

About a year ago my phone rang and there was an agitated gentleman at the other end. He explained that he'd bought a baby parrot several months ago and lovingly hand-raised it with the intention of taking it back to his own country. But with Bird Flu still rampant, no airline would carry the parrot. His own ticket was confirmed and he had to leave in a week. There was a long, pregnant pause as I considered the implications of yet another creature in the compound.

"Bring it over," I said resignedly.

To this day I've never purchased a pet, they just seem to keep turning up. Chiko arrived the next day with a big cage, a travelling cage, a supply of toys and a permit. We examined each other with interest. Chiko is an Eclectus, an Eastern Indonesian parrot who'd been bred at the parrot ranch in Singapadu south of Ubud. He is a sleek, brilliant green with scarlet underwings piped in turquoise and a bright orange beak tapering to yellow at the tip. Chiko's a pretty bird, and he knows it.

At first I thought he was a perch potato, beautiful but somewhat lacking in personality. It turns out that he was just biding his time. Chiko is a thoughtful bird. When offered a peanut, it can take him a couple of minutes of deep deliberation before he accepts it. And for the first six months after he arrived I was out of Bali for long periods of time looking after my parents. My staff and house sitters tried to play with him but he remained silent and aloof. His only words were a very soft, polite "Hello" and what sounded like "Monk".

Only in November did we really begin to get to know one another. He'd been hand-raised from a chick and missed human company, so I began to include him in my activities. I brought my computer outside and worked at the table on the patio, and he would sit for hours on my shoulder like a statue, watching my fingers on the keyboard. After a few weeks of this he began to gently groom my hair and I understood that he'd accepted me as his Person. Chiko became more demanding. If he felt he wasn't getting enough attention he would pull out my earrings and take off my reading glasses. When I was drinking tea, he wanted to sip from my cup. If it happened to be arak, that was fine with him too. I had to banish him from walking on the table because he was obsessed with pecking the keys off my computer and nipping through all the interesting cables.

Wayan Manis and I learned to clip the long feathers from one of his wings so he could leave his cage. He became a resolute walker, strutting around the garden for considerable distances. We had to curtail this activity when he took to climbing trees; a gust of wind would easily blow him down the undercliff where he'd be impossible to find. Even when he's perched in the hibiscus bush, he is so perfectly camouflaged as to be invisible.

I place him on bushes close to where I'm working in the garden and he poses there for hours, pondering the ways of the universe and muttering to himself. If I move out of sight, he will often swoop down to the grass and chug around the garden until he finds me.

Rama the bald cockatoo resents my attention to the newcomer. "I love you!" he reminds me when I play with Chiko. If they happen to be placed on the same bush at the same time, the much smaller Rama menaces the Eclectus with bony outspread wings and threatening hisses. "Monk," responds Chiko peaceably.

He's become much more vocal recently. I live next to an elementary school, and in the mornings Chiko manages to sound like a whole classroom of screaming children. He joins in when the dogs bark. I hear him quietly practicing some complex monologue in which I think I recognize a few words. I'm waiting for him to surprise me with a perfectly articulated sentence some day.

Just a few weeks after Chiko arrived there was another agitated phone call. It seemed that another Eclectus needed a home. Unlike Chiko, this male was older, wilder and rather thin. I immediately applied for a permit, named him Darius to empower him, and set to fattening him up with nice things to eat. He'd never interacted with humans and nipped me hard with his sharp beak if he felt I was taking liberties. Only after months of patient interaction would he gently accept a peanut from my fingers and tickle my finger with his tongue. I was planning to slowly tame him so that he, too, could join us in the garden. After a year, the permit to keep him finally arrived. We all celebrated with roast chicken (parrots are very partial to chicken). The next morning Darius was dead in his cage.

Parrots can be most contrary birds. Full of beans one minute, dead the next. The evening before, Darius had been well and happy and had in fact polished off half a cob of corn and most of a passion fruit. Twelve hours later he was a sad splash of colour on the floor of his cage. The ants had already found him. I buried him in the orchard with every flower in the garden. At least he died legal. The next day I remembered that we were supposed to send the identifying ring around his ankle back to the parrot ranch for their records. When the staff arrived, we dug him up.The ring was too tight to slip over his foot, and none of us could bring ourselves to cut his foot off. Nyoman suggested we let nature take its course for a couple of weeks before trying again. We buried him once more.

The other birds don't seem to notice that Darius is gone. Rama continues to lord it over the household from his highest perch. Chiko is content as long as I'm in sight. Visitors tell him he's a pretty bird, and he placidly agrees.

Electric Adventures

It began in April 2008 when all the petrol stations in Bali suddenly ran dry. I was up at Candidasa, and on the way back to Ubud every station sported a hand-written sign 'habis' (finished) at the entrance. It got me thinking about how very inconvenient life would be without wheels.

My friend Kathy has been muttering under her breath about electric bicycles ever since I met her. Recently she announced that they were now being assembled in Java and a few were actually available in Ubud. My staff and I tracked down the tiny dealership and went in with a list of searching questions. They had the newest model—a sporty looking electric motorcycle with two batteries. Nyoman took it for a spin, and I left him bargaining with the owner. The next morning he drove up (silently) on my new steed.

Although it seemed like a bit of an impulse buy, the electric option had been on my mind for a long time. Besides the fuel issue, Ubud's once-clean air grows more polluted by the day. (Emissions, caused not only by the steeply increasing number of motorcycles and cars, are made worse by the recent invasion of huge tourist buses which spew their stinking fumes into the streets and cause endless traffic jams on our village's tiny roads. But that's another story...)

I have to admit that the new purchase unnerved me at first. The last time I'd driven a motorcycle was on the almost-deserted roads of the east coast of Malaysia... could it be 40 years ago? It doesn't sound like much if you say it quickly, but the comparison with Ubud's busy streets of today was daunting. I hadn't even been on a bicycle since then. It took me several days to find the audacity to actually get on the thing. It's garnet red and rather flashy looking (I am more drawn to the profile of a Lambretta), with a misleading decal of a wildly racing horse on the front.

Wayan tied an offering around one mirror and I augmented this with a stick of incense, some flowers from the garden and an ardent prayer that all journeys on this new set of wheels would be safe ones. That done, Wayan unlocked the imported bicycle chain, wheeled my steed into the lane, showed me where the accelerator and brake were and waved me rather apprehensively aboard.

I set off, wobbling alarmingly, along the deserted lane with Wayan trotting anxiously alongside. This triggered a flashback to my very first experience on a two-wheeler with my nervous father standing by. I managed to stall the bike, hauled it around and went up the other way with a particularly exciting wobble that made Wayan shriek. Pak Mangku came out to see what the excitement was all about and called for his wife to hurry and see Ibu Cat learning to drive a motorcycle.

Up and down the lane I teetered before an increasing audience of neighbours, small children, chickens and dogs, hanging on very hard and squeaking pathetically at intervals. It was all quite humbling. The speedometer hovered between five and ten kph, which seemed unnecessarily brisk. The brake and accelerator were fiendishly close together and I soon demonstrated that it was quite possible to activate both of them at the same time.

I had to go lie down after that while Wayan stabled the bike. But from then on I took an increasingly confident turn up and down the lane every evening. Finally I careened left at the top of the lane and daringly teetered along the gang to the temple parking lot, where I went round and round under the jaded eyes of the men who always gathered late in the day to eat spicy pork satay.

It was evident that my bike had already been the subject of some discussion in the neighbourhood. I pulled up next to a group of young guys who were trimming the temple garden, and they were full of questions. Was it imported? How fast would it go? Was it true that it needed no petrol or oil? What did it cost to recharge the batteries? And—most importantly—did it not require registration or a drivers' license?

They were surprised to learn that the machines are now assembled in Java and retail at half the price of a new conventional motorcycle. My model, the Trekko Nexus, had two batteries and could scream along at 35 kph on the flat (steep hills can be challenging). This is fine with me; I'm seldom out of second gear even in the car. I keep it plugged in to recharge whenever I'm not using it to prolong the life of the batteries. The only sound is a low hum. And it's true... these machines are considered electric bicycles and currently require neither a driving license nor registration. This enchants my staff, who envision themselves sailing silently past the early morning roadblocks thumbing their noses at the police.

The bike is smartly designed to look just like a motorcycle, which is actually a bit of a disadvantage as other drivers expect it to have a motorcycle's speed and agility; it does not. It's a bit awkward on corners. And it's so quiet no one hears it coming, although it sports a loud horn. The only downside is that there is no service centres for them in Bali.

I took my maiden voyage into Ubud early one morning before the traffic was heavy. Soon I found myself roaring along at 20 kph with the wind in my hair, bugs in my teeth and a big grin on my face. Weeks later I was confidently driving myself to the edges of town and trying to persuade the bike to climb the hill to Penestanan (it declined). There was lots of interest from the street, which intensified when the price of gasoline rose almost thirty percent a few weeks later. Every time I parked, people would wander over to take a look. Friends dropped by to take it for a spin. Balinese husbands talked about getting one for their wives. High school students gathered in front of my parking space to look the flashy red machine over. "Keren," they nod to each other. Cool.

I didn't know at first how people could tell it wasn't a regular motorcycle, because it looks just the same to me. Nyoman tells me it's the absence of number plates that floors the onlookers. This is a big selling point, apparently, along with not needing a driving license. Wheels without Indonesian bureaucracy or gasoline. Imagine. Nyoman carved me a vanity plate for the back bumper and constructed a woven bamboo basket with a lock.

At that delightful time of day between the parentheses of five and six in the afternoon, there is nothing more pleasant than tootling down the back lanes of Ubud very slowly on a motorbike. Lots of other people are tootling too; three pretty young girls squashed onto one bike, a grandfather holding a baby in front of him, a mother with several children tucked onto every flat surface. With the end of the rains, the vines have exploded into bloom and the lanes are strident with bougainvillea and alamanda. Neighbours chat at open gateways. Puppies wallow in the warm dust. Chickens march along the tops of walls and scrabble crossly in the shade. This is the energy of back lanes all over Southeast Asia in the late afternoons of decades gone by. I'm so grateful to find it still, right outside my garden gate.

I am beginning to understand why people ride these things for pleasure. The dogs don't know what to make of this electric business. Perhaps there's a high pitch in the motor that we can't hear, but they look startled as I approach and see me off with a baffled flap of the ears. Othello, the big black Doberman who lives down the lane, always races out to check when I pass—he is almost at eye level, which is disconcerting. Perhaps he finds me disconcerting too.

Out on the open road it's a different story. Even on the side streets there's a lot of vehicles zooming back and forth to say nothing of piles of sand, children, slumbering dogs, men playing with their roosters and women on their way to temple. Like the coward I am, I wait politely for everyone to pass before venturing out and tiptoeing along the verge of the road at ten kph. Balinese I don't even know call, "Careful, Ibu Cat!" as I zoom silently by. It's a completely different dimension to driving a car, where you are higher up, sequestered and contained from what's happening outside. On a bike you're part of the life at street level, right out there in the thick of things. Once I got over the sheer terror, it was wonderful. Could it be that little blast of ozone? Maybe because I'm not behind tinted windows (even rolled down), there's an immediacy to my passing through on two wheels. People meet my eyes and smile, and the children wave.

When there is no traffic, dogs, children or roosters on a straight stretch downhill, I've cranked it right up to a dizzying 35 kph. "How fast is that in miles per hour?" asked an unmetricated American. There was a long silence after I admitted that it was about 18 mph. But it feels pretty fast when you're out there doing it.

Riding my electric bike brings back memories of 1970, the year I spent on the east coast of peninsular Malaysia with my family. I had a motorcycle there that I used to ride to the kampongs and the beaches. There was very little traffic in those days and I remember roaring along as fast as I could go, taking corners at an acute angle and frightening my mother half to death if she happened to be driving by. Those were the days.

Reptilian Revelations

I don't live alone, exactly. Besides two or three or four dogs, I'm completely surrounded by reptiles at any given time. The inside of the house teems with cecaks and tokays. Skinks, chameleons and monitor lizards prowl the garden and the undercliff. I'd like to think there were some gliding lizards out there in the trees as well. It's a herpetologist's fantasy come true.

Ted the tokay moved into my new house the same day I did. I paused in unpacking the kitchen to watch the minute, newly hatched little lizard make its unsteady way along the counter. The house was barely finished—how had the precious egg remained hidden from 14 busy workmen? As I approached for a closer look, he danced up on his tiny feet and threatened me with an inaudible roar before starting the long and hazardous climb to the roof beams.

I didn't see him again for about a year, though evidence of his presence was visible every morning on the same patio tile. (You may have noticed that tokays are very regular in their habits.) I frequently heard his repetitive call of "Toe—Kaaaay'" as he patrolled the house in the dark. Then I arrived home late one night to find that he had got himself thoroughly stuck on a piece of fly paper. The little house lizards often did this and were easy enough to free unharmed with a cotton bud and some vegetable oil. But Ted was not content to wait for me to come home and release him. He'd thrashed around until he was wrapped up like an eccentric parcel, now firmly stuck to the counter.

His furious roars were a bit daunting, and tokays can deliver a nasty bite. But there was no choice, I couldn't leave him there all night at the mercy of the ants. Ten tense and very messy minutes later Ted was free, hissing indignantly. He was completely covered in oil, and so was I.

According to Ron, my consulting herpetologist, tokays are very territorial. "There is rarely more than one male tokay in a house or on a tree," he notes. Only males make the distinctive call. Tokay couples share their space with immature young, but adult sons have to move on and establish their own territory. A healthy tokay can grow to 30 centimeters and continue decorating the same patch of floor for a couple of decades. That's longer than most dogs and marriages last. Maybe we should be developing deeper relationships with our resident tokays, or at least progress to first-name terms.

In my previous house in the rice fields, I'd often been woken at night by what sounded like large mammals dancing on the roof beams and thundering around on the woven bamboo ceiling. I learned that tokays were the source of the nocturnal noises. They filled the hours of darkness by raiding rats' nests, fighting with each other and perhaps engaging in tokay races with exciting prizes, not very endearing at four o'clock in the morning.

Tokays are particularly attractive members of the gecko family, sporting suits in stylish shades of blue with yellow or red spots. They dine on insects and baby rodents (in England, Ron fed his pet tokay 20 newborn mice twice a week), which make them useful household members, and are in turn consumed by Chinese as food or medicine. My father had a bottle of medicinal Chinese wine with a preserved tokay floating in it. He took great pleasure in offering a glass to dinner guests.

They always declined.

The more numerous but less dramatic cecak or common house lizard is probably the most widely distributed lizard in the world. In the absence of TV, Daisy watches them unblinkingly for hours as they patrol the kitchen wall at night, and has to be carried away protesting to her cushion at bed time.

Our ubiquitous cecak has become an exotic item in Europe. Thousands are exported from Indonesia as pets every year. In England it's become a popular hobby to breed them at home. Cecaks and skinks lose their tails when startled, a clever survival tactic that distracts predators long enough to allow an escape. Some varieties actually slip out of their skin when grabbed, which must be disconcerting to the grabber who is left with a flaccid lizard-shaped wrapper but no lizard. Geckoes can't blink, so they lick their own eyes to clean them.

Ron says there may be something poisonous about cecaks, because cats that eat them invariably vomit them straight back up again. He claims they've adapted remarkably well to city life in Indonesia. He's seen the little forest animals clinging to the outside of high-rise buildings in Jakarta, presumably feasting on high-flying bugs.

Ron is a gold mine of information about the common lizards I've spotted in my house and garden, but I suspect that his real passion is snakes. He grows quite tender when he talks about them. Over the past two weeks he's flushed several young cobras from near his house and relocated them away from habitation, to the relief of his less admiring family."Cobras are so misunderstood,"he mourns. He grieves that people kill snakes automatically, when most are harmless. Balinese snakes are not aggressive as a rule and seldom bite unless cornered or threatened.

Snakes have a larger range, so you're unlikely to strike up a lasting relationship should one slither through your garden. But do commune with your resident tokay. You never know, he could be with you for a long, long time.

The Cult of Canine

Blackie is a fairly typical Bali dog, spending his days busily trotting the dusty back roads of Ubud, dozing in the gateway of his compound and making fearsome noises at apprehensive tourists. He is fully employed as his family's watchman, enjoying regular meals of rice and scraps. He probably has a couple of bald patches. Of course he is a male, because female dogs have the annoying habit of producing puppies regularly and are expensive to neuter. Blackie will either have survived a brutal village castration or still celebrate his unaltered masculinity with blatant sexual congress by the roadside, to the amazement of Western tourist children who are quickly hustled along by their parents. At night he sounds terrifying, but is in fact rather a coward.

The lot of the Bali dog has improved tremendously in the past few years as owners begin to take more responsibility for their pets. Many dogs in Ubud these days wear a collar. As a tourist to Bali ten years ago, I remember being afraid to walk to my homestay at night because the packs of mangy dogs were terrifying. Now, thanks to the Yudisthira Foundation and Bali Animal Welfare Association, tens of thousands of dogs have been sterilized and thousands of Balinese children have been educated in the proper care of companion animals. The recent rabies epidemic has also thinned the ranks of street dogs dramatically. Most dogs in Ubud these days appear to enjoy a fairly comfortable life. I've seen Balinese walking their dogs on leashes, taking them for joyrides on the motorcycle and tying kerchiefs around their necks.

This is still light years away from a dog's life in the West, of course. In the past few years, the North American dog has been elevated to a cult-like status undreamed of in developing countries. Single people, childless couples, the gay community and empty-nesters have embraced canine companionship with unprecedented enthusiasm. A whole industry has sprung up to accessorize The Dog.

In the old days, all a dog needed was a collar with an ID tag, a leash, a bowl and, if he was lucky, his own blanket and a couple of toys. He ate commercial dog crunchies (now known to contain all sorts of rubbish) and relished the occasional bone. How times have changed.

Someone recently sent me a slick magazine called 'Modern Dog'. The tagline reads, 'The Lifestyle Magazine for Urban Dogs and Their Companions'. On the cover, Pamela Anderson clutches a rescued hound against her astonishing bosom. Inside are perfectly serious articles about what kind of coat your dog may require in the winter, whether playing tug might be harmful and how to brush his teeth. The fashion spreads feature models in expensive frocks embracing large Huskies with pedicures.

While Blackie enjoys his boiled chicken feet, his American cousin Ebony dines like a raja. There are recipes for liver biscuits (take pork liver, wheat germ, flax seeds, brewer's yeast…) and an ad for Power Bars for the active dog. The full-page, glossy ads are for specially formulated gourmet-quality, holistic dog foods containing venison, lamb and organic chicken, allergen-free grains and chelated minerals, delivered to your door. One small firm sells hand-made, organic, grain-free dog biscuits. Dog treats come in charcoal and peppermint, peanut butter, cheese and chicken finger flavours. Did I mention the smoked salmon skins?

There is a special pet seatbelt for Ebony to wear in the car, and a small alarm for his collar to alert you if he falls into the swimming pool. Ebony slumbers on a wide variety of pet beds ranging from contoured cushions and minimalist Scandinavian teak to a four-poster with a tasselled tuffet. Several ads for dog coats include a goose-down jacket, a hooded raincoat and serious cold-weather coats in arctic fleece and Lycra in a full range of canine sizes. Someone has developed all-weather dog boots with non-skid soles that fasten with Velcro tapes. For more formal occasions, tuxedo ties and collars can be rented by the night. The House of Lolita (Discriminating Wear for the Diminutive Dog) provides an exclusive line of hand-knit dog sweaters. On the same page is an ad for tasteful cremation urns in maple and cherry wood, ranging from

$150 to $525, so Ebony's ashes can always be with you.

Full-service dog spas are beginning to appear, offering grooming, hydro massage, open plan day care, pre-warmed towels, swimming, TV, mineral water, and a limo service. Ebony enjoys canine spa products that include aromatherapy, spritzes, a selection of shampoos and conditioners, natural ear wash and paw balm.

If Ebony is on the small side, he probably has his own carrier bag in a choice of beaded silk, faux fur or leather. Or perhaps a Burberry tote? Big Ebony has a backpack to carry his stuff when you go on hikes together.

Then there are the social aspects. You'll want to attend all the best dog shows to make sure you're au courant with the latest trends and to see what the other dogs are wearing. And Ebony will naturally attend a prestigious training academy to learn his manners with positive reinforcement and the most modern psychological techniques. If he's a bit of a handful, then a weekend at Doggy Boot Camp will help him focus. Don't let's even start talking about medical insurance.

Bali is still a long way from these excesses, you may harrumph. But last week I saw a Bali dog that belonged to a batik shop on the main road, wearing a t-shirt. "Where did you get that?" I enquired. The proud owner directed me to the new pet shop near my house. There I found a rack of dog accessories including t-shirts in several sizes, a wide range of collars and—wait for it—specially designed knickers for Mrs Blackie to wear at that time of the month. Another little shop in my village is dedicated to small dogs and includes a grooming table with all the right combs and a hair dryer. It sells tiny harnesses and little clips for your poodle's coiffure. Yes, there's a poodle in Ubud.

So hang in there, Blackie. With a little practice you could start wearing a batik sarong and a hibiscus tucked into your collar. The Bali Dog look may someday be a fashion statement. Hold the paw balm.

Coffee Break at the Warung

I was out of sugar. Contemplating a cup of bitter morning coffee, I strolled the hundred metres of unpaved lane and around the corner to my local warung, one of the informal coffee shops/general stores that punctuate every street corner in Indonesia.

As Old Ibu carefully filled a plastic bag from a big sack of unbleached sugar, insect parts and dust, I ordered a glass of Bali coffee and took my place on the unpainted bench. It's a long way from Starbucks, but the coffee culture is well established here. This unprepossessing establishment is an energy centre for the neighbourhood and the nearby temple. Old Ibu dispenses gossip and groceries, Pak Mangku hangs out between ceremonies, the young guys shoot pool and the babies chase the chickens. The bench that runs the three-metre length of the warung is never empty. Even at this early hour, several youths in temple gear lounge around smoking pungent clove cigarettes and drinking black coffee out of little glasses. Everybody except the babies drinks coffee.

You won't find this particular brew on the menu boards of fancy coffee houses. This is very local coffee indeed. A glass costs about ten cents, extra if you want milk. Wayan Manis insists that home-grown coffee in Bali is all organic. Who would bother wasting expensive chemical fertilizers on the compound's garden? Someone might throw a little cow manure around the coffee bushes now and again, but for the most part they are left to themselves, shaggy and unpruned. I've been looking forward to drinking my own coffee, but Wayan tells me not to hold my breath. She points out that the two dozen coffee bushes in my garden are still a few years from bearing fruit.

Recently she brought me a bag of little grey beans from her own garden that I didn't even recognize as coffee. She'd picked them a few days before, removed the red covering by hand and dried them in the sun. It didn't look much like coffee and didn't smell of anything at all. We spent a companionable hour picking through the beans and discarding the small, discoloured ones—about a third of the volume. Then she poured the remainder into my grandmother's cast iron frying pan and started to roast it over the flame of the gas stove. I was left in charge of this operation, which took an hour of constant stirring with a little bundle of twigs. Finally the beans took on a dark mahogany colour and began to smell like the real thing. The picking, cleaning, drying, sorting and roasting of about 500 grams of this politically correct, shade-grown organic coffee had taken about a week. I'd like to report that it tasted remarkable, but in fact it was pretty ordinary.

There's a legend that a goat herd in North Africa first became aware of coffee's potential when he noticed his flock frolicking around wildly after consuming fallen coffee berries. He tried some himself and experienced the world's first caffeine blast. It's a charming tale but almost certainly fiction. Coffee berries taste awful, and most of the caffeine is in the seeds inside them.

But someone in the Arab world must have looked at those pretty red berries a millennia ago and thought, "I bet if I picked those berries, tossed away the fruit, dried the seeds in the sun for a few days and roasted them black, ground them to powder and brewed them in hot water, I'd get a buzz."

That powerful buzz was initially thought to be sacred. Coffee was first consumed as a beverage in the Arab world about 1,100 years ago, when it was linked with doctors and mystics. Drinking coffee was said to produce sensations ranging from exhilaration to religious ecstasy. Physicians dispensed it as an expensive medicine and it was used as part of religious ceremonies; Sufis would stoke up on it before a night of whirling. Then coffee's interesting side effects began to trickle into the secular community and it was adopted by scholars, artists and other night owls to help them stay awake. Coffee went mainstream when the world's first coffee houses opened in Mecca around the 15th century. The trend was well established in Europe 300 years later, about the time the Dutch started to establish plantations in Bali.

Both Robusta and Arabica still grow here, though Wayan just calls the small bushes in my garden kopi Bali (ordinary coffee). Unpruned coffee trees can grow to almost 10 meters in height, though they bear much more heavily when tightly pruned. In India, pepper vines are trained around the coffee bushes, which in turn like to grow in the shade of taller plants. In parts of Indonesia I've seen vanilla orchids being cultivated on coffee trees.

The argument about coffee's effect on health continues, with over 19,000 studies undertaken on the subject. One faction insists that coffee in any quantity is unwholesome and leaches vitamins and minerals from the food we eat. It's touted in the industry as an anti-depressant and a performance enhancer. I suppose it depends on who is performing what.

Probably the most interesting coffee in the world comes from Vietnam and, more recently from Indonesia. A species of civet cat, presumably depressed, eats the fallen coffee berries. The beans are passed in the civet's droppings and are then carefully collected, washed, roasted and sold as a niche product.

Talk about a specialized occupation... I've been hearing about this coffee for years, but never met anyone who would confess to trying it. Of course, it is very expensive.

I ask my neighbours on the bench why they drink coffee. They variously reply, "Because it tastes good," "It helps me stay awake when I've been up all night," "Because I always do." A random survey in any Starbucks would reveal the same. Addiction to the little black bean seems to span all cultures and tastes.

Please pass the sugar.

Snake Oil

I avoid the medical profession on the principal that doctors always seem to find something wrong with me when I go to see them, and I'm perfectly well when I don't. Many Balinese and expats tend to treat minor physical malfunctions themselves. My garden is full of plants to treat everything from fever to wasp stings and mental sluggishness, and the pantry is lined with jars of infused oils and home-made tinctures.

Wayan is delighted with this do-it-yourself attitude and constantly adds to our pharmacopoeia. When I get a cold, she plasters me in pungent pastes and presents me with slimy green drinks. When she starts to sniffle, I bombard her with Vitamin C and Echinacea. It all seems to work.

In between home remedies and the standard medical profession lies the grey area of what my father used to call the 'Snake Oil Men'. For centuries, if not millennia, this subculture has sold mysterious patent medicines for what seem to be mankind's three major embarrassments: baldness, hemorrhoids and sexual dysfunction.

The Javanese equivalent of Viagra was brought to my attention during an Indonesian language lesson. It was a particularly grueling class in which our teacher was trying hard to help us understand the tricky verb prefixes. We had just read a simple story about bus schedules when one of her more unruly students pulled out a recent copy of the Bali Post and asked her to translate an ad. It featured a photo of a grim-looking granny and some text with many exclamation marks.

Komang welcomed alternative learning tools and encouraged lively discussions about all kinds of things. On this occasion she shifted seamlessly from transitive verbs to penile enhancement as she helped us put our newly acquired language skills to use.

"Memperbesar…. to make bigger. Memperpanjang… to make longer." Those damn verb prefixes were starting to pay off. "Sampai 15–20 cm." Penny pulled a tape measure from her purse; Americans still think in inches. "Ejakulasi dini… the only thing that is early in Indonesia," explained Komang airily. This was a lot more engaging than bus schedules. There were several of these ads, all with photos of unsmiling men and women which were probably meant to be reassuring. Prices ranged from $45 – $65.

A whole new world was opening up. We scanned the other pages, alerted to what was evidently a major industry. Quite a lot of advertising rupiah were dedicated to this very subject. Here was another big ad for Renaissance Oil, Formula Special for Men, Imported, featuring a large picture of a charging bull. It promised the usual improvements to dimensions and performance. ("Snake oil," I could hear my father snort.)

Kencing, for instance, can mean urine, kidney stones, blood in the urine, sexual intercourse or to be urinated upon. Indonesian can be a very tricky language, and you'd want to be sure of your prefixes before you embarked on a discussion of this nature.

When I got home I showed the ad to Wayan Manis and Nyoman, who viewed it with casual interest. "If the Balinese have this problem, they go to the balian (Balinese shaman) and pay Rp10,000 (about a dollar)." Of course, the Balinese had to have the last word and get a better price as well.

(All this thinking had made me tired and I went to lie down. When I woke up, I found that Wayan Manis had finished all my homework about bus schedules. "We learn this in elementary school," she explained kindly.)

For stress and depression, I swear by a visit to Cokorda Rai, a balian who lives about 20 minutes from my house. A friend took me to see him after a terrifying house fire left me depressed and off balance, a condition later diagnosed as Post Traumatic Stress Disorder. I certainly felt out of order. The wise old man looked at me, then at the air around me, then palpated my skull rather ungently. After that I lay down on a woven mat as he took a sharpened twig and poked under my toes. "Heart, liver, spleen," he murmured as he prodded. There was no discomfort. "Kidneys, lungs…" Suddenly I arched my back and howled from a pain that was profoundly deep. "Ah," he intoned with satisfaction. "The Story Body is sick."

It was interesting to learn that the mind was considered a physical organ like any other and to be found on the same menu, so to speak. Western medicine puts them in completely different restaurants. But Cok Rai said, "Your mind is frightening your body. and…" he glanced around my head, "… there are holes in your aura; I can see the colours leaking out. I will fix it." And he did, with gestures of his hands that I could feel from several feet away. A few minutes later when he poked the same spot under my toe with the pointed stick, there was no pain at all. I immediately felt much better, and was quickly back to normal. I've taken several people to see him since then, all with the same results. A major mental tune-up with no medication, all for about $20. ("Expensive," points out Wayan Manis. "Cheaper for Balinese.")

So we try a little of this, a little of that. Working in the garden one day when I had houseguests, Nyoman was stung by a scorpion. We brought together the accumulated wisdom of our various cultures to treat him. Whether it was the paste of crushed limestone, the urine, the antihistamine, the ice or the Reiki, within an hour the pain and swelling had disappeared. Or maybe it was the Snake Oil….

Walking on the White Side

Almost every foreigner who lives in Bali has some kind of recognition of the intense magic that moves over the land here. Some can feel the energy, some see it, some hear its voice in the night. Not everyone is allowed to live here, a non-negotiable fact that has nothing to do with the Immigration Department. A visiting Buddhist nun once stated that she thought Bali was a karmic vortex; people come here to meet their karma. Even the most prosaic expat will know of the dark events that haunt some foreigners on the island before Bali spits them out, dead or alive.

Those in synchronicity with Bali are among the happiest people I have ever known. They acknowledge and respect the swirling smoke of magic that only the balians can harness.

I learned much about balians from Madé Surya, eldest son of a Hindu priest and is an authority on Bali's healers. Surya was senior researcher in Bali for the Society for Study of the Afterdeath. He is now working with Professor Dr. Adi Putera on the first book in English to be written about traditional healing practices in Bali.

Surya has observed many strong healings which can't be explained by medical science. He conducts one-to-five day workshops on balians which include visits to selected healers (danu@earthlink.com).

According to Surya, there are four kinds of healers in Bali. They are not necessarily priests, although they may dress like one, make offerings and visit temples. Balinese people tend to be more comfortable if the healer is also a priest.

Embracing magic is dangerous work. The black and white checks of the traditional poleng cloth remind us that good and evil walk side by side here. The healer must be pure of intent, empty of ego and have the permission of his or her spirit guide for the strong protection necessary before undertaking this work.

The first kind of healer is called a Balian Ketakson. These are usually channelers who take the position as a kind of middleman between god and the patient, or a dead person and the living. Many use trances to obtain information. The Ketakson will invoke the spirit of a dead person. The spirit enters the channeler, and the family can converse with it and ask practical questions about what kind of offerings and gifts should be made for the cremation. The healer will often take on the voice and mannerisms of the spirit.

The Balian Ketakson can also channel for living people, helping to locate stolen items or giving guidance about the client's work. A trance is not necessary for this; the healer directly contacts his or her spirit guide for the information. There is no set fee, but people usually put between $5 and 10 in an offering. Later, if results were good, they may additionally give an umbrella for the healer's temple as a punia gift. A client who has benefited from the healer's information will often present a ring or cloth for the healer's temple.

The second kind of balian is called a Balian Pica. The Balian Pica receives physical objects or spiritual power, and will not necessarily be a formal student of magic. These mediums may receive objects which appear spontaneously and are used during healing sessions. "I've seen a kris (wavy ceremonial dagger) suddenly materialize during meditation, standing on its point and rotating by itself," reports Madé, who has been highly educated in both the Balinese Hindu and Western traditions. "The object may be a ring and might not necessarily be beautiful. It may be an ordinary-looking piece of cloth." The object is dipped in holy water which the client may be sprinkled with, drink or bathe in with traditional herbs. These ritual objects appear and disappear of their own accord. The longest Madé has known one to manifest is five years.

The third kind of healer is called a Balian Usada, who has the intention to become a balian and studies with recognized healers. The disciplines include ethics, anatomy, traditional herbs, meditation, yoga, tantrism and other subjects. They study both black and white magic, which are very similar except for the intention of the practitioner. Although all balians walk on the white side, they need to understand the other aspect as well.

The last kind of healer combines all of the above (Pica, Usada and Ketaksan). He or she may receive divine knowledge during a severe illness, and then decide to study formally. Many will appear crazy or psychotic while the wisdom is entering them. Cokorda Rai, my favourite balian, used to be a car mechanic; he suffered insomnia for eighteen months during this process of receiving the knowledge. Now he is serene with a wisdom not of this earth, and he sees beyond our physical edges to heal our souls.

The World According to Wayan

Wayan Manis, my housekeeper, is a unique window into Balinese culture for me. Sometimes when we're companionably chopping vegetables together in the outdoor kitchen, she'll bring me up to date on community buzz that I'd never otherwise be aware of. These occasions push my Indonesian language skills to the limit, but somehow I seem to get the gist of the story even when I don't understand half the words.

There seem to have been a lot of sudden deaths lately. Granted that the night temperature can plummet to an arctic 18 C at this time of year, but even in Bali that's not quite life-threatening. Wayan reports that there have been three deaths in as many weeks in her village alone. What did they all die of, I wondered. "They weren't old. They weren't sick. They just came home from work, sat down and died," said she.

Pak Mangku next door concurs that there seems to be a lot of it going around, whatever it is. He's told her of several recent deaths he's heard about where the people have not been sick at all. One was a man of 60 who sat down at a coffee shop on our very street, ordered a glass of coffee and promptly fell over dead. There was no suggestion that the quality of the beverage was at fault.

Wayan approves of these rapid departures. "That's good, they're happy now," she nods, briskly chopping garlic. "It's good to be dead. Being alive has a lot of problems."

Her insights into the local fauna and flora can be illuminating. Several times I offered her the seeds from a particularly succulent papaya that grew in my garden, and she always refused them politely. Finally she felt she knew me well enough to confide the reason, which was rather startling. "We can't have papaya trees in our compound, or ghosts will hang around them," she stated. I glanced around my yard at the seven or eight trees heavy with fruit. "There are no ghosts hanging around my papaya trees," I declared indignantly. She agreed that I ran a tight ship in that department, but she would get them for sure. "It's a problem."

A few weeks ago Nyoman flushed a huge black scorpion from the garden near my unglazed bedroom window, the second we've found (only then did Wayan tell me that she sometimes finds their children under my bed and in the bathroom when she cleans). He put it in my best tupperware container and took it back to their village that night to try and sell. Could there really be a market for big black scorpions? Yes, indeed; he had seen a man on a motorcycle with several of them crawling around in a container. The man was taking them to the market in Denpasar where they would sell for Rp20,000 each. The buyers, using some technology that was beyond my language skills, brewed the scorpion venom with coconut oil and sold it as a remedy for rheumatism.

This was big money. We discussed the possibility of breeding scorpions as a business initiative, but agreed that it might have a negative impact on our social lives. Besides, how did you tell a male scorpion from a female scorpion? What did they eat? How often did they breed? As so often in Bali, the production issues were daunting. Nevertheless, when he drove me into Denpasar the next day Nyoman brought along our new acquisition. While I ran my errands in Jalan Sulawesi, he visited the bazaar to do some market research. Alas, there were no takers. We drove back up the mountain with a large scorpion noisily scrambling around its container in the back of the car. It was released back into the jungle, at what I hoped was way beyond walking distance to my yard.

I told my staff a scorpion story I'd recently heard from India. Roadside stalls in Gujarat feature aluminum pots full of just this kind of big black scorpion. Wealthy clients pay $7 to allow a scorpion to sting them on the palm of the hand. Apparently the initial pain quickly subsides, leaving a feeling of euphoria that lasts several hours. Wayan and Nyoman scoffed at this nonsense ("Crazy people!"), and I had to agree I didn't think it would catch on here.

Then there were the walking catfish. "Sometimes I'll be standing in a dry rice field talking to a friend, and I'll see some lele (catfish) walking to the river," Wayan confided as she swept around my office chair.

"Walking?"

"Truly." In fact, I had heard elsewhere that catfish can make their way overland between waterways in the dry season. "But when I looked again, they'd disappeared. They are really the children of the River People, so we're afraid to eat them or we'll have a lot of problems."

Wayan stopped buying red apples for my morning juice. "Poison," she intoned darkly. After a big ceremony a few weeks ago, rumours started to fly that the red apples from China were poisoning people. "After people brought the offerings back from the temple, they would eat the fruit. When they ate the red apples, their mouths swelled up and they would die." How many people had actually died? After some discussion, my staff agreed that at least four people had expired in this unpleasant fashion. A fairly serious public relations issue for the Chinese apple marketing board. I'm now only allowed to use the sour little green ones from Java.

I hadn't been in Bali very long before I realized that this part of the island was prone to gentle earthquakes. "It's the rain," Wayan told me. I wasted quite a lot of breath trying to explain the relationship between live volcanoes and earth tremors, and she listened with patient attention. "Maybe that happens in other places," she conceded when I finished. "But in Bali the rain causes earthquakes."

Determined that Western logic should prevail just this once, I tried to keep track of the tremors. Annoyingly, they did seem to occur in the rainy season. Finally, early one morning, I was woken by the gentle rocking of my antique Madura bed. Although overcast, it hadn't rained for weeks.

"There was an earthquake this morning, and it wasn't raining," I informed Wayan when she arrived from the market. She tipped a bag of chicken heads into the pot to boil up for the dogs. "But Ibu, it must have been raining somewhere, or there wouldn't have been an earthquake."

Later that morning a neighbour's housekeeper arrived to borrow our ladder. There was a rapid exchange in Balinese. As the dogs escorted the visitor to the gate Wayan turned to me with a triumphant smile. "It rained last night," she announced, "in Mas."

I've decided not to be a warrior for logic any more. After all, I'm living in a world of walking catfish, haunted papaya trees and rain-induced earth tremors—the world according to Wayan.

It's About Time

It would not be an understatement to declare that the Balinese have a different sense of time than Westerners.

Those who have come straight to Bali from the frenetic West often feel they have been drop-kicked into a different dimension. They have. There's never been a sense of urgency in everyday life here, and the Balinese decline to adopt one. They open their shops and warungs at a certain time each day—ceremonies permitting—but it seems more a matter of habit than adherence to a schedule. A watch is a fashion statement, not an essential tool for living. The rhythm of the Bali day is dictated by much more than the remorseless march of the clock.

Modern thinking enjoins us to live in the moment, a skill we try desperately hard to achieve for the sake of our mental health. It's not easy to shed decades of multi-tasking and deadlines. The Balinese live richly and effortlessly in the moment. When there's too much to do or problems with money, they claim 'stress'. There was no word for this condition before we came along.

I lost my watch a few months after moving here and never bothered to replace it. Last year I was given one while out of the country, and it ran perfectly until I arrived back in Bali. A few days later it stopped and could not be persuaded to run again. For months it sat on the bathroom shelf staring at me with its blank face and baleful unmoving hands. Then I planned another trip and began to pack my bags. The watch came to life suddenly and started to keep perfect time.

When I pointed out to Wayan that it had begun running again, she was unsurprised.

"It wasn't necessary here. Now you need it again,"This seemed perfectly logical to her.

"Will it run while I'm away?" "Probably."

"And when I come back?"

She shrugged expressively. "Maybe."

She and Nyoman arrive promptly at nine each morning, although they rarely wear the watches I gave them. They are somewhat less punctual about leaving at three, their designated departure time. Sometimes they don't go home till four, which makes me late for my nap.

At first I kept a much closer eye on the clock than they did, concerned that they were working overtime. I tried to balance their work schedule; when I needed them a few hours longer one day I would give them time off later. They gently resisted this by appearing as usual on days I had declared holidays and turning up with plants for the garden on Sunday, their day off. It took them a long time to train me, but finally I succumbed to their concept of 'when'. It's not about what the clock says, it's about what we do in the day and how much time that takes. There are no sharp edges.

They appear to enjoy coming to work. I suspect they find me more entertaining than television. Occasionally they take a day off for a ceremony or I need to be picked up at the airport at night. Their philosophy seems to be that it will balance out if we are all reasonable. We are and it does. Nobody looks at their watches during these unspoken negotiations, because no one is ever wearing one.

In Indonesian class I learned that besok doesn't necessarily mean tomorrow, it just means 'not today'. Lusa, the word for the day after tomorrow, can be loosely interpreted as sometime in the more or less immediate future. Two weeks is approximately equal to infinity. I learned a long time ago that most Balinese don't think two weeks ahead, and there's just no sense getting cross about it.

My Indonesian teacher reminded us that invitations to weddings and tooth filing ceremonies arrive only two or three days before the event, because the Balinese might forget if the interval was longer. I used to panic about these abrupt summonses, translating them with the aid of a dictionary while Wayan dressed me in my ceremonial clothes and actually arriving promptly at the stated time. Invariably it was all over by the time I got there and everyone was lounging around dreamily eating smoked duck. Only recently did I learn that the printed invitations give the time the reception is over, not when it begins. It all bears a bit of thinking about in terms of cross-cultural expectations.

Another interesting wrinkle in time is the tendency, not just in Indonesia but elsewhere in Asia, to agree to make a certain item in two weeks. The unsuspecting foreigner turns up fourteen days later to collect it, at which point the vendor actually begins the work. Why do they wait until they see the whites of our eyes before they start the project, I wonder. Are we so unreliable? Didn't they believe us? Was two weeks just too long?

After 20 years of living in Southeast Asia, I've developed a philosophy that has been very helpful—sooner or later, something will happen, one way or the other. What time does the bus leave? In the west, four o'clock means just that, give or take ten minutes. In much of Asia it can mean six o'clock, midnight, when the bus is full, or "What bus?"The bottom line is that if you get attached to what you think should happen at a certain time, you may be disappointed. Despair is futile.

I seem to have struck a happy balance between the two worlds of Bali time and Western time. I can turn up at exactly 9 o'clock for an appointment if that is required. But if a procession suddenly blocks my path, I turn off the car engine and slip across into that other dimension.

The cymbals clash, the women sway gracefully under their towers of fruit and the pretty children run to catch up. In Jakarta, it's demonstrations that make people late, in Bangkok it's gridlock.

Here it is ritual and music, which is not so very hard to take. The rest of the day will unroll itself a few minutes later, that's all.

I recently returned from a trip to Singapore, wearing my new watch. I checked it when the plane landed and it was still working when Nyoman drove me up the mountain in the dark. Gradually the traffic thinned, the air cooled, the road began to climb steeply. The dogs greeted me ecstatically as Nyoman unloaded the bags and departed. I pottered around contentedly, unpacking and making a cup of tea. By the time I took off the watch, it had stopped. I smiled as I put it away; I wouldn't be needing it for a while.

Hazels' Begonia

My paternal grandmother was a woman of considerable character. She crossed Canada in her teens, fell in love with a handsome entrepreneur in Vancouver and brought up three children during the Depression. In the childhood summers I spent with my grandparents on their little farm, she never seemed to rest. She cooked delicious old-fashioned food on a big wood-burning stove, bullied the chickens into laying more eggs and kept an eye on her many grandchildren while making jam and mending socks.

Hazel was a born gardener. Nothing she planted ever failed to thrive and in the summer her front garden was a chaotic jungle of flowers and herbs. She always had a big pot of begonias which was put out on the long south-facing porch in the spring and brought in before the frost. My parents moved into a new house when I was four. There was a wooden divider between the living and dining room and along the top was a row of Hazel's begonias in pots. Even my mother, whose fingers were far from green, was not able to quench their hardy survivorship.

Decades passed, we grew up, Hazel left us and the begonias kept growing.

When we daughters moved out, we each took a begonia cutting with us. They were easy plants for starting gardeners, tolerating neglect and remorseful over-watering. This variety had serrated leaves which were dark red underneath and dark green with silver spots on top. The potted begonias went with us from apartment to apartment, house to house. When I moved to Singapore 20 years ago, I brought a few inches of withered begonia stem with me. It sprouted and grew. Hazel's begonia loved the tropics, perhaps having a deep cellular memory that this was where it all began for begonias. Like plants, people transplant to the tropics with varying degrees of success. Some adapt quickly, putting down deep roots and tolerating the heat, the wet and the cultural bafflements with ease. Others struggle to be comfortable, seeking a balance in this demanding new environment that is by no means automatically acquired.

I was once asked to speak to a class at an International School about adjusting to life in Asia. I declined, because I don't think it is a skill that can be learned. Like the cellular memory of a begonia cutting, I believe we are born with the potential to thrive in different climates and cultures. If we don't have that, no amount of wishing or training will make it so.

Perhaps there is whole set of genes the scientific community has yet to discover. There must be an Adventure Gene. Some kids spend their young years reading exciting travel books and planning incredible journeys, and others would rather not stray far from the house. Are these instincts hard-wired? It begs the question of whether the expatriate (expat) is born or made. I've known expats born in Asia or Africa who loved their birth country and never wanted to be anywhere else. Yet their siblings dashed for the West and the white picket fence as soon as they could, and never looked back.

Those of us who settle happily and permanently in foreign countries are not necessarily from families with old colonial or sea-faring traditions; most of us are first-generation expats. And when I ask my staff if they'd like to fly with me to Lombok or Java some day, Wayan Manis lights up with excitement. Nyoman hates the idea. He has a dominant White Picket Fence Gene.

The Tropical Gene is even more mysterious. So many of my western friends here share my inappropriate freckled Celtic skin, yet we love the heat. What on earth are we doing here? What drew us from frosty northern climes to this steamy environment and why do most of us eschew air conditioning? The Tropical Gene must have an Arctic option. I've known many Asians who claim that their best memories are from winters in Ottawa or Oslo. An elegant Thai lady described eating bangers and mash in an English pub during a snowstorm as one of the highlights of her life.

Then there's the Cultural Challenge Gene. Most people in most places are most comfortable among their own kind. They like the familiarity of language, cuisine, culture, religion. The maverick few can't wait to hurtle themselves into another cultural context, the stranger the better. Many marry locally and dig in for life. Is it the Gene that causes this behaviour, or are they reincarnations of their Balinese neighbour's great-great-great Aunt Ketut? The Balinese seldom carry the Cultural Challenge Gene.

Oh, and the Wildlife Gene. I'm not the only person on this island with an affection for reptiles and big crunchy bugs. When I spot a green pit viper in my garden these days, I have a list of three guys who want to know immediately. (Now that Bali's Green Pit Viper has been declared a distinct species, they all have to have one.) There are no Balinese on this list yet, just crazy expats.

No wonder the immigration departments of so many Asian countries don't know what to do with us. They think we're foreigners. We feel that we are home. It's confusing for all of us.

When I moved to Bali 10 years ago I brought another sprig of Hazel's begonia. It languished in a pot for years before I had the wit to tuck it into a corner of the garden. Now it's thriving in the dense green shade, its roots deep in the rich Balinese soil. Like mine.

Cuisine Unseen

You can tuck into all kinds of different food in Ubud—fusion, Mexican, vegan, Japanese, Italian, Padang, French or Indian. But the search for authentic Balinese food usually dead-ends at overpriced smoked duck with all the trimmings at 24 hours notice. Smoked duck is divine, but it's hardly everyday fare.

Why is the local cuisine so elusive? Janet de Neefe's book *Fragrant Rice* recounts her passionate love affair with its aromas, tastes and textures and reminds us that preparing it is a slow labour of love. There's no written history of Balinese cuisine, no ancient recipes handed down on the lontars on which so much Balinese cultural wisdom is recorded. Pungent, savoury and multi-dimensional, the distinctive dishes were passed down the generations by word of mouth. It's also very labour-intensive. Traditionally the spice mixtures are blended in a stone mortar with a pestle, meat is minced finely, vegetables are reduced to microscopic dimensions and all ingredients are mixed by hand. Short cuts don't seem to work. Wayan Manis was delighted with a new blending wand but we both found that the Balinese food didn't taste the same; the flavours were too homogeneous, less distinct. We soon went back to the mortar and the blender is gathering dust under the sink.

Most dishes are built around a bumbu or spice paste, and I'm intrigued that so many basic bumbu ingredients also serve as medicines in their own right. Garlic crushed in hot water with lemon juice and honey treats colds and flu, and the raw bulbs swallowed whole combat intestinal parasites. Ginger is taken for indigestion and nausea. Turmeric is known to be a potent natural antiseptic and antibiotic, whether taken internally or applied to the skin. The juice (popularly known as jamu) is taken as a general tonic and for menstrual pain. Kencur, a related rhizome, is ground with rice and water to make boreh, a paste that is applied to the head and body for fever. Lemongrass and onions cool the body and tamarind purifies the blood. The chili arrived in Bali fairly recently, some time after the Portuguese brought it to India in the 16th century. It contains capsaicin, which releases endorphins (the body's natural painkillers) and thus reduces stress. Chili also thins the blood and speeds the metabolism. With all of these ground to a paste in the mortar, the bumbu is an amazing amalgam of flavours as well as a formidable pharmacy for the diner's wellbeing.

There are some interesting parallels with other cuisines. The ancient Romans valued a seasoning they called garum or liquamen. (In Indonesian, garam is salt.) This mixture of fish or shellfish and salt (to inhibit bacterial growth) was left in an earthenware pot in the sun for several months until a clear golden liquid could be drawn from it. This singular liquid somehow found its way to Vietnam and Thailand where it's widely used today under the names of nuoc mam and nam pla. The residue was compressed and dried into a hideously pungent block and by a similar mysterious route arrived in Indonesia where it's known as terasi. Minute slices of this noxious seasoning are roasted and added to the bumbu, which does not seem to suffer from the addition.

While I was in the pantry curling up my nose over the household jar of terasi, Wayan volunteered that the Balinese made a different, even stronger variation from rotted garden snails which is called black terasi.

"It smells very bad when you're making it but if you add just a little bit, the food is delicious," she insisted.

Another menu item favoured by many Balinese is blood. "You can boil it or fry it," Wayan instructs. "Not in this house," I demur. Blood is a key ingredient in lawar, a ceremonial food prepared by men. If offered lawar, it may be strategic to enquire whether it is red lawar (with blood) or white lawar (bloodless). Blood has been a traditional food for nomads through history, requiring no packaging or cooking if taken in small amounts from the living animal. The Irish ate blood boiled with milk, butter and herbs. In France in the 1890s, ladies would drop by the local slaughterhouse for a bracing glass of fresh blood. The Masai of Kenya drink it fresh from their cattle and blood sausage is still popular today.

Since we were on the subject of interesting food, I asked Wayan if she had ever eaten dog. "I don't really know," she admitted. "I'm not brave enough to try it. But sometimes if you're sick, people will give it to you to make you strong and tell you it's cow meat." As an afterthought, she added, "People who donate blood and feel weak should drink dog's blood."

As everywhere else, people in Bali are busy these days. Many women are too busy to cook from scratch. The shift from traditional foods to white bread, processed food, instant noodles and the ubiquitous fried rice have had a dramatic negative impact on the health of the Balinese.

Largely unknown to the outside world, Balinese food is appetizing and unique. There are several cooking schools in Ubud, all offering different menus and teaching styles and all well worth a visit.

Puppy Love

You can always tell when there's a puppy in the house.

All the shoes are on a shelf off the floor. The older dogs are hanging out in shady parts of the garden, looking resigned. The floor is littered with a miscellany of well-chewed items: an old toothbrush, a young coconut, a rawhide bone, a carrot, a cob of corn, the knuckle of a deceased pig and a rope tied to the railing. The puppy looks perky and well rested. The owner looks exhausted. And there are puddles.

I'd never had a tiny, straight-from-the-mother pup before. I intended that this puppy would grow up to be a big, scary, well-adjusted, obedient guard dog. Before he arrived I sat up nights studying manuals on puppy care. Crating, feeding, house breaking, bathing, discipline, obedience training; it all seemed very complicated. I tried to think like a dog, not a person. I practiced being Alpha Dog with Kalypso, who rolled her eyes and took off for the bamboo grove.

I visited the litter when it was three weeks old, picked up two likely pups and held one against each cheek. "I'm the one," murmured the puppy on the left, exploring my ear with his damp nose. His eyes were exactly the colour of imperial topaz, a rich golden brown. I visited him once or twice a week after that, bringing treats and carrying him into a nearby garden to play away from the rest of the litter. Topaz was already a fearless little fellow. His manners were good; he would politely amble off to piddle on his feet every two or three minutes and then return for another round of tug.

I brought him home the day he was eight weeks old and too small to get up the stairs by himself. The only time I ever heard him cry was when he couldn't see me; for the first week I was not allowed out of his sight. It's very tiring to be adored, especially when you are sitting on the loo in the middle of the night.

Kalypso, who is fed up to the back teeth with my insistence on bringing new dogs into her house, tolerated his bumptiousness for about half an hour. When he went to explore her dinner dish, she bit him on the face and he ran to me screaming, dripping blood all over the floor. I cradled his trembling little body, staunched the blood and felt as indignant as any mother. Late that night in heavy rain when out for a pee, he became disoriented and wandered into the pond. I went straight in after him, through the rose bushes, and we emerged soaked, scratched, shivering with cold and hung about with duck weed. He was fine, but I felt rather shaky.

The first week was intense. He screamed hysterically if I moved out of sight, wouldn't eat unless I sat with him and had to get up three times during the night to go outside. I had many opportunities to study my garden by moonlight as Topaz sleepily watered his toes. I'd resisted the idea of a crate as a method of housetraining, but after the first night (known thereafter as The Long Night of the Puddles) I asked Nyoman to make a portable wire cage for the pup. Dogs are den animals by nature and Topaz immediately loved his crate. He retired there to nap and kept his favourite toys in it. Sometimes he'd break into the house during the day just to doze in his crate, and slept in it in my bedroom at night.

Just as I was about to expire of sleep deprivation, he doubled in size overnight and grew out of it all. Suddenly he was sleeping through the night, wandering around the garden all by himself and wolfing down his meals of minced chicken heads and hearts mixed with red rice and vegetables. Best of all, he regarded me more as a manager than a goddess, watching me carefully and trying to figure out what I wanted him to do. Then he tried hard to do it.

I chose Topaz to be a fearsome guard dog, so it's ironic that the only collar I could find in Ubud that fit his young neck was a pink one with rhinestones. "It will help him get in touch with his feminine side," said my female friends. "Poofter," muttered my male friends. He was oblivious to all this. He knew he was a mighty warrior doglet with the kind of genes I preferred not to meet on a dark night. At least he would be on my side.

Within a month he'd learned to sit, lie down, pee outside most of the time and break into the house three different ways. The week after that he taught me throw a bone across the patio while calling, "Go get it! Bring it back! Drop it! Good dog!" until I was hoarse. We are pretty pleased with one another's progress. He has the makings of a fine dog, and I'm learning a thing or two myself.

The View From a Small Town

I grew up in a suburb of Vancouver, and after that I always seemed to live in cities. When I moved to Ubud, I became part of a small town for the first time. What a revelation... smile, and everyone smiles back. If you don't have the right change at the shop, you can pay tomorrow. When a neighbour has a big ceremony, a basket of food often appears in my kitchen later. I send the basket back afterwards with a succulent papaya from my garden.

Singapore was never like this.

When I visited Canada one summer, my father and I took a walk early one morning. At first I thought it was just pleasantly quiet, then I began to realize it was much too quiet. No cars drove past. There wasn't a person to be seen anywhere; no one was sitting on a porch, sipping coffee behind a kitchen window or pottering in the early morning gardens. And where were the children? When I was a kid we played outside from June until September, reluctantly reeled in by parents only to eat and sleep. This was spookily like walking through a deserted movie set, with no sign of life. Everyone is too busy, over-committed; even the kids today have tight schedules and hardly play outside any more.

I couldn't help contrasting this with my early morning walks in Ubud. My compound is private and tranquil, but as soon as I pass through my gate into the little lane in front of my house I'm part of the warp and weft of the community. Busy dogs nose along the motorbike tracks, ignoring the indignant chickens. Pak Mangku's wife calls a greeting on her way to the temple. At the warung on the corner Old Ibu is opening up for the day. She lifts her chin in greeting, then tidies the piles of produce and collects the coffee glasses from the night before. Parents are driving their children to the elementary school next door, three deep on the back of a motorbike. In the community hall opposite the temple, a squadron of Balinese in white track suits practices Tai Chi. I wave, and they grin in unison as I pass.

I turn into the main road, already crowded by seven in the morning. Public vans disgorge women on their way to market. The boys in charge of the mobile snack carts are already comparing notes on the corner beside their steaming pots. The policeman at the market corner gives me a thumbs-up when I break into a trot. He's been monitoring my fitness routine for months.

It really is a very small town. Saturday night finds the parking lot of Delta supermarket jammed with motorcycles and cars. In the absence of a mall, this is really the only place to hang out. It's a wild scene. Courting couples, young guys and families cruise the aisles, check out the latest flavours in instant noodles and eye the bizarre foreign groceries. By ten o'clock the town is tucked up for the night, apart from a few roadside vendors selling snacks by the light of hissing gas lamps. The sidewalks are punctuated by dusty, slumbering dogs.

Until recently the foreigners who chose to live here tended to be eccentric, creative and reclusive. I'm astonished by the range of skills in this small, loosely knit community. Whether you need a computer genius, psychologist, systems analyst, pattern maker, engineer, chef, early learning specialist, photographer, yoga teacher, graphic designer, business consultant or any kind of artist, there's probably a world-class example living within a couple of kilometres. And when trouble strikes, they all come together to provide an instant platform of caring support. There's not a lot of cash around, so services may be exchanged for jewellery, Tarot readings, organic chickens or computer lessons.

In a big city, you throw things out when they break. In a small town, odds are that someone can fix that flashlight, juicer or desk lamp. Discard a torn skirt and it turns up a week later as a smart new shirt on your housekeeper's little boy.

My staff take me to pray with them when they think it's a good idea. Telephone numbers have six digits. If I don't feel well, I examine my symptoms before deciding whether to go to a doctor, a balian, or have Wayan Manis concoct a remedy from the garden. Once a month or so I get a piece of mail, and for the first few years the postman brought it right into the kitchen because he didn't recognize the function of my mailbox. I often drive past a smoldering corpse at the cremation ground near my house when I come home with the groceries. It's all very interesting.

There is a downside to this charming lifestyle. After a few years here, a trip to Denpasar an hour away becomes downright unnerving. And one becomes alarmingly easy to amuse. I went to a deli in the south a while ago and after listening to my squeaks of excitement ("English muffins! Lamb chops!") a jaded shopper turned to enquire, "Are you from Ubud?"

As I sink ever deeper into bucolic contentment, I find I'm losing my big-city social skills. An old friend from Canada watched me de-tick one of the dogs at the dinner table recently and announced, "You know, you're never going to be able to come back." He was only half joking. I only half care.

Snakes Alive

Trendy folk have a personal trainer. I have a personal herpetologist. Whenever I spot a new reptile in the house or garden I fire off an email to Ron, who responds enthusiastically with identification and advice.

Snakes have an unfortunate reputation for being vicious, poisonous and giving people bad dreams. This is quite unfair.

Balinese snakes are very shy and law-abiding. They probably tell their offspring scary stories about huge, violent homo sapiens who will club them to death with big sticks, which explains why we hardly ever see a serpent if it sees us first.

Not everyone shares my admiration of the reptile race. Phobias slither right across cultures; Wayan is terrified of snakes. I explain that not all snakes are poisonous. She looks dubious. I tell her that some people keep snakes as pets. She lets it be known in three languages that this idea gives her the willies. As far as Wayan is concerned, the only good snake is a dead one. Her adoring husband used to oblige by killing every hapless serpent they saw, despite my pleas for mercy.

My previous house was near a rice field and we often saw black, brown and beige rice field snakes. Although I'm now only a kilometre away, we get much less variety. There's a dainty little black and brown pond snake with white ears that keeps the frog population in check by grazing on newly hatched tadpoles. I asked my staff if it was poisonous. "Probably," Wayan said, on principle. "Only in the afternoon," corrected Nyoman. I'm told that there are pythons near the river but we've rarely seen one. Apart from that, the snake population here seems to be limited to green pit vipers.

There are a lot of them. During construction of the house, the workers killed two. Shortly after I moved in, Nyoman killed a few more. After that there was a hatching and we found tiny juveniles all over the garden for several weeks. By this time I had persuaded Nyoman to pick them up between two sticks and toss them gently over the riverbank. "Go to the river," I hissed to the little ones. "Don't come into the garden; it's dangerous here."

The green pit viper is a pretty snake. Fluorescent green with a dark red tail, the ones around here seldom exceed about 60 cm in length. They don't actually live in pits; the name refers to a little temperature-sensitive dent between the nostril and the eye. It's true that they pack a nasty venom and can deliver a painful bite, but they're not aggressive by nature. When I meet one in the garden, it invariably slips away in embarrassment as soon as it sees me.

I don't see them very often because I'm not looking for them. But Wayan is convinced that they're afraid of me and only approach the house when I leave town. This could be true. When I was gone one July, there were three green pit viper dramas. Wayan was sitting in the pantry ironing one day, dreamily glancing at the palm tree outside the unglazed window, when she focused on the unblinking gaze of a palm-green serpent that was watching her from a metre away. Then my house sitter was having a massage on the terrace one day when the masseuse noticed a green viper in a tendril of flowering vine that grew against the house. Then there was another one in the mango tree.

"I don't know how you can sleep at night with all the snakes around here," declares Wayan darkly. None of the windows have glass in them, but after one of my dogs was bitten my staff insisted on stapling mosquito net over all the openings. It made them feel better. Actually, according to Ron's research, deaths from green pit viper bites are very rare. Even if the snake bites you, chances are it won't release its venom. Only the extremely young or old might succumb.

As development continues to cover Bali's verdant rice fields with villas, shops and restaurants, a less visible change is also taking place. The many small creatures which live in these areas are driven out of their native habitats and are increasingly to be found in houses and gardens. I've lived here ten years and never heard of a single sighting of the very poisonous banded krait until recently. But in 2010 there were several sightings and two fatalities.

Frogs, insects and especially snakes play an important role in the health of Bali's rice fields (sawah). Frogs and toads eat mosquitoes and other pests. Snakes prey on the rats which decimate rice crops all over Bali. As snakes continue to disappear, killed by nervous humans and harvested for the fashion industry, the rats are getting the upper paw in Tabanan and Gianyar Regencies. A cobra can consume up to 5,000 rats in its lifetime and a python about half that, so each snake can reduce the potential population of destructive rodents by tens of thousands.

It's a vicious circle. The snakes get killed so the rats eat the rice, the farmer becomes discouraged because the harvest is poor and sells his land for development, therefore taking one more rice field out of production and driving the snakes into – guess where? The new villa! Dear reader, please think several hundred times about building a house on rice land, and then do it somewhere else. Not only will you avoid taking another bite out of Bali's rapidly shrinking agricultural land bank, but will be helping preserve the also quickly diminishing wildlife population.

Rapid loss of habitat due to development has resulted in a predictable increase in the number of snake sightings, and this situation will probably result in more snake bites in future. "Don't blame the snakes," says English herpetologist Ron Lilley, whose specialty is Indonesian reptiles. "Bali's serpents are shy and retiring, and much prefer not to encounter humans. Snakes don't want to bite people. They are only interested in two things, food and sex, and you can offer them neither. So snakes are not going to seek you out but if they are cornered or frightened, of course they will defend themselves."

Bali has about 35 species of snakes, only three of which are poisonous – the green pit viper, the cobra and the krait. (Well, the sea snakes are venomous too, but there is no record of anyone ever being bitten by one.) Besides the green pit viper, the most common venomous snake is the cobra, which can range in colour from beige through all the shades of brown to black. They are also shy and will not rise up, spit or bite unless threatened. King cobras are found only in West Bali. The local krait, usually marked with alternating black and white bands, is the most venomous snake on Bali and its bite can be deadly.

Very few people are known to have died of snakebite in Bali, and if you're bitten it's important to remember that the snake was either probably not a venomous one, or didn't release much venom into the bite. Never cut into a snake bite or try to suck out the poison -don't touch the bite at all. It's important to lie quietly to prevent the toxin moving more quickly through the bloodstream. For neurotoxic cobra and krait bites, apply a pressure bandage and immobilize with a splint if the bite is on an arm or leg. Viper bites should be splinted but without pressure. Take the bite victim to Sanglah, Prima Medika, SOS or BIMH immediately. Krait and sometimes cobra venom can affect the respiratory system, so it's important get to medical professionals who can recognize and deal with this appropriately. Alcohol enhances the effects of snake venom; don't drink it or pour it over the bite.

Size is not an issue with venomous snakes; a newly hatched snake has fully developed venom glands and can pack the same punch as its mama. A snake may not inject much or any venom during the course of a bite which is why medical observation is important, especially before giving anti-venom.

Biofarma, an Indonesian company in Bandung, produces 40,000 doses of a polyvalent anti-venom each year which contains serum (ABU) for krait, viper and common spitting cobra (but not king cobra) bites. But anti-venom is very specific, and it's not clear whether the farmed Javanese snake venoms from which the anti-venom is made are effective against Balinese species. There is a possibility of allergy, so a skin test should always be done before administering ABU.

Pythons have no venom but will still bite if threatened.

We recently found a spectacular python lying on top of the high wall between the coffee garden and Pak Mangku's yard, its gleaming coils brilliant against the grey concrete. We stood watching it and its unblinking golden eye watched us back. There was a brief discussion about how this snake would drop by every couple of weeks and help itself to a small chicken, which Pak Mangku didn't seem to mind.

But there was no telltale bulge in this snake; it just lay folded rather awkwardly on the wall. It took us a while to realize that it was badly tangled in the string netting we'd erected in a vain attempt to keep Pak Mangku's chickens out of our yard and the deadly jaws of my killer dachshund. The python had tried to push its way through the small mesh and was doubled back on itself, trapped and unable to move.

"We will have to cut it free," I said.

Nyoman sighed. He knew that 'we' in this context meant 'Nyoman'. Over the years he's been with me he's become much braver about snakes, guiding them into bottles or releasing them over the cliff. This one, however, was over two meters long. He fetched the ladder and a knife, and soon we were standing on the grass around the trapped snake and several metres of netting, strategizing the release. None of the Balinese wanted to touch it even after I immobilized the back half, so we gently laid a bamboo across its neck to hold it down. Nyoman gingerly cut away the netting without damaging the skin, looking as though he wished he was somewhere else.

The reticulated python is a beautiful animal, gold and silver and black. Its scales glowed in the sunlight as its strong tail groped around my arm, making Wayan squeal. Nyoman clipped the last confining strand and the lithe, muscular body stretched to its full length in relief. Suddenly realizing its freedom, it glided through the grass to the wire fence, pushed its way though and dropped down the wall on the other side. We ran to the fence in time to see its tail disappear into the jungle.

"I don't like snakes, but that was a pretty one," admitted Wayan. A well-fed Bali reticulated python can grow to four meters, although they seldom live long enough near habitation to attain that length and most of the ones we see are about half that size. In Malaysia, pythons have been known to grow to almost ten meters and to consume calves and even the occasional unfortunate passerby. But Bali's pythons dine largely on small birds and rodents.

Wayan continues to believe that my presence keeps the compound snake-free. I have a sneaking suspicion, though, that there's quite a colony of green pit vipers down by the river, giving their kids nightmares with stories about a man with a machete.

Chop Wood, Carry Water

There's been no running water in my village for five days now. Repeated attempts to call the water authority have failed; the staff has obviously taken the phone off the hook. Consultations with neighbours in my lane reveal a consensus that something is probably broken somewhere. They sigh and shrug, go to bathe in the river and let the laundry pile up. Many rural Balinese haven't had modern conveniences long enough to grieve when they disappear. They still have a foot in each bathroom, so to speak.

But it's a terrible inconvenience to members of the privileged minority who have always had all the water they could consume—like me. We read stories about millions of people who live without access to clean water, but it doesn't actually mean anything until our own taps run dry. You don't realize how many times a day you turn on a tap to wipe down a counter, wash your hands, brush your teeth, rinse the veggies, wash the dishes, wash your smalls … until you can't. To say nothing of flushing the loo or having a shower.

I'm fortunate in having guttering and two large rain water tanks, so I haven't been completely dry. But I've had a chance to learn what it's like to carry every drop of water you need, even though it's only for a few meters. Water is heavy and messy to haul around. You have to be strategic about how you dip it out of the big container on the kitchen counter so you don't contaminate the whole thing. You also learn to bring in all the water you'll need for the night before it gets dark. You begin to feel lucky that you don't have to scale a steep river bank every time you need to do this, as so many Balinese women still do. And now the rainwater tanks are getting very low. Wayan and Nyoman are only here six hours a day. I'm learning to cope.

Hauling a slopping bucket into the house, I am vividly reminded of a journey through Rajasthan 15 years ago. The desert women were tough and straight in their vivid saris, striding through the sand with gleaming brass water jars on their heads. It was a timeless, romantic scene. I even took a few pictures, may the goddess forgive me, before the radiator of our old Ambassador started to hiss and we ground to a lurching halt.

A circle of women gathered around the stranded car talking among themselves, their bold silver nose rings glinting in the sun. Our driver opened the hood and addressed the eldest one authoritatively. The women looked at us and laughed rather unkindly, but they all set down their water jars. As the radiator cooled one of the women challenged me to pick up her load. It was so heavy I couldn't even lift it off the hot sand. And they walked several kilometers twice a day to bring the precious water to their huts. These jars, too heavy for a soft foreign women, contained pathetically little water to meet the needs of their families.

Without expression, each woman tipped some of her water into the radiator. I was horrified at the value of this gift, knowing that the rupees I gave them were meaningless in the desert where the only currency was their own energy. Since then, I've regarded water with something like awe.

As simple as breath, it is always there. When it is not there, we can't survive.

Over forty percent of the world's population lack basic sanitation and access to clean water. One billion people drink unsafe water—contaminated with animal and human filth or toxic chemicals. A mindboggling 675 million people in Asia still draw their water from polluted rivers and lakes. When small children grow ill from drinking bad water, they usually die.

There was a scandal in Ontario, Canada when many people fell sick and even died from a polluted civic water source. Things like that aren't supposed to happen in the so-called developed world. But pure water is very easily polluted. Clean water sources, once fouled, are difficult and expensive to rehabilitate. In parts of Russia, access to clean water has actually declined in the past few years as civic authorities lose the will or ability to safeguard supplies. Conditions in some North American cities are also deteriorating.

The water situation probably adds an extra hour to my day, because I can still draw from the rain water tanks. But in many countries, hauling water long distances to meet the washing, cleaning, cooking and bathing needs of a family is a full-time job. There's a special relationship between women and water. In most cultures, women and girls carry it. Pregnant women, women with babies and toddlers, elderly women, sick women. In developing countries, little girls are routinely pulled out of school to haul water for the family. Because nothing is more important to survival.

Nothing is more important—not status, power, money, possessions, politics, religion or technology. The elemental simplicity of clean water to drink, air to breathe and fuel to cook our food is taken for granted... until it disappears.

And when it does, we're drop-kicked back into a time where we have to chop wood and carry water to survive, if only for a week. These may be useful skills, I remind myself as I wake to another morning of buckets and dry taps. But I'll be a lot more aware of the blessings of running water when I have it again.

To Dye For

As I learn more about Bali's environmental issues, I discover that even the most prosaic products can be problematical. Next time a beach vendor offers you a brightly coloured sarong, give a thought to all the textiles produced in Bali for the tourist trade and for export each year. Those inexpensive garments carry a high price tag for the environment.

Chemical dyes arrived in Indonesia over a hundred years ago and quickly became popular because their colours were bolder than traditional plant dyes. Most of the textile dyes and associated chemicals used in Indonesia today are very harmful to the environment. Cheap, harsh chemical dyes, many containing heavy metals, are routinely flushed into Denpasar's waterways. This effluent, with its extremely high pH of between 10 and 14, quickly kills any fish or plants that come into contact with it.

In 2007, environmental engineer Gede Sugiarta surveyed 234 dye factories in Denpasar as part of a project to find a solution to this seriously polluting industry. At that time, 90 of these businesses were considered large—each producing over 50 cubic meters of effluent each day. Gede experimented with several possibilities including anaerobic wastewater treatment plants, using chicken manure to create a soup of dye-consuming bacteria and adding more chemicals to the effluent to remove the colour. None of these methods was effective, mainly because they could effectively treat only a fraction of the effluent at any time. Companies that wished to add treatment facilities found the cost of the infrastructure and chemicals prohibitive.

"Because of the very high alkalinity of the dye waste water, hydrochloric acid is used to neutralize it," explains Gede. Even at that time, industrial grade HCl cost about $50 a drum, and large amounts were needed to cope with the huge volume of effluent being produced every day. And neutralization is just one of the steps.

"There's no easy solution. The dye factories need serious government support; they don't have the resources to put in treatment systems. Bali can't handle even a small polluting industry. It's better not to allow it at all if the factories can't treat their effluent."

A crackdown was imposed on the hundreds of dye factories that line the river in Denpasar. The factories were given two months to put settling ponds and filtration systems in place, or face permanent closure. Many of the small, cottage-industry level factories working on lean profit margins were unable to afford these improvements. Meanwhile, the factories released their effluent at night, in concealed drains or waited until government inspectors are out of sight.

"When I saw the conditions people were working in, I was truly embarrassed to be part of the demand that creates these factories," says an American agent who sends sarongs to the United States. "Closing them is good for the environment, but what about the livelihoods of the people involved at all levels of the industry? There are hundreds who are stirring dye vats, stamping patterns, washing and stretching cloth, the owners of the factories and shops, the shop workers, cargo workers, buyers, agents…"

What are the alternatives to using harsh chemical dyes? Natural plant dyes from Indonesia and India and high quality, non-polluting chemical dyes are available, but the costs are high and the colours are softer than local dyes. I talked to William Ingram about the possibility of returning to Bali's natural plant dyes which were used for hundreds of years before chemical dyes arrived with the

Dutch. With his wife Jean Howe, William is co-founder of Threads of Life, a certified Fair Trade business that helps traditional weaving communities in East Nusa Tenggara maintain their heritage of natural dyes. (www.threadsoflife.com)

"The biggest issue with using a natural dye like indigo, for example, is the sheer volume of plant material that's needed to dye a relatively small amount of fabric," he explained. "It takes twenty kilograms of indigo leaves to dye a single scarf or sash. Indigo grows like a weed in the dryer parts of Bali but the amount required for commercial production would require huge plantations. With the price of land rising as it is, that's not viable." And plant dyes are hard to standardize. The colours produced by a single plant can differ according to variables like soil type, amount of water available and freshness of the material.

Indigo as a dye is environmentally benign. It thrives in poor soil and reproduces readily every three or four months. A vat of indigo dye has a pH of between 7 and 10 and can be kept going indefinitely as long as it's kept fermenting. "The fermentation process releases the indigo from the leaves and reduces the oxygen in the solution, turning it a yellow-green colour. When the thread is dyed and oxidizes in the air, it turns blue."

Before chemical dyes were invented, most of the world's flags were some combination of blue or red on white—plant-derived dyes that were colour-fast and weathered well.

Sediment is a serious issue with chemical dyes. It can make up as much as twenty percent of some dye wastewater, especially from the batik dyes used in Java. This sediment contains high levels of heavy metals and is very difficult to dispose of. Some dyeing processes require a mordant which attaches the dye to the fibre. Much of the commercial batik industry uses waterglass (sodium silicate) as a mordant, which further complicates the witch's brew of effluent. By contrast, the natural dyes that require a mordant also use plant materials.

What's the solution? "Better chemical dyes," says William firmly. "Natural plant dyes can't begin to meet commercial needs."

But the office, collections, dyeing shed and gardens of Threads of Life and its sister organization, the nonprofit Yayasan Pecinta Budaya Bebali (PBB), hold their own fascinating story—the country's living heritage of over two hundred natural plant dyes. Indonesia's ancient traditions of labour-intensive hand-tied ikat textiles vary from island to island, but one common thread runs through them all. They use a wide range of plant materials for dyes and mordants in these complex ritual and sacred weavings, some of which take years to complete.

Threads of Life and PBB help traditional ikat-producing communities in East Nusa Tenggara maintain their heritage of natural dyes, with projects in remote communities of Flores, East Sumba, Sulawesi, Timor, West Kalimantan and Bali.

East Nusa Tenggara is a cradle of expertise in complicated tying, dyeing and weaving techniques. Its ikats are fiendishly complex in strategy and construction, with many taking years to complete. The weavings' motifs are rich in cultural lore, ceremony and tradition. Many are still used as bride-wealth and in ceremonies for house-raisings and funerals. "The traditional textiles of Indonesia reflect a deep engagement with nature and the community that has sustained its indigenous people through the centuries," says William. "The beauty of these textiles is selfevident, but their deepest gift is in the stories they tell. The motifs are rich in cultural lore."

Young women today aren't interested in spending years producing a single piece of cloth, leaving that labour-intensive task to their mothers and grandmothers. But as the older women die, the rich tradition of spinning, tying, dyeing and weaving ritual textiles in this country could disappear within a generation.

There's another reason the traditional weaving has been laid aside. The ripple effect of Indonesia's monetary crisis that began in 1997 soon reached even the remote shores of East Nusa Tenggara. The impact would have been slight a generation ago in these communities where barter economies were the norm. Barter is still common, but now people need cash to send their children off-island for schooling and to purchase essential commodities. Not only have the women begun to sell their traditional ritual textiles for much-needed cash, they are now too busy producing cheap weavings for both the tourist and local markets to create the time-consuming heritage textiles. The market demand now is for cheap, small weavings using chemical dyes and pre-spun fibre.

With support from Threads of Life, traditional weavers can continue to create heritage textiles using natural fibres and dyes. Threads of Life provides advance payments for important pieces that may take years to complete, finds Indonesian and international markets for weavers' work and helps remote communities network, share and build on their knowledge of natural dyes.

There are many different dye plants in the palette of Eastern Indonesian textile artists. Indigo, mangrove bark, causurina bark, eucalyptus alba, mango and teak leaves, and annato are among the more common ones. Many are rare, hard to grow or difficult to harvest. Morinda (also known as tiba or noni) for example is used as a red dye, but the part of the plant used is the bark of the root. It's very difficult to sustainably harvest this delicate plant material without stressing or killing the tree. The bark from the roots of two trees is needed to dye one small cloth and it must be used immediately.

"Tying, dyeing and weaving a textile over many years brings a lot of life-force energy to the piece," says textile expert Madé Lolet, who has been studying Indonesian dying and weaving for years. "The finished textiles hold a lot of power." There's a good market for these textiles among wealthy Indonesians and foreign collectors, and Threads of Life facilitates this.

The intricate process of creating a traditional textile is almost unbelievably labour-intensive. The fibres are selected, spun, placed on a frame, then meticulously bundled and tied off to create the desired pattern. The weaver does this by imagining the three dimensions of the entire finished piece as she ties each group of threads to resist the dye. Then the dyes and mordants are collected and prepared. When using red tones, Morinda root bark is put in the dye vat and then various other plant products are added as a mordant, which connects the dye to fibre. Mordants must include three elements – a protein, a tannin, and aluminum salt or other metal salt. Many Indonesian communities use kimiri nut oil as the protein, which gives the final textile a distinctive texture and aroma. The tannin is often viloca, and the aluminum salt is extracted from plants of the symplocos family, which contains up to fifty percent of the material.

The tied threads stay in the dye bath at least four months, but longer exposure improves the colour significantly. "Doubling the mordant time from one to two years makes the colour much brighter," William explains. "That's why we pay part of the cost of the finished textile up front—to enable the family to live during the long dyeing process and so they won't be tempted to rush this critical step." When the dyeing is complete, the threads are unbundled and sorted so that the weaving process can begin. A skilled weaver can complete about five centimetres an hour, but due to the highly concentrated nature of the work can't weave for more than four hours a day. Depending on the size of the textile and the complexity of the pattern, the weaving alone may take over a month to complete.

Threads of Life has become an international centre of excellence for traditional textiles from East Nusa Tenggara. The Threads of Life Textile Arts Centre in Jalan Kajeng in Ubud not only displays these rare textiles for sale, but serves as a museum and education centre for the ancient art of Indonesian ikat production. It also offers short classes on Indonesian textiles and a seasonal full-day workshop on indigo dyeing when the materials are available. The organization's headquarters includes a dye garden which contains a growing number of traditional dye and cotton plants with an adjacent dyeing laboratory. An air-conditioned room in the office houses the herbarium—a collection of about a hundred of the dye plants used in East Nusa Tenggara.

Threads of Life is a valuable cultural catalyst, ensuring not only that this precious aspect of Indonesian heritage remains alive, but that the women whose hands create it are generously compensated for their art.

Communication

Breakdwon

Anyone who has undertaken activities requiring exact communication in foreign lands has stories to tell. Often they have a few more gray hairs than usual, too. There seems to be an interesting and sometimes disastrous disconnection between what is said, what is heard and what happens next. No matter how much detailed instruction is given, there is always room for individual interpretation.

Of course, giving less instruction leaves much more space for interpretation. I remember a story told to me by a Canadian diplomat posted to Delhi a couple of decades ago. She lived in a big old house and the kitchen was in a hut at the foot of a large garden.

Weather permitting, she liked to have breakfast on the garden terrace, savouring the exotic ambience and the excellent tea. Only one tiny flaw rendered her breakfasts imperfect. The toast was always cold.

Those of us of a certain age and raised in the traditions of the Commonwealth are familiar with the dubious British practice of serving toast in little silver racks. Although attractive, it ensures that the toast is cold and flabby. Very disappointing if one is looking forward to a slice of crisp, hot toast with butter melting into it.

This lady's cook was an elderly Brahmin who had been trained in strict British tradition. The leap from cold toast to hot seemed too great. He gazed in puzzlement down his elegant nose at her as she tried to explain the concept, but the silver toast rack continued to bear its limp payload every morning.

Then one day the bearer proudly presented toast that was actually warm. Not hot enough to melt butter, but appreciably warmer than previously. The lady was delighted, and decided to reinforce her approval with a visit to the kitchen hut. She strode through the garden and paused at the kitchen door. The cook, bare to the waist and perspiring in the hot kitchen, was frying her breakfast eggs. He was carefully holding a slice of toast under each arm.

This example of imperfect communication may suggest that extremely detailed instructions will circumvent such misadventures. However, it seems that there will always be room for the listener to add some individuality. This appears to be especially true in Bali, as anyone who is involved in production can attest.

One can direct the workman to make an item exactly like this, paint it a certain shade of yellow with a special brush and have it ready on Tuesday. When he delivers it (on Friday) he is quite hurt by our cool reception. After all, we didn't tell him not to paint little blue hearts all over it. The lady didn't tell the cook not to keep the toast warm in his armpits. Since we didn't give them a complete brief, they don't consider themselves in the wrong; they have merely been imperfectly instructed. After a while you become a little neurotic about giving obsessively detailed instructions and wondering what can still go wrong. It's amazing how a producer can add individual touches in ways that would never in a hundred years occur to you. I've heard stories from designers and exporters who have ordered several thousand somethings all exactly the same, and come back later to find that they were either not the same as each other or measurably different from the sample. This can be disconcerting when you are packing a large Christmas order on deadline.

The Balinese have these issues too, when making products here. Wayan Manis and the women in her village weave stunning laundry baskets from lontar palm. Wayan was delighted to get an order for six big baskets, and we carefully planned the production. I took a photograph of the sample basket to show the design, enlarged it and had it laminated. Wayan bought the correct materials and I made a sketch of the finished basket with exact measurements. Wayan delivered all these to her friends and gave them full instructions.

A week later she arrived at work with a stricken expression, sat down and put her head on the table. "What's the matter with these people?" she wailed. They had made the baskets in different sizes, with the wrong motif and had added a few hot pink touches of their own. But it was rather gratifying to learn that the communication gap spanned all communities.

So I was particularly careful when instructing Nyoman about my gate before I went away for a few days. He had carved a nice sign that said 'Ibu Cat', and I asked him to repaint the double Balinese gate and attach the sign. Even after all this time it did not occur to me to say, "Do exactly this and no more. Do not use your initiative. Do not try to make it better. Just paint the gate and hang up the sign."

I don't know where he found that particular shade of red, but it certainly makes the house easy to find. The Balinese are sensitive about balance, and Nyoman was evidently uncomfortable that one panel of the gate had a sign and the other did not. So he carved a companion piece that said 'house' and hung it on the other panel. He was terribly pleased with himself. I still can't bring myself to explain that my bright red entrance declaring 'Ibu Cat House' now resembles the door to a bordello. It wasn't his fault; he had been imperfectly instructed.

A Sense of Humus

My staff find me vastly entertaining in a general way, but my bizarre gardening techniques astonish them.

A well-kept Balinese compound is bare dirt, swept remorselessly several times a day until every atom of topsoil has been removed. When I moved into my new house eight years ago, it took us several weeks just to clear away the debris from the construction, exposing a vast expanse of virgin soil. I rubbed my hands in anticipation of a lush organic garden. Wayan Manis picked up a broom and began to sweep.

"No sweeping," I implored, replacing the broom in the kitchen.

"But Ibu, it needs to be clean."

"We will plant grass," I announced.

They absorbed this radical concept with mistrust. No matter how many times I explained that I intended to plant over every inch of bare dirt on the garden, they couldn't believe that I meant it. "It will be cooler," I explained. "The house will be cleaner because the dust won't blow in. The dogs won't bring in mud during the rainy season. And it will keep the earth from blowing away during the dry season." Wayan shook her head. "It's not usual, Ibu."

It took almost three years to grass in the whole compound, one blade at a time. Wayan and Nyoman were very suspicious of this activity. At first they would actually pull the new grass up again when I wasn't looking, or cut it back to the ground during the hot season so it would die. But finally I achieved my goal of a cool, grassy garden. My staff at last conceded that indeed our garden was several degrees cooler than the street, and the house was indeed easier to keep clean. Then they told me that they were slowly introducing the concept into their own compound, lifting the broken old concrete a few centimetres at a time and slowly replacing it with grass so that Nyoman's mother wouldn't notice.

Next came the Battle of the Mulch. Nyoman subscribed to a scraped-earth policy in the flower beds and around the shrubs and trees. When I explained the principles of mulching, complete with nifty coloured drawings, I could see that his Balinese sense of order was outraged. Mulch does look untidy, true, but it also cools the roots of the plants, distributes nutrients as it decays and keeps the earth beneath it moist for weeks after the last rain.

"It is not usual, Ibu."

"In other countries, it is usual," I assured them.

They looked at each other and refrained from rolling their eyes as I built little bamboo fences around the trees and heaped straw and grass cuttings inside. I watered the tomato plants well and piled on a foot of rice straw. Nyoman observed all this with an expression of deep disapproval. When I asked him to mulch, he would scatter a handful of grass clippings around to humour me, but I could see he thought I was barking mad.

Then came a long dry spell. In some parts of the garden plants wilted, leaves drooped. In others, the same plants bloomed and flourished. When I pulled away the mulch from these, he couldn't help but be impressed by the rich, moist humus underneath.

Now he mulches deeply where I ask him to and hauls home truckloads of dry straw and rice husks to humour me, but I know he won't be taking this technique back to the village. It's just too messy looking.

My gardening eccentricities escalated alarmingly after I took a tropical organic gardening course from a master gardener who came to Bali from Australia once or twice a year. She delivered intensive courses covering garden design, soil chemistry, composting, natural pest control, companion planting and yes—mulching. I came home with all kinds of peculiar new ideas.

"We will no longer dig in the earth to plant vegetables," I announced. Nyoman winced and Wayan Manis sat down abruptly. They carefully avoided looking at each other.

"Ibu, we have to dig," explained Nyoman patiently.

We went into the garden and I demonstrated Diane's no-dig garden. First I placed about ten sheets of newspaper in a sunny spot right on top of the grass and weeds, and watered it well. Then went a layer of nicely rotted cow manure, also well watered, then a few handfuls of rice straw and lots of compost. I finished it all off with a thick layer of rice straw and gave it all a good soaking.

"There", I said. My staff stared at the pile without expression.

We made a bamboo tripod and planted some bean seeds and spinach. I never did figure out how to explain that digging destroys the structure of the soil and buries the rich culture of micro-organisms that populate the top two centimetres. They wouldn't have believed it anyway. But seeing is believing. Within a month they had to admit the vegetables were growing faster than usual. By the time we were eating the harvest, they had become used to the strange appearance of our vegetable garden. When the plants died back, we put another layer of mulch and compost on top and planted in that. "Organic," Wayan explains kindly to visitors.

I have already signed up for a class on pruning and grafting. I can't wait to see Nyoman's face when I graft an orange branch onto a lemon tree. It will be good for his sense of humus.

Bringing Home the Bacon

Everyone warned me that the piglets would get car sick on the long drive from East Bali. But they were remarkably restrained, given their tender age and the fact that they were in unfamiliar territory, namely the floor of the front seat of my car. The newspaper on which they were lying was perfectly dry.

We peered through the passenger window at the two little creatures, who peered woefully back. They were eight weeks old. Nyoman had stopped every 20 minutes to give them water, but now they were hot and nervous. As soon as they had been gently decanted into their paddock they both squatted for an urgent pee. I was impressed by their manners.

On my first trip to Bali in 1969, these little black sway-back pigs were everywhere. They rootled by the dusty roadside and slumbered under the benches of the warungs. Industriously they dealt with the garbage and, in those days before plastic, kept the villages clean. Since then they have largely been replaced by huge pink hybrid porkers which require large amounts of expensive commercial feed laced with growth hormones. Today, the Bali pig can hardly be found.

For months I had toyed with the idea of re-introducing the Bali pig to Ubud as a sort of ambulatory household composter. Much of the waste generated by homes in Bali is organic. In the old days when everyone had a little pig, it wasn't an issue. Today, when keeping a pig entails a considerable investment in livestock, a concrete sty and purchased feed, many people can't afford one. Leftover food ends up mixed with other rubbish in a plastic bag or thrown down the riverbank. I wanted to see just how much food a Bali pig needs, and whether they might have a place in a contemporary compound or foreigner's garden.

I did a little research on potbelly pigs on the internet. Of course there was a huge website, based in the United States, for the hordes of people who presumably keep these pigs as pets. I learned that they were as intelligent as some dogs, could be house trained and liked to share their owner's beds. (Wayan and Nyoman refused to believe this.) In fascination I browsed pig accessories like harnesses and leashes and viewed the photo gallery of happy champion porkers with ear ribbons and lace collars in exotic Ohio. But where were the little piggies of my memory? These were all huge. A little more research revealed that little piglets could grow to 75 kilos. The males were vicious and the females went into heat frequently and could manifest fearsome PMs symptoms. Of course, my pigs wouldn't be like that.

Contrary to general opinion, they are also said to be extremely clean if given the space. Imprisoned in a small concrete pen as they are in Bali, pigs can hardly help but smell. So would we, in the same circumstances. Part of my experiment would establish the pong factor of two Bali pigs kept in humane conditions. In fact, they were pong-free.

Nyoman had fenced in a large, cool corner of the garden under a stand of bamboos and built a shelter cushioned with rice straw. I thought it was Pig Heaven. The piglets were not particularly impressed. Disoriented by the long journey and new surroundings, they promptly went to sleep under a giant yam leaf.

I went out a little later, leaving them snuffling around their luxurious quarters with my rapt staff in attendance. Then about six o'clock, in the middle of a meeting across town, I suddenly had a strong urge to go home. Driving back a little too fast, I parked the car just as dusk began to close in. Indeed, there had been a jailbreak. As I opened the gate, two little black pigs trotted across the garden path, a highly curious Kalypso at their heels.

I had a feeling I wasn't going to be very good at catching escaped pigs, so I locked up the dogs and called Nyoman, who took about 20 minutes to arrive from a temple ceremony. Darkness fell. It was astonishing how well camouflaged little black pigs can be, I thought, as I followed them around the garden with a torch. I knew that if I lost sight of them, they would disappear into the rapidly deepening shadows. I couldn't leave them at large all night because of the dogs. When Nyoman turned up I was sitting on a plastic stool, torch trained on two exhausted, slumbering piglets.

A spirited chase around the garden followed as we raced through the pitch-black yard after two pitch-black invisible piglets, our torch beams waving wildly. Sensing excitement, the dogs barked hysterically inside the house. We caught one escapee in the crossed beams of our torches and Nyoman threw himself on top of her, muttering about snakes. It is amazing how strong a very small pig can be. We bundled her into an empty aviary and went looking for the other, who broke through the cliff fence and declined to be caught until the following morning.

An experienced pig person pointed out that our wire fence was absurdly inadequate for the likes of these wily escape artists. The piglets spent three days in the aviary while we built sturdy cement block walls. During this time the girls began to settle down. I could hear them snuffling away together as they burrowed into the fragrant straw of their quarters, no doubt discussing the merits of their new accommodation and diet.

The Bali Buddha Café had generously entered into the project with daily contributions of leftovers. The piglets dined enthusiastically if messily on organic greens, bagels and other exotica, tufted tails wagging. Paolo the manager dropped by frequently to check the menu and we named the little creatures after our mothers. Paulette and Peggy continued to thrive. Life in Karangasem was never like this.

I'd read that pigs were amiable and intelligent. I'd heard that they were nice creatures with tender hearts. Someone told me they were gentle and obedient. My observations thus far confirm none of these characteristics.

A pig lives for just one thing—food. There is no room for sentimentality in their tightly focused lives. Pigs are eating machines. Even after a heavy meal when they were slumbering in the cool dust with their bellies distended like footballs, they would heave themselves up on to their little hooves when I appeared, just in case I had a tidbit for them.

My staff strongly disapproved of feeding the scraps from the restaurant straight to the pigs. "I feel sorry for them, Ibu," said Wayan Manis reproachfully. "The food is too hard. How can they eat it?" I looked at the heap of organic greens, soft bagel ends and noodles, then at the tough yam root the piglets had demolished in their paddock. "They seem to be managing," I pointed out.

Wayan never argues with me but somehow has her way in the end. The next day I found that my staff had built an ingenious little brick stove near the paddock, and were cooking up the scraps in a big old pot over a flame of bamboo scraps. "They like the food to be warm," Wayan explained, scratching Paulette fondly behind her hairy black ears. Paulette grunted agreeably into her lunch. A few days later I saw Wayan making her way down to the 'farm' with a bowl of white powder. "Salt, Ibu. It makes the food taste better." Next it will be chili sauce.

I've often thought that certain phrases in our language demeaned this noble animal, but closer observation reveals some home truths. Fat as a pig… just like us, pigs increase in girth according to the amount they consume. And because a pig is obsessed with food and will eat everything in sight, even a Bali pig can grow alarmingly large.

Eat like a pig… alas, the pig is not a dainty diner. Paulette and Peggy are served their warm mélange de jour in a large plastic tub, which they immediately and joyfully jump into up to their knees. Because they are always rootling around the paddock, their dirt-caked snouts add an element of mud to the meal which does not in the least diminish their appetites.

Your room is a pigsty... also true. In a couple of days, these two little animals had churned their large and pleasant paddock into a mud hole, trampled their straw bedding into it, uprooted all the plants and were sleeping in a hollow between two banana trees instead of in their tidy house.

Pig-headed...no contest here. Pigs are creatures of strong character. It is very difficult to confine a pig if the pig would rather be somewhere else. At first they pushed up the wooden gate to their enclosure in their quest to graze on the lawn. Later, after we had strengthened the gate, they simply broke it down. When apprehended, Peggy becomes implacably stubborn in her refusal to leave my vegetable beds unploughed by that busy snout. Even lured by a buttered bagel, she returned to her paddock when she is damned good and ready and not a moment sooner.

Smell like a pig... this is a wicked lie. Pigs themselves have no odour and are very clean in their habits, always relieving themselves in the corner of their enclosure furthest from the feeding area. When fed real food, their droppings resemble and have less smell than a dog's, and it's easy to cover them with earth or leaves. (It's a different story when they are confined in a concrete pen and fed commercial swill.) Wayan bathed the pigs every couple of days, which they enjoyed.

What did undeniably smell was the leftover, muddy, trampled pig food. We removed this immediately and composted it under fragrant rice straw. I could proudly claim that my pigs are as pongless as we could make them, despite my staff's insistence that pigs just had to smell.

In late afternoon I sometimes rambled down to the 'farm' with a cup of tea, and sat on the bench Nyoman made in the pig paddock to spend some quality time with Peggy and Paulette. They declined to commune with me, however. After a thorough snuffle revealed that I was not carrying anything interesting to eat, they ignored me. I tossed a yellow ball to them, but this activity was evidently beneath their dignity. I began to despair that our relationship would ever reach its full potential.

I learned a lot about Bali pigs from a fellow countrywoman who lived on the north coast. She nursed a fantasy about riding her pig along the beach and even had an appropriate harness made. When the pig was small, she massaged it daily and took it for short walks around the yard. The fantasy was building nicely. But then she had to go away for three months, which is a very long time even if you are not a baby pig. Their tender bond was broken. This pig now weighed 70 kilograms. She eats puppies and baby chicks that wander too close, and chased my friend around the yard when she was in heat, snapping at her heels.

A farmer from the Prairies told me that the huge pigs bred there sometimes exceed 200 kilograms. It has been known to happen that a farmer may trip and fall in the sty, only to be remorselessly consumed by the behemoth he had been fattening for bacon for so long. Talk about irony.

So I look at Peggy and Paulette more thoughtfully these days as I served them their warm, nicely seasoned breakfast. There's a look in those alert brown eyes that bears watching.

I must get Nyoman to put another bolt on the paddock gate.

Pigs in Love

Those of you who have penetrated the back roads of rural Bali may have glimpsed a unique local art form; a hand-painted sign featuring two pigs sharing a tender moment. I used to find these signs merely engaging, but when my own pigs were growing up I took a deeper interest in the niche market of the stud for hire.

My Pig Project was conceived as an income-generating activity for my staff. When I bought two female Bali piglets from East Bali, they were about the size of my dachshund. Our plan was that when they grew up, we would breed them (I didn't give much thought to the technical details) and Wayan Manis and Nyoman would sell the piglets. After they paid me back for the breeding stock, the profit would be theirs. This seemed a happy arrangement for all of us until Peggy and Paulette reached the full glory of hirsute porcine maturity. Suddenly we were faced with the technical challenge of impregnating two large, pure-bred swayback Bali sows in the heart of Ubud.

This was new territory for me. I'd sort of drifted into the Pig Project without thinking it through. As the girls grew older I began to grapple with two pressing issues. When is a Bali swayback pig in heat? And how on earth do you find her a boyfriend? I launched the subject at a local watering hole one night on the off-chance that someone at the table might be a closet pig farmer. It turned out that no one had actually met a pig personally, but everybody had an opinion. On the subject of when a girl pig might be receptive to a boy pig, the consensus was that she would begin to wear a lot of make-up. This was not particularly helpful (perhaps it was the gin). Later, a visitor from Sumba stated that when she was ready to mate, the female swayback pig would vocalize loudly for three days. More helpful, but still begged the question of finding a male.

The black swayback Bali pig went out of fashion a decade or two ago when the government brought in huge white hybrids from Australia. When I started to ask around and follow up rumours, I found just two or three of the right species around Ubud, all females. Then Nyoman found a boar in Gianyar. I began to think through the logistics. First, make sure my pigs are in heat, monitoring them for loud cries and eye shadow. Quickly send Nyoman with his truck to Gianyar. Bring back the male pig. somehow get a fully grown, disoriented boar out of the truck, through the gate and walk it through my garden ("Just tie a string around its neck", suggested Nyoman helpfully) to the pig paddock. What if he wasn't in the mood? What if the girls didn't fancy him? Hope that nature would take its course, then reverse the whole process, pay the $3 stud fee (and travel expenses?) and wait two months for the happy event.

It seemed very daunting, so I decided to explore the high-tech option. I knew there was an agricultural office near Ubud and encouraged Nyoman to track down an official. Much of the information he elicited was beyond my vocabulary, but Wayan was advised to mix papaya leaves with the feed every day. This would apparently get the hormones moving. When the hormones moved (check under the tail, we were advised), then someone would come around with the equivalent of a turkey baster and Do the Deed.

This raised a whole new list of mind-boggling questions. Where did they get the sperm? How did they get the sperm? Who obtained the sperm and how did they choose the lucky boar who got to father all the swayback piglets in the regency? This is presumably one very contented pig.

Meanwhile, Peggy and Paulette continued to lumber around the paddock and luxuriate in the mud with no sign of raging hormones, but every once in a while they got a faraway look in their little brown eyes. They would probably prefer the Gianyar option.

Did I mention that pigs have ten to twelve piglets each time? It just occurred to me that I could go from two pigs to twenty pigs overnight...

Fishnapped

Imagine for a moment that you're an untroubled reef fish in a warm tropical ocean.

The thinking box of even quite a large fish is rather small, so you will not be agonizing over world affairs, your relationship or your cholesterol levels. Life is simple. You spend your days loitering around the reef, grazing on lower life forms and avoiding predators. You enjoy the occasional uncommitted amorous interlude with another of your kind. Your borderless world is full of colour and sounds and interesting flavours.

Then one day a diver appears from above, squirts a solution of cyanide in your face and you wake up inside a plastic bag. You spend the rest of your life in a glass box in a dentist's office, eating synthetic fishflavoured flakes when someone remembers to feed you. The things we do to other species would read like science fiction if we did them to each other.

The aquarium trade is huge and Indonesia has been a major exporter of reef fish since the 1960s. This lucrative industry is unregulated, and until the present there has been no way to manage collection activities, keep records or establish statistics on ornamental fish populations.

The Balinese fishers who collect aquarium fish come from poor, isolated communities with no real alternatives for generating income. About 500 collectors depend on the ornamental fish industry to support their families. Once a local resource is depleted, collectors rove in search of fish. Taking their small boats to Lombok, Sumbawa, Flores and Sulawesi, collectors from the north coast of Bali will stay away up to three weeks on each collecting trip.

The trade is hard on the collectors who risk their lives for a meagre income, and on the fish which can suffer mortality rates of more than fifty percent during capture and the stress of handling and transport. But placing a ban on reef fishing is not the answer. There is little incentive to captive-breed, as wild-caught fish are still so cheap in comparison. As long as people are hungry and there's a market for their wares, the communities will continue to sell the fish at ridiculously low prices, even after they've been trained in 'best practices'. The challenge is to make it sustainable for both collectors and marine species through communitybased resource management programs and the adoption of fairer trade mechanisms.

Ten years ago, the Marine Aquarium Council (MAC), an international organization based in Hawaii, started working with collectors and exporters in Indonesia to help create a sustainable and responsible industry. In 2003, Marine Biologist Gayatri Lilley, the MAC Indonesia Coordinator, opened an office in Bali and created programs with the collectors of North Bali with her husband Ron providing technical support.

The Lilleys presented the concept of the MAC program to the fishcollecting community in Tejakula in North Bali in 2004. The fishermen, who had seen their only resource dwindle in a single generation, quickly agreed to take part in a community-based resource management program. The program received support from the local and central governments and the resorts along the beach, which saw the advantage of maintaining the natural resources that attract tourism.

But change is slow, especially in the developing world. In 2007 MAC Indonesia closed when funding dried up, and Gayatri set up the Indonesian Nature Foundation (LINI) a local Indonesian not-for-profit organization. Using the skills learned with MAC and retaining the small group of dedicated staff, LINI continues the work.

Training the fishers in sustainable collecting techniques was an early priority. The Lilleys researched extensively to find a softer netting material to reduce damage to the fish, and it is now used by all the collectors in the program. The use of cyanide is being phased out as fishermen are trained to snorkel and use face masks and fins, which give them greater visibility and mobility in the water. The collectors can see for themselves that it's cheaper in terms of time, money and effort not to use cyanide. Collectors have also been taught to dive more safely. Several have visited the decompression chamber at Sanglah Hospital, which is now available to them. And training in post-harvest management has lowered the mortality rate of the fish significantly.

Two of the most experienced collectors from Tejakula are now training collectors in other Indonesian coastal communities in 'best practices'. LINI's programs have expanded from Bali to Lampung, Padang and the Mentawai Islands in Sumatra, several collection areas in Sulawesi, and the Thousand Islands off Jakarta.

In 2011, LINI's program includes development and improvement of reef fisheries management, surveying and monitoring coral reefs, providing training in collecting, handling and transport of fish and in safe diving, village-level economics and development of village cooperatives. Developing community-based marine ecotourism and a responsible and sustainable marine aquarium trade, where the fishermen have direct links to the exporters, is a core objective.

LINI continues its main work with communities in North Bali and the Banggai Islands where certain areas have been selected for protection. It is in the process of developing No-Take Zones where the fish can breed in safety. The results are already impressive. "Fish stocks come back in about two years, and collectors report the return of species they have not seen for a long time," Gayatri points out.

With LINI's help the communities have started reef rehabilitation schemes in front of their villages. They made and installed low-tech artificial reef structures that attract fish and other marine organisms, which make the once-trashed reef flats productive again. Special structures were also designed to provide breeding areas for ornamental shrimp, and the sale of these provides another source of badly-needed income for the communities. Finally, some of the villagers decided to open up their reefs to visiting tourists, who can snorkel or dive there, and see the results of these collaborative efforts for themselves. These sites serve as a testimony to what can be achieved by the communities themselves in terms of resource conservation, with a little help from outside.

The Lilleys also work with the middlemen who buy fish from the collectors and sell them to the exporters. LINI is working to shorten the trade chains between the suppliers and the final buyers, which significantly reduces stock mortality during the long journeys overseas.

The North Bali and Banggai Islands areas where the Lilleys are working were surveyed in 2003, 2005, 2007 and 2010.The abundance and variety of fish is good and continues to improve in the No-Take Zones. Although the aquarium trade has been active for decades, no catch records were ever kept. Now the middlemen and collectors groups are trained to record every fish they buy and sell, and the collectors are encouraged to catch only what is ordered, as long as it remains below an agreed total allowable catch. The Indonesian Department of Fisheries and Marine Affairs supports the program by funding training for the collectors, and has asked LINI to train its own staff in data gathering and management.

LINI's eventual goal of sustainable resource management is still a long way off. But the wheels are slowly turning, especially in the communities which have taken on stewardship of their natural resources. So the next time you pause by an aquarium, take a moment to wonder where the fish came from, send them a little blast of sympathy and tell them the Lilleys are on the case.

Accidental Jungle

In 2002, I launched myself into the great adventure of tropical gardening. The land around my newly-built house was an empty palette—actually a wasteland of uprooted banana plants and broken bricks from the construction. I bought Madé Wijaya's inspiring Tropical Garden Design book and visualized glorious landscapes, artful little garden accents and plenty of fruit and cut flowers for the house.

Somewhere along the line it all got out of hand. The first priority was to cover a large expanse of bare dirt. Without a plan, a budget or any idea what I was doing I planted dozens of seeds, filched cuttings and uprooted every unattended plant in the neighbourhood. In this folly I was abetted by Wayan Manis, who brought daily offerings from her own compound. With the first rain, all these plants took root and began to follow their own agendas.

Forests of papaya trees appeared overnight as if sown by a ghostly hand. Carefully planted herbs and flowers declined to thrive; uninvited vines, shrubs and grasses quickly overcame them. Heliconia plants spread as if on steroids. Turmeric bloomed rampantly in the undergrowth. Down on the undercliff the night-blooming jasmine grew leggy and unlovely, but periodically delivered the most ravishing perfume after dark. A pink flowering creeper overwhelmed a coconut tree and gained a determined foothold on the roof. Nothing was where I intended it to be, but most of it was too pretty to pull out.

In the first flush of enthusiasm I planted some trees, mostly but not always around the edges. Now it's too late to change my mind and there's too much shade to plant vegetables. I learned that six avocado trees is too many and one mulberry bush isn't enough. A large mango tree that delivered a superb crop shortly after I built the house declined to do as much as flower ever since, and no one can tell me why. The frangipani cuttings I planted so enthusiastically have sprawled into messy if exuberant trees because I didn't know how to prune them properly, and now it's too late.

Then I decided to integrate some food production into this disorder. We started raised beds, laid on the mulch and were generous with the organic fertilizer. Tomato vines climbed up papaya trees and bean plants disappeared into the hibiscus, but crops proved elusive. Pumpkin vines roared around the garden like trains, growing at a rate of a metre a day. Every morning I would do the rounds, trying to match female flowers with male flowers in hope of actually generating some vegetables. But pumpkins are contrary creatures; a vine will produce only male flowers for weeks, then only female flowers, then up and die. Sometimes I would strike it lucky with the pumpkin sex and sometimes the bugs would. Pumpkins dangled from trellises, ripened on the roof and hung from the highest trees. If we didn't find them in time, they'd suicide spectacularly on the path.

When I built the house I didn't have enough money to put a proper roof on the car park, so Nyoman cut bamboo from the edge of the cliff for the struts and nailed pieces of thin plastic sheeting over them. We planted a profusion of flowering vines against the walls and within months had a living roof of passion flowers, thunbergia, bougainvillea, alamanda and green pit vipers. Now the plastic and bamboo have largely rotted away and the foliage is about two metres thick. But we hesitate to replace it. It's much prettier than an ordinary roof and, as Nyoman points out, better to leave sleeping snakes lie.

As the garden becomes wilder, the boundary between my territory and the undercliff becomes indistinct despite the fence. Creatures from the river climb the trees around the edge of the garden and fall inside it—a porcupine, civet cats, metre-long water monitor lizards. It's not always easy to persuade them to leave again, even with the whole pack of dogs nipping at their heels.

The only part of the garden that doesn't revert to jungle is the paddock under the bamboos where the pigs used to live. This shady and fertile corner is now a little coffee garden and also home to a small flock of Muscovy ducks. With any luck we'll be drinking our own kopi Bali sometime soon, after a dinner of roast duck.

To enhance the general jungle ambience, a python was recently discovered on a garden wall. Nyoman persuaded it into a sack and I suggested it would be an appropriate addition to the family, tasked with managing the rat population in the roof. My staff, however, found this solution unacceptable and it has now rejoined its relatives down by the river.

Everything grows so fast and profusely I sometimes think if I hesitate too long between sentences as I type in the garden, that I will succumb to the remorseless embrace of some vigorous jungle vine myself. Nyoman and I spend several hours in the garden every day trying to bring some order to the chaos, but we never get very far. It seems that we hack back a corner here and there to let in a little light, and it grows back by the time we return from lunch. And the garden has in eight short years written its own story. Every plant has a history—a root extracted from a muddy river bank, a branch clipped from a friend's garden, cuttings smuggled from Sulawesi. It's become a green story book, living testimony to the supremacy of chlorophyll over human will.

A Bowl of Honest Rice

"This rice is excellent," I declared to a fellow diner at a restaurant one night in my early days in Ubud. "I wonder where it came from?" He tasted his and shrugged.

"Rice is rice," he said.

Years later, I realize that little non-event triggered what has become a passion to discover and conserve Bali's heritage rice varieties, and to encourage farmers to grow them.

Rice is not just rice. Like potatoes, this staple comes in many varieties, each with a distinct flavour, texture and aroma. We're lucky to have an excellent variety of rice available in Bali—local varieties of brown, pink, white and red rice, black and white sticky rice, jasmine rice from Thailand, risotto from Italy, Indian basmati, short-grain Japanese rice and the ubiquitous flavourless, aroma-less, tasteless commercial hybrid white rice that comes in those big bags and probably has the nutritional profile of a piece of cardboard.

At a community fund-raiser in Ubud in 2002, people crowded around a table selling freshly harvested organic rice. It was presented in drawstring cloth bags of unbleached cotton with a little window so buyers could preview the fat, glossy grains of padi cica within. Where did it come from? "I grow it," said Ed modestly. "Near Tampak Siring." Intrigued, I drove up the mountain to find out why an American artist is trying to re-introduce traditional rice culture in Bali.

About 40 years ago, a new rice hybrid was introduced to Bali to address the country's food security issues. Gradually this higher-yield, faster-growing crop replaced the indigenous varieties as the island's main rice crop. It required chemical inputs, however, which gradually depleted the organisms in the soil and caused the rich, living topsoil to float away with the irrigation water. As a result, these days most commercial rice in Bali is grown in the subsoil—dense, infertile clay which the growers plough in an attempt to distribute the burned or half-rotted rice straw from the last harvest which is the only organic addition.

Ed set out to prove to his neighbours that he could grow organic Bali rice more profitably than they could grow commercial rice with chemical fertilizer. He proved his point with his latest harvest of 50 kilograms of husked rice from three are (30 square metres) of land. Top yields for commercial hybrid rice growers here were 20 kilograms of husked rice per are but few get that much. Ed expected to increase his yield by up to forty percent as his land became increasingly fertile. Padi cica takes only ten days longer to grow than hybrid rice.

"It took about 18 months to recondition the rice fields I've used as a test area," he explained. "There was lots of trial and error before I figured out it was all about bacteria."

The kind of bacteria that provides nutrients to plants requires oxygen to thrive. Between crops, Ed dried out the field for a month, topdressed it with composted cow manure or rice straw and then gently raked the surface. Most of the bacteria live within an inch of the surface and the topsoil is friable, so there's no need to plough. Then he planted his rice and went away for about four months. His padi field teemed with eels, frogs, snakes and other creatures feeding on the many insects and each other, and providing nutrients. Every once in a while he pulled out the weeds and composted them. After harvesting, all the rice plant roots were cut out and composted too.

This was Ed's third harvest. "My first harvest was only 18 kilograms per are because the land wasn't in good shape and I let the gardeners plough it. The next crop was nearly 30 kilograms. Then I took advice from some of the older farmers around here and went from 30 to 50 kilograms in one crop, using the same seed. There's very little algae in my fields compared to my neighbours' and the soil is much cooler. Not only that, but the hybrid rice crops around here all failed recently because of a virus. The Bali rice is more resistant to disease and drought and doesn't fall down when it rains."

To demonstrate the thick layer of topsoil that's been established in just two years, Ed plunged his arm halfway to the elbow in the rich muck of his padi field. As a farmer's granddaughter, I appreciated the gesture. The earth looked good enough to eat.

Later, over organically grown herb tea, Ed detailed the economic facts of growing rice organically compared to using chemical-dependent hybrids. "There's no money for small holders in growing hybrid rice with chemicals. If local growers kept track of their outlays and benefits, they would all go organic overnight," he argued. Ironically, some farmers then go out and pay for traditional rice because they don't want to eat the tasteless hybrid rice any more than we do.

Two huge bags of rice—the harvest from a larger field—had been delivered that afternoon from the miller. Ed opened one bag and we plunged our hands deep into the living, fragrant grains, still warm from the milling. Honest rice.

Several years later, I've become a committed advocate of helping Bali's rice farmers restore their ancient fields that are no longer productive due to decades of indiscriminate chemical use. Bali has been producing rice for over 1100 years. Its naturally fertile volcanic soil and abundant water made it one of Indonesia's most productive areas, and its spectacular terraces are among the island's leading tourist attractions. Rice cultivation became an integral part of the Bali Hindu religion, with rituals which evolved to ensure a good harvest and placate Dewi Sri, the rice goddess; these practices continue today.

Bali's rice terraces are sculpted by hand from steep volcanic slopes and the rice (a variety of grass) is still grown on small family plots instead of on an industrial scale. Each family cultivates less than half a hectare (an acre) of rice fields, usually divided into several terraces. Rice is grown by land-owners, tenant farmers and sharecroppers in a small scale, labour-intensive way. Ploughing may be done with cows or a small mechanical plough but planting and harvesting are still done by hand in most areas.

These small, traditional family farms are grouped into subaks, or community rice-growing associations which include men from every farm. Subaks have existed in Bali since at least 986 AD. The subak shares the local water supply for irrigation, which is carefully engineered to ensure that each rice terrace receives enough water. From antiquity, Balinese rice farmers have worked together in these groups to bring water from sometimes distant sources of springs, rivers or lakes. Sophisticated hydraulic engineering systems consist of continuously maintained, hand-built aqueducts, small dams, canals and underground tunnels dug through solid rock. The ancient system is now breaking down in places as water grows more scarce.

From antiquity, the Balinese grew and ate traditional varieties of rice known as Padi Bali, a generic term which includes at least a dozen different varieties which may be red, pink or brown in colour, growing to a height of two metres and taking up to 150 days to mature. The traditional rice was fertilized with natural compost and animal manures.

The 'green revolution' began in the late 1960s, when food security in Indonesia became a serious issue. The Indonesian government and World Bank introduced a hybrid white rice called Ir36 which was designed to mature in 120 days. All Indonesian farmers were ordered to grow this new crop, which was heavily dependent on chemical fertilizers and pesticides. (In remote areas, some farmers continued to grow a little traditional rice for their own use, keeping a priceless seed bank alive.)

Initial results were spectacular, as the rice instantly responded to the chemicals (like snorting cocaine, one agronomist explained to me— the effect is dramatic, but temporary). Briefly, Indonesia became a leading rice producer and even became self sufficient for a short period after 1984. In 1986 a supra-intensification system was introduced using a limited variety of seeds, and more chemical fertilizers and pesticides. By 1985 over ninety percent of Bali's rice land was planted in hybrid rice. In a few remote pockets, farmers still continued to grow the more flavourful Padi Bali they preferred to eat, becoming seed banks for varieties that would otherwise have disappeared. One large area of Tabanan called Jati Luih has never adopted the use of chemicals and continues to grow Padi Bali to this day.

As the use of animal manures and organic composts stopped, so did the slow, continual enrichment of the soil. Rice quality and yield declined. Soon farmers began to need more and more chemicals to get the same yield, and the economic returns of growing rice with artificial inputs started to drop. Productivity leveled off, became stagnant and in some places went into decline. It became evident that rice production was failing to keep pace with demand.

The use of chemicals was also upsetting the ecological balance in irrigated rice fields. Biodiversity disappeared. Naturally fertilized rice fields are home to snakes, eels, frogs, fish, dragonflies, freshwater crabs and a regular zoo of insects. All of these animals contributed to the health of soil and water systems which in turn produced high rice yields. But the biomass, no longer held together by the creatures that once lived in the terraces, began to float away with the irrigation water. Within a few decades, the topsoil was gone, along with the protein sources that poor farming families relied on.

Chemical fertilizers, pesticides, herbicides and fungicides are widely employed by Balinese farmers who have little understanding of their correct use, application and potential health hazards. Many can not or do not read the instructions. Safety equipment is virtually never worn. Increasing incidences of cancer and birth defects in agricultural areas are probably due to excessive exposure to toxic agricultural chemicals, but there is no formal data on this that I am aware of. (My information comes from farmers, healthcare givers and midwives).

Because a single water source is shared by the entire subak, any chemicals or other elements introduced to the water will contaminate all the fields downstream. This means that no one farmer can decide independently to stop using one or more chemicals, because they are an integral part of the irrigation system.

Traditionally, Balinese rice farmers would alternate every second rice crop with peanuts or other legumes to replace depleted nitrogen in the soil, and allow the land to lie fallow between crops. Under the pressure to grow more rice, these practices were dropped. Crop rotation now seldom occurs and the understanding of the importance of crop rotation and nitrogen fixing is being lost. Hybrid rice has been grown continually on much of Bali's rice land for over forty years, and the land has become so exhausted that even large chemical inputs no longer ensure a healthy crop in some areas.

The conventional cultivation method of growing hybrid rice in Bali is to plant about a dozen rice seedlings in a bunch about 20 centimetres apart, flood the field and treat it with chemical fertilizers, pesticides and herbicides.

The System of Rice Intensification (SRI), a technique developed in Madagascar about ten years ago, saves farmers money and increases yield dramatically in several ways. Seeds are tested for viability, then just one seedling is planted 30-40 centimetres apart instead of a bunch together. This single seedling does not have to compete for sunlight or nutrients, and so grows more strongly. The ten-day-old seedlings are set out in late afternoon, so the plantlets aren't stressed by the sun, and planted at an angle so as not to damage the root. The fields are shallowly flooded only two days out of seven when the plants are young, encouraging deep, strong roots and saving eighty percent of the water used in conventional rice cultivation (a serious issue in times of dwindling water supplies). When grown without chemical inputs, the farmer saves this cost. Manual weeding two or three times after planting ensures a better crop. If ducks are released into the flooded fields when the plants are two months old, they take over the weeding, pest control and fertilizing until harvest. Returning to the traditional cycles, the field is rested and sown in peanuts or other legumes after two harvests. This cash crop enriches the soil before it's planted in rice again, and additional income can be earned from the ducks and eggs.

This method saves ninety percent of the cost of seed. The strong single rice plants can set over 70 (some reports in India claim 100) grain-bearing shoots (tilars) instead of the usual 25 to 30 from conventional methods. When correctly practiced over several harvest cycles so that the natural biomass has a chance to build up again, SRI yields at least twice as much rice as conventional rice cultivation. Individual rice grains are also heavier. The Indonesian government now endorses the SRI and encourages rice farmers around the country to adopt it.

There is increasing interest among Bali's rice farmers in growing traditional varieties of rice without chemicals, as they can see the demand for this product and the higher prices it demands. Organic heritage rice is become a boutique food item in Bali and abroad. There is also a slowly growing understanding of the health impacts of uncontrolled use of agricultural chemicals.

In 2007, I started working with I Madé Chakra, a young Balinese farmer, to write a proposal for money to train farmers in the SRI. With money from The Funding Network in England, a pilot program began in November 2007. Chakra initially trained farmers from 32 subaks in the SRI, and then spent the next few months making dozens of site visits to ensure that the farmers were following the technique correctly. When the first harvest came in, the advantages of the system were clear. The usual yield from one are of rice land was five bags of threshed rice; the farmers who used the SRI harvested eight bags, and each bag was three to four kilograms heavier because the rice grains were fatter.

No pesticides, herbicides or fungicides were used, so the farmers ended up with more rice while incurring fewer expenses. Yields should continue to increase with subsequent harvests as the condition of the fields improves. Neighbouring farmers who had mocked the experiment became interested in learning the new technique.

Some of the farmers opted to grow heritage rice as well by the SRI. This was more problematical because the non-hybrid traditional varieties don't yield as much and are targeted by pests like birds and rats which vastly prefer it to the commercial white rice. Chakra is helping seek solutions. Farmers can get a much higher price for the heritage varieties.

There's a lot more interest in chemical-free heritage rice these days. Chakra has trained over 200 subak leaders in the technique. Chefs in Bali's hotels and restaurants are starting to feature it on their menus. If you know who's growing it, you can put in an order for limboto, mansoor, mangkok, gago or one of the many other unique varieties now available. Each has a subtly different flavour and aroma. Walking through the rice fields, it's easy to distinguish the terraces with SRI white rice because the plants are further apart and more lush than those in the neighbouring fields. The heritage rice is even more distinct, growing over two metres tall. It stands like a sentinel in the subak, towering over the puny hybrids around it—a proud testament to a thousand years of rice culture that is coming full circle.

Feeding Frenzy

Dawn broke. The frogs turned the volume down and the song birds and roosters geared up with the sunrise. I stretched under the mosquito net, enjoying the feeling of being not quite awake on a luminous tropical Sunday morning. Then the sounds began to sort themselves out and I recognized the increasingly insistent squeals of hungry pigs and honking geese. The parrots started screaming. The dogs barked.

It was time to get up and feed them all.

"Is this a zoo?" a friend's young son asked recently. Well, no. But I often felt like a zookeeper as I devoted my first hour of wakefulness to ensuring that all my animal companions were appropriately fed and watered. My staff don't come in until ten, an unacceptably late hour for breakfast.

The pigs came first, because they are the largest and I harboured a dark suspicion that if breakfast was late they would push down the concrete block walls of their paddock and come raid the kitchen. Carrying a bucket of rainwater, I made my way to the 'farm' where two black snouts snuffled at their gate. I was always greeted warmly. Standing on their hind feet and braced against the wall, they watched anxiously as I uncovered the blackened pot of food that had been cooked for them the previous afternoon. My staff had made a little brick stove here, where food scraps and stale bread from the Bali Buddha kitchen simmered over a flame of bamboo sticks to the colour and consistency of mud. Peggy and Paulette considered this the pinnacle of fine cuisine. Still half asleep, I poured the slop into a big square bucket, added water and braced myself. As I leaned over the wall with breakfast, the pigs rushed the bucket, scrambling to insert as much of their chubby selves into it as would fit. Black snouts ploughed blissfully through the stew, tufted tails wagging happily.

One species down, five to go.

In the next paddock Richard and Rosalind honked insistently, spreading their broad white wings as reminders that geese get hungry, too. They were acquired as a young pair about a week after the pigs, since there was a big empty enclosure right next door. From the beginning they refused to eat anything but rice, despite my research which declared that they were foragers. So we cut up greens very small and sneaked bean sprouts into their feed. Repeated lectures on nutrition failed to move them; anything except white rice was regarded with imperial disdain. They marched around their paddock with great dignity and made noisy goose love in their little pond.

At that time I had set up a rest home for cockatoos with Parrot Beak and Feather Disease. This virus manifests in baldness and grossly overgrown beaks. The breeder of these captive-bred parrots had tried every treatment mainstream science could provide, and had lent me a few birds to try alternative therapies. The disease is said to be incurable, but we refused to give up. The patients looked like plucked chickens, with random tufts of feathers sprouting here and there. The occasional bird would achieve full featherhood, usually with strange little curls on the wings and tail. Then just as you congratulated yourself that he was cured, he'd fall off the perch for no obvious reason. This could be very discouraging.

The dogs followed me around to keep me on schedule. They knew they were next in the queue when I opened the fridge door. The refrigerator was a small one, each rack filled with containers of food for the geese, food for the dogs, food for the birds, offerings, holy water, the occasional dead parrot awaiting burial, pots of herbal potions and spices. There was very little room for people food.

I peeled fruit and vegetables for the juicer. apples, carrots, beets, turmeric and parsley went through first. The residue was mixed with the usual dog food of chicken heads, vegetables and red rice lovingly prepared by Wayan Manis and sometimes supplemented with tofu or scrambled eggs. Kalypso was a very selective diner when she first came to me, but has relaxed her standards slightly over the years. Daisy hates vegetables and had to have hers mixed well with the rice and napped with a splash of rendered chicken fat or coconut oil. They both wished I would order smoked duck from the village more often.

Despite their pathetic appearance, the sick cockatoos ate like wolves. The screaming for breakfast started at dawn. (In the afternoon they screamed just for the hell of it.) Every two or three days I cooked up a mash of red rice, peanuts, and mung beans with red palm sugar. This was mixed with the rest of the residue from the juicer with added unhusked rice and millet. They were also given a variety of nutritious snacks during the day by Wayan Manis, who feels that food is always the best medicine.

Four species down, two to go.

The fish swam in patient silence while I brought out the stale bread. It's a pleasant interlude to sit on the steps and toss them crumbs. They prefer bagels.

Just one species left now. I added ginger, turmeric and oranges to the juice (I'm the only species that likes citrus) and sat down at the computer to begin my day. Contented silence reigned for a while. But by the afternoon they would all be hungry again...

Home Leave

Once or twice a year I returned to Vancouver to visit my family. It was always a huge leap—geographically and culturally—to find myself half a planet away from my life in rural Indonesia.

I stood in the garden my sister had carved out of the Canadian wilderness, surrounded by dense cedar forest. Eagles wheeled overhead. Bees hummed in the herbs and garter snakes rustled through the dry grass at my feet. There was no other house in sight. After the vibrant hustle of life in Ubud, the vastness and silence of the temperate rainforest was shocking.

Robin found her land on the British Columbia coast and started building about the same time I built my house in Ubud. There the resemblance ends. My house went up in under four months, in tropical weather, with plenty of help and no building code. Robin moved onto her land alone in late winter, without electricity or running water. Every step of building the house was an obstacle course of bad weather, delays, expensive and unreliable workers and officious inspectors measuring the height of the balcony railings in millimetres. When at last she could sleep under her own roof, the mammoth task of clearing the land was still ahead of her.

My sister has three big axes. She chops a cord of firewood every winter to feed the little wood stove that keeps her warm. Every free moment when it isn't raining, she's in the garden growing food and herbs and fighting back the relentless tide of the forest that seeks to reclaim the clearings. It rains too much, or not at all. The well water is meagre and undrinkable. She drives her old truck several kilometres to fill 25litre bottles with fresh spring water from a neighbouring property.

Robin's rambling garden is a small organic jungle of vegetables, berries, fruit trees and the many herbs she grows for the market.

Each garden is fenced against deer, which can devastate a crop in a single night. Bunches of fragrant herbs hang drying in every corner of the house, waiting to be weighed, bagged and labeled.

We drove up an abandoned logging road to harvest St Johns Wort on a vastly silent summer day. We left the truck doors open and frequently scanned the clearing for bears. Bears and cougars were a constant presence in Robin's life. She didn't have a barbecue or a salmon smoker. When we ate lamb chops, the bones were buried far from the house. "Bear bait," she explained. The bears here are bold. Local stories abounded of bears tearing open the trunks of cars and the lids of outdoor freezers, drawn by the tantalizing aroma of fish and meat. Last fall, her little apple tree was heavy with its first ripening fruit. When Robin spotted a mother bear and two cubs strolling up her drive toward the orchard she erupted furiously from the house, shouting rude things and banging two pot lids together. "Bloody bears," she mutters.

I am awed by her courage. When I visit Canada people sometimes say, "You're very brave to live in Indonesia." They must be kidding.

I try to pass for normal in the city of my birth, but am constantly betrayed by little things like not knowing how to get off a bus or fill the car with gasoline. I look like any ordinary Canadian on the outside. Under the shell is a person who seldom leaves her small town in Indonesia where the pace is slow and the choices few, and who likes it that way.

After re-calibrating from jet lag, I wander out into the neighbourhood I grew up in. I stand in line at Starbucks, fairly confident that I can order a cup of coffee. After all, the selections are clearly listed on a board on the wall. I'm third in line. The woman at the counter places her order. "A soy latte, half sweet, three quarters froth, grande, to go."

This seems outrageously persnickety to me, but the waitress (pardon me, barista) calmly scrawls an arcane code on a piece of paper and passes it to the operator of a complicated stainless steel machine which gushes steam, hot milk and black coffee.

I mentally review my order and rehearse it a couple of times while the bearded man in front of me steps up to the counter.

"Decaffeinated Cappuccino, Arabica berries plucked from an eastfacing mountain slope by an Ethiopian virgin at the full of the moon, twenty five percent camel milk, seventy five percent goat milk—Swiss goat—venti, 170 degrees, one and a half centimetres of foam, to drink here, black mug."

Then it is my turn. The pierced and discreetly tattooed barista turns her unblinking pale blue gaze at me and poises her pencil.

"A tall Americano, please," I order apologetically. There is a long pause.

"Here or to go?" she asks sternly. "Umm... here."

"Is that all?" I am painfully aware that I'm letting down the side, but don't know enough of the jargon to pass for a local. After quite a long time I'm handed a mug of coffee and then have to decide between white sugar, raw sugar, brown sugar, stevia, cocoa powder, vanilla powder, skim milk, semi-skim and half and half, stirred with a recyclable plastic spoon or politically correct fast-growing softwood stick. It is rather daunting. In Ubud we can order fancy coffee too, but our regular fare is plain kopi Bali with sludge at the bottom of the cup. Hold the soy milk.

My other sister lived in a suburb, near our parent's house where we grew up. This world now was almost as exotic to me as Robin's. I was amazed by the wide, deserted streets of the suburbs. There were no dogs or children in the empty gardens. I cast back a few decades to when these same streets buzzed with kids on bicycles or playing games in their yards.

Traffic was rare, and the drivers were usually elderly. Where was everybody? "At work, at school, in front of the computer," Beth explained.

She juggled a job, a family, a house and garden and an endless stream of boarders. Somehow, she found time to throw a party for our parents. About 30 elderly folk tottered up the front walk on a sunny Sunday afternoon, supported on canes and each other's shoulders. No one arrived in a taxi; they had all driven themselves, often with the aid of a Google-generated map. They consumed an astonishing amount of wine and food before tottering off again.

Even here in the 'burbs, there was wildlife. Cheeky raccoons nosed in through the cat doors to raid the pet food bowls. It was not unusual to find my mother in the front garden, flapping a tea towel at the large deer grazing on her geraniums. Bears wandered in from the many forested creeks. Last year, a young bear was found happily foraging through the produce warehouse at the back of a local supermarket in broad daylight. Wildlife officers sedated it with a dart gun, carried the slumbering bear to their van and took it into the forest. It must still be dreaming of imported figs and cherries.

The dogs here are uniformly well-behaved and very clean. Never do they strain at their designer leashes or snap at innocent bystanders. Their toenails are invariably neatly clipped, and they never have bald bits or engage in sexual activity on the sidewalk

Beth and her family had two foreign language students living with them. I felt empathy with the two boys from Japan and Mexico, as, dazed with jet lag and culture shock, we navigated the intricacies of everyday life in Canada. Bali seemed like another world.

The supermarkets were overwhelming. I met up with a friend living in another Asian country who was also here on holiday, and we spent almost two hours buying groceries. Enchanted, we lingered in front of the endless displays, goggling at the obscene variety and excess of food. I picked up a huge, crisp, perfect cauliflower and we admired the magnificent vegetable under the suspicious eyes of blasé shoppers. We looked like normal Canadians, but we were not. After so many years away our country had become exotic, full of wonders.

Out of the Dust

People sometimes say to me, "Surely there can't be poverty on Bali." Indeed there is. Bali's arid northeast is home to thousands of people living at a subsistence level, without permanent water supplies or access to productive employment. The only sign of poverty in the more prosperous parts of Bali are the women and children who beg by the roadside in Kuta, Denpasar and Ubud. They are among the 5,500 people from 35 poor villages high on the slopes of Muntigunung in Karangasem, the driest area of Bali. A few years ago I visited one of these villages to see the situation for myself.

Contrary to rumour, there is no 'mafia' behind the beggar women. They come to town when the money runs out. First they walk for several hours down the mountain to a road where they can catch a bemo to their destination. They organize themselves into small groups because it makes them feel more secure and they can keep an eye on each other's children. In Ubud, they know the best places to beg, where to bathe and sleep, and where to hide from the police.

They're very shy about having to beg and don't like to talk about it. When they've made enough money, they make their way back to the mountain to buy food and necessities for their families.

Situated on the steep slopes between Tulamben and Tejakula on the rugged slopes of Mount Batur, the 28 square km district of Muntigunung ranges between 200 and 900 metres above sea level. There are no springs or rivers here, and the soil is too dry to farm for 8 months of the year. Thirteen of the upper villages have no road access and are too remote for government education or health services. Malnourished and without education or resources, these people are outside of the development mainstream. Years ago they turned to begging as their only means of generating cash. Now it's become part of the village culture.

Begging women and their children used to be a common sight in Ubud. These days the numbers are much reduced, thanks to a multifaceted Swiss-funded project. Futures for Children (FFC) is providing water and income generation activities to these impoverished villagers for the first time. The project's first strategic priority is to build a sustainable water supply for each village. Then a capacity-building process begins, teaching villagers income-generating activities using local commodities and services. Eventually, as health and nutritional profiles for the children improve, an educational component is being integrated.

We drove around Kintamani and south past Tejakula, then headed up the mountain. The road was increasingly steep, narrow and rough, and finally faded out altogether. Leaving the car at the end of the road, we pulled on knapsacks and started hiking up the almost vertical path toward Cangkeng, the first village the project began to work with in October 2006. Now that I could see the distances and difficulty involved in obtaining water, I began to understand more fully how people who have to struggle so hard for the basics of life have little energy for anything else.

Access to water was the most crucial of their needs. One woman told me that she would leave her house at 5 pm when the sun was low and walk to the bottom of the mountain, fill her 15-litre bucket and hike the steep trail back to her home in the dark. That one small bucket of water was all her family had in the dry season for drinking and cooking. There was never any left for washing clothes or bathing. Today, every household has a secure rain water tank and the village shares a 250 cubic meter community rainwater cistern, ensuring plenty of water throughout the year for all.

With water provided for, the next step was to bring sustainable income generating activities to the village. FFC strongly believes in the philosophy that if you give a poor man a fish you feed him for a day, but if you teach him how to fish he can feed himself for life. "We wanted to prove that begging was not a tradition, that there was a way to solve this," the Ubud-based FFC founder explains. "If the villagers could be taught to earn a sustainable income, there would be no need to beg."

In fact, the women embraced the concept with relief. They were embarrassed to beg and much preferred not to leave their villages. The first project was to develop a three-hour trek with the village women guiding visitors through the remote and spectacular landscapes of East Bali to their villages. Marketed through the Bali Hotels Association, this project has proved very popular with European and North American tourists who are delighted to have access to a part of Bali they would normally never see. Hundreds of people have taken the trek to date. Part of the money earned from the treks is paid to the women in cash, part is held for them against times of need and part is saved for the education of their children. The women are very happy with this arrangement. The trekking activity was recognized with a global Ecotourism award in 2011.

The next project was the production of woven lontar hats and baskets. FFC procured a contract from one of the large hotels for several hundred hats, and the women quickly learned to produce them. The day I visited, we could hear the women long before we could see them. the sounds of women talking and laughing grew louder as we climbed up through the village toward the big community water tank. Over 20 women sat companionably working together under the aluminium rain-catching roof of the tank, surrounded by slumbering babies and toddlers. I recognized several of these women from the days when they would crouch outside the Bali Buddha in Ubud with their hands outstretched for coins, and we exchanged smiles.

Every family of the village was represented. The women now make as much as they did from begging and are at last above the poverty line. The older children,who used to beg alongside their mothers, were helping to cut and beat the lontar. Why weren't they in school? There wasn't one at that time, but since 2010 about 60% of the children from this village attend school, despite the fact that they have a long way to walk.

The children see their mothers working and have positive role models to follow for the first time. FFC has begun to help families register with the local government, which is a prerequisite for obtaining government services. Every person over the age of 17 who has a KTP card benefits from a health program for the poor. For the first time, the health of the villagers will improve through training in hygiene and nutrition.

FCC has built a Development Centre further down the mountain where training and commodity processing take place under the management of Dian Desa, an Indonesian NGO with wide experience in village-based sustainable income programs. The Centre's goal is to improve the value of existing products in Muntigunung and market them in Bali and abroad.

All of the villages were offered the opportunity to grow Rosella flowers, which are easy to cultivate. The villagers who agreed to try this new crop had very good harvests. In 2010, 80 tons of flowers where harvested; 40,000 boxes of tea and 4,000 boxes of a new product, Rosella Sweets (similar to dried cranberries) were produced. The Rosella growers earn money by selling the flowers to the Centre, and up to 30 people are employed for three months to cut out the seeds, dry the flowers in the Centre's solar dryers and package them for sale. Roella tea, sweets, syrup, soap and salt are now produced and research is underway to produce fibre from the branches.

High quality palm sugar powder has a high market value. The sugar is made from the lontar pine, of which about 3,500 are growing in the villages. The sugar is processed in a hygienic kitchen at the Centre and packaged for sale.

During the cashew season, villagers bring in the nuts and sell them to the Centre where they are dried, cracked and peeled, dried again and packaged for sale to participating hotels. In 2008 two tons of high quality cashews were processed at the Centre and 29 people were employed for four months. In 2012 the Centre processed ten tons of product, employing 50 people year round.

All of the products are of the highest quality to meet the exacting standards of the five-star hotels which buy them.

Employment opportunities have improved to the point that several young men who had left the villages to work in Kuta returned to work in the small village of Cangkeng. About 220 villagers are working with FFC programs.

It's a very slow process, but eventually all 35 villages will have access to water and income generation options. Thirteen villages now have rainwater catchment tanks. Besides Cangkeng, six additional villages have employment for at least one member of each family. They are cracking cashewnuts and producing lontar baskets, gourds and women's handbags made from traditional textiles. FFC brings in international designers to help create stylish, high quality hand-made products from natural materials that ensure ongoing orders.

The villages use a lottery system to decide which will be the next to get water. At each lottery, one village with road access and one without is chosen.

The FFC water supply projects have been on hold since 2010 when the government started a project to pump and pipe water from Lake Batur to Muntigunung which is still not operational. The FFC has built two more water tanks since 2012.

The remaining beggars still to be seen in Ubud are from different villages of Muntigunung which do not yet have water access and jobs.

How to help? Buy the Muntigunung project's products and send your visitors on the trek. Creating a robust local economy is the best way to help these people rise out of the dust.

For more information on Futures for Children please visit www. Zukunft-fuer-kinder.ch

No Parking

Ubud is laced together with small lanes meandering off from narrow roads, apparently leading nowhere much. But whole villages buzz with life just off the main streets.

The entrance to our lane is almost invisible, and a stranger would never guess there was anything between Jalan Sukma and the river. But it is a comprehensive little village of about fifty family compounds, two schools, shops, home stays, warungs, tailors and three modest bungalows belonging to foreign women. In the mornings the lane is jammed with motorcycles driven by teenagers on their way to school, dodging the elementary school kids, mobile food wagons, ducks, chickens, dogs and women coming home from the market. At noon the lane is impassable as 600 children on foot, bicycles and motorbikes make their ways home from school. It's usually blissfully quiet after that. Women in pakaian adat (ceremonial dress) walk up to the temple with their offerings, holding toddlers by the hand and with the family dog ranging ahead. In late afternoons, young men take their baby nieces for slow joyrides up and down the lane on their motorcycles. When I step out of my gate, I'm often greeted by name.

But it has taken some recalibration for me to live here. I'm still getting used to the different concept of boundaries, real and perceived, and of privacy. Your space and my space. Where I grew up in Canada, most of our big suburban front gardens are unfenced to the street. Although back yards are carefully enclosed, it's considered somewhat unsociable to fence the front. But no one would dream of resting on a stranger's unfenced lawn just because there was no barrier to prevent it. In Ubud, family compounds are vigilantly walled and usually accessible from the front through one small gate. But that gate is usually open. Anyone with business with the family or foreigners with impertinent questions about the neighbourhood are free to wander in unannounced.

I built my house on a vacant piece of land that was separated from the lane by a low wall. Pak Mangku, my landlord, formally broke a narrow gap in it for me to step through the day I came for the first land ceremony. Later, when I began to build, the gap was enlarged to accommodate the trucks unloading sand and bricks. When I moved into the house three and a half months later, the yard still looked like a building site and there was a three-metre hole in the wall. I woke up the first morning under my own roof and looked out to see a small truck, nine motorcycles and several bicycles parked in my yard. I was bewildered. Couldn't they see that this was a private house? Well yes, shrugged Wayan Manis when she arrived. But there was no wall, no gate. So when all the interlopers had driven off ,we placed a single slender bamboo pole across the gap. That fragile barrier was enough—no one ever crossed it after that.

The garage was an afterthought. Out of money and ideas, I walled off a corner of the garden open to the lane. I had intended the garage to shelter my little car, the staff motorcycle, a few sacks of composted duck manure and a feather duster. But it soon became clear that I'd generously provided the village with parking, recreational and courting space.

The high school kids were convinced that my shady garage had been constructed for their own personal convenience. It's taken years to establish my ownership. Polite signs asking students not to park their motorcycles in it were ignored. I'd return from shopping to find ten motorbikes parked there, or I would leave the house to find several motorbikes parked in front of my car so I couldn't get out. Unparking a locked motorbike is bloody difficult; Nyoman would wrestle them across the lane and I'd write crisp little notes on labels and stick them firmly over the ignition keyholes. One morning, already late for a meeting, I found my car blocked in. Fed up, I stormed down the lane, up the steps of the high school, along the path and straight into the staff room, much to the alarm of the teachers relaxing there. Politely requesting their assistance, I returned to my garage like the Pied Piper with half a dozen teachers in train. As they wrestled the motorbikes away in the hot sun I could see that the parking issue would be high on the agenda at tomorrow's assembly.

Privacy is at a premium in Balinese compounds, and after school I would sometimes find a young couple courting in the back of my garage. They murmured quietly, heads bashfully tilted toward each other as they clutched their textbooks, and sprung apart with guilty giggles when I appeared. Sometimes they'd be wearing their motorbike helmets.

The animals of the street appreciate the cool shelter of the garage as well. Pak Mangku's ducks frequently rest in the dust under the car, quacking indignantly when I disturb them and crossly waddling home in a row. Chickens roost on the car roof and scratch around the tires. Dogs have been known to have torrid affairs here. Once a year or so when the temple at the corner hosts a community fundraiser, I'll roll home late to find my garage full of men gambling and smoking, none too happy to be interrupted.

The flowery roof of the garage has become a repository for the chicken bones and satay sticks that can't be buried with the compost because the dogs dig them up and choke on them. Waiting until staff and guests have departed, I position myself in the garden and hurl bones up onto the roof, where a whole subculture of cats, birds and insects has undoubtedly grown up around them.

After eight years we've reached a balance, the lane and I. The school kids would grin at me as they parked a careful distance away. The village still buzzed around me, although it acknowledged my space. Still, there were issues. The neighbourhood dogs were gathering there to relieve themselves. School boys would occasionally help themselves to the mirrors from my staff 's motorbikes. And after the purchase of my new electric bike, I became more security conscious. Nyoman ordered and installed a decorative iron gate. At first I thought the neighbours might be miffed, but they nodded with approval when they saw it. It's all about boundaries.

Dancers on the Wind

Bali in July and August is an island of wind. Candles blow out. Trees flex and stretch over rippling grass. Cooling breezes flirt along heated skin, bearing whispers of night-blooming jasmine.

Bali in July and August is an island of kites. Their silhouettes soar overhead, dancing on the wind and humming eerily. Almost every tall tree holds the bamboo skeleton of a kite that danced too close.

July and August are busy months in my garden; every kite in the neighbourhood seems drawn to my trees like moths to a flame. Each year I meet a new generation of small, grubby boys who gather around my gate with anxious faces, piping "Layang (kite), Ibu!". Usually their little kites get caught up in the frangipani trees and together we delicately disentangle them. One landed on the roof once, and another had to be cut out of the mango tree.

Sometimes we catch a real monster. One Sunday afternoon the dogs began baying hysterically and I ran out to find a really large kite sinking into the jungle at the edge of my cliff. Soon half a dozen boys hastened single file along the business side of the wire mesh fence that keeps my dogs in the garden and the larger creatures of the undercliff out. Together we surveyed the damage.

Four metres of fragile black plastic attached to a split bamboo frame had fallen into a tall banana plant right on the cliff edge. The largest boy began to edge toward it. "Careful, it's dangerous!" I warned. His smaller companion regarded me bleakly. "I've been playing here all my life," he stated, putting me firmly in my place as an outsider who had usurped their territory.

Penitent, I offered a range of long bamboo poles I keep for the purpose. Eventually we freed the kite almost undamaged and manhandled it carefully over the wall onto the road. The very next day there was a loud pealing of the bell at the front gate, where yet another herd of small boys waited to rescue their kite from my chempaka tree, its long string hopelessly tangled in Pak Mankgu's electricity line...

Wayan Manis gets dreamy in the windy season. One day she pointed to a white mango tree about fifty metres tall that towers across the river. "When I was small, we kids used to climb right to the top of a big tree like that," she remembers fondly. "We stood on the highest branches as they swayed in the wind, screaming with delight." Where was her mother? "Screaming at us to come down!"

Wayan's fearless streak has been passed on to Kadek, her daughter. When she was barely five, little Kadek would wander off alone into the rice fields or the forest for hours at a time and thought nothing of visiting a friend's distant house on her own. Although it's very unusual for girls to fly kites, she developed a passion for them.

"She asked me to help her make one but I don't know how," Wayan related. "It's not something women do. So Kadek followed the boys when they flew their kites in the rice fields and came home hours later, covered in mud. Now she knows how to make her own kites."

Boys begin to play with tiny home-made kites when they're young, then graduate to the huge, traditional community kites when they become full members of the banjar (village). These legendary Balinese kites are inspired by mythology, nature and modern cultural icons. Blending ancient and contemporary techniques and materials, some of these fabulous flying images have tails over seventy-five meters long.

Kite making and flying has a long history in Asia, where it's recognized as a traditional art and sport. There are written records of contests in Malaya going back to the 15th century. Long before that, bamboo kites were used by the Chinese during battles, humming and shrieking in the wind to frighten the enemy. Some were large enough to carry spies above enemy territory. Kites are used as a fishing aid in Indonesia and in Korea to announce the birth of a child.

Bali's ceremonial kites may be the most spectacular in the world today. The entire process, from conception to flight, is enveloped in ritual. When a village decides to build a kite, the priest selects an auspicious day to start its construction. A traditional kite is very costly to make. When it's finished the team prays; a ceremony marks its readiness to fly and gives it life. After the kite has flown it's tenderly put to rest until the following year, often in the rafters of one of the temple buildings.

The annual kite festival at Sanur sometimes attracts dozens of teams.The enormous kites are loaded onto trucks and driven to the beach accompanied by supporting truckloads of team members and gamelan players, causing endless traffic jams on the way to the highway.

Once at the beach, the kites are launched after a final prayer. It takes about ten men to hold the flying rope and control the kite, while several more lift it into take-off position. The gamelan plays lustily and increases in tempo as each kite leaps into the wind. Sometimes ten kites are launched at once in a deafening cacophony of gongs, drums and cheering crowds. Vast dragons, butterflies and gods soar and dance in the energy of wind, wild music and human excitement, tethered to the earth by only a slender filament of rope.

Less than a decade ago a women's gamelan was uncommon, and now nearly every village has one. Perhaps one July day I'll open my gate to a group of anxious little girls piping, "Layang, Ibu!" And maybe a few years after that I'll follow them to Sanur to watch their giant kites dancing in the wind.

High Finance

When people ask where I live, I tell them I'm close to Ubud's Financial District. This raises eyebrows until I point out the row of banks all huddled together at the east end of the main road. If Ubud has a Financial District, surely this is it. Not that you see many suits and ties, mind you. The dress code around here runs to sarongs and flip flops.

I've been patronizing the same bank for over five years now. I selected it because it seemed to be a stable national institution and it was ever so convenient, being located just a two minute stroll from my house. I didn't have to visit very often, but it was nice to know it was there. Then one day about six weeks after my latest visit I went to make a withdrawal. The bank was gone.

The ATM had been ripped out and the huge generator that used to take up most of the parking area in the front had disappeared. A metal gate was locked down over the entrance; so much rubbish had blown against it that the place looked as if it had been abandoned for years. On the gate was a small, torn, hand-written sign, "Pindah ka Andong".

Well excuse me, but it seems a bit casual for a national bank to just slip away in the night like that. I felt quite indignant as I mounted my electric steed and headed up Jalan Andong to see where my financial institution had washed up. Fortunately it wasn't very far along, or I would have been forced to transfer my affections and modest transactions to a bank closer to the downtown core. Andong was the sticks. (Readers in Bali's fashionable south may feel that Ubud is the sticks. So now you know that even the sticks have sticks.)

Going to the bank has changed a lot in the past ten years. There are computers now, and you take a number from the machine when you come in. A polite man with a billy club and a pistol escorts you to your seat under the television so you can watch the soaps while you wait. Service is big factor when choosing a bank, and in Ubud it ranges from the discourteous snarls of the tellers at the largest institution in town to the heartfelt can't-do-enough-for-you at a smaller bank at the edge of the Financial District. Ibu Snarl has been known to interrogate foreigners about their immigration status and finances and rudely deny them bank accounts if they didn't hold a resident's visa. At the other end of town another bank is delighted to open an account for you, visa notwithstanding, no extra charge for the smile.

Then there was the little hole in the wall bank Kathy used to patronize. It was so tiny only a couple of clients could be served at any time. The staff was so transfixed by the high drama of the soap operas they watched constantly on television that no transactions could be completed until after the denouement. Once Kathy entered the bank at a few minutes before three o'clock, needing some money for the weekend. The teller apologized and told her the bank was already closed because the manager had a ceremony. "But I need the money urgently!" Kathy told him. "How much do you need?" he enquired. She told him, and he lent her Rp 300,000 from his own pocket on the spot. Try that at Citibank.

When I first came to Ubud, few Balinese had bank accounts. If you wanted to contract land or pay a builder, you withdrew bricks of cash and carried them around town in a brown paper bag. No one seemed to find this odd, and no one was ever mugged that I heard of. These days you can transfer rupiah into other people's bank accounts in heartbeat with internet banking.

But things are not always so straightforward. My bank has plenty of computers and I know I'm in there, because every time I turn up they know where to find me. So when I arrived one day to make a withdrawal and discovered I'd forgotten my bank book at home, I thought this would be no problem. I was in the computer, right? I went up to the Customer Service Lady, and told her the situation. She regarded me with alarm; she was not allowed to give out bank account numbers. But this was ME, I pointed, one of the handful of foreigners with an account in this bank and well-known to all. Muttering, she consulted the bank manager, who indicated that she might just this once be allowed to entrust me with my own account number.

First she consulted a hand-written ledger for about ten minutes, until I indicated that I was pretty sure the information she sought was in her computer. Another five minutes passed before she motioned me to sit down at her desk. In a whisper she walked me through all my security questions. Full name, nationality, birth date, address, phone number? Mother's maiden name? Colour of maternal grandmother's eyes? The bank manager observed all this impassively from the next desk. Finally, finally, the lady wrote my bank account number in very tiny figures on a piece of paper and passed it reluctantly over the desk to me.

So I filled in my withdrawal form and took it to the teller, who asked for my bank book. I told her I'd forgotten it. Sorry, she says, you can't make a withdrawal without your bank book, period.

Now, the manger and the Customer Service lady both knew I wanted to make a withdrawal and they both knew I couldn't do it without my book. Yet they let me go through the whole process of obtaining my account number anyway. I mulled this over as I walked home to get the book. The longer I'm here, the less I understand.

Mother Goose

Evenings in Bali are meant to be tranquil and dreamy, touched with the fragrance of jasmine. I tried to remember this as I dodged through my dark, wet garden with a sick goose under my arm. The fragrance was decidedly not floral.

Rosalind the goose came late to motherhood. Her other siblings were raising their second batches of goslings while she was still puzzling over how to lay her first egg. Once she got the knack of it, though, she couldn't find the 'off' switch. Even after two charming balls of yellow fluff appeared, she continued to lay one huge egg after the other. Perhaps the constant presence of her amorous spouse over-stimulated her.

Now, a goose appears to be a bird of dignity and deep intellectual insights. This is a façade; there is not much going on in a goose's thinking box. Also, the Bali goose is singularly lacking in family feeling. From the day the chicks appeared their parents completely ignored them, except for knocking them out of their way at feeding time. They just kept making more babies without paying any attention to the ones they had.

Rosalind stopped eating as soon as she began to lay the first clutch. For weeks she rarely appeared at the feeder and grew very thin. One morning I noticed that she was sitting in the mud and by the end of the day she still hadn't moved. Then it occurred to me that she had been laying eggs and not eating for several weeks. She probably had so little calcium left in her body that she was too weak to stand. Don, our Ubudbased bird expert, agreed with my diagnosis and came to catch her.

As a child I'd been terrorized by my grandfather's hissing geese, which used to chase me around the farmhouse and corner me in the orchard until I hollered for rescue. Bali geese are very polite in comparison. although they make a lot of noise, they don't peck. We caught Rosalind and deposited her in a spare aviary, bedded down in rice husks, then poured nourishing concoctions down her long throat.

She was pathetically thin, her breastbone as sharp as a knife, and too weak to stand. Geese are foragers and would normally live on tender grass and weeds. But in the compound where Rosalind and Richard grew up everybody ate white rice—the Balinese, the dogs, the geese and the roosters. Grass and weeds contain calcium; rice does not. But Rosalind had turned up her beak at greens and had to be trained to eat them now.

Six times a day I mixed fresh chopped greens with corn, bean sprouts, red rice, calcium supplements and honey in rain water. She nibbled on this and slept a lot. Every few days she'd lay another egg. The last one weighed 200 grams, the equivalent of delivering a 10 kg baby. I sent it home with Wayan who later reported that, when scrambled, it had fed the whole family.

After a week of intensive care Rosalind looked pretty dingy, but was able to stand up for a few minutes at a time. I thought she would benefit from spending some time in the little pond in the front garden, where she could preen herself and do other gooselike things in the water. She leapt into the shallow pond happily and began to bob around. Nearing dark I went out to check and she was still in the water.. she wasn't even strong enough to get out of the pond, and was shivering in the cold water. I caught her and put her back in the aviary, and ran to call Don. Hyperthermia was dangerous, he told me. Bring the goose into the house, warm her up any way you can and get some warm food into her, fast.

By now it was dark and rainy. I tried not to think of pit vipers, which have the run of the garden after sunset, as I made my way to the aviary. Rosalind was huddled shivering near the back wall and I crawled in and grabbed her. The cold rain poured down on both of us as I splashed back to the house through the mud with the goose under my arm.

She regarded me bleakly as I toweled her dry but was surprisingly tolerant of the hair dryer. Nested down on a pile of newspaper in the shower, she finally stopped shivering. When presented with a bowl of warm feed she consented to eat. The next morning I was almost afraid to get out of bed in case she hadn't made it through the night. But the goose was standing up and the food bowl was empty. Her smoky blue eyes were bright and enquiring.

However, my shower would never be the same. Whoever coined the phrase 'loose as a goose' certainly knew his waterfowl. Rosalind's misadventures had not resulted in constipation. The volume and projectile nature of delivery were particularly noteworthy. I decided that she was well enough to go back to the aviary—besides, I had to clean up the mess before Wayan Manis arrived.

The goose was getting used to being carried around and settled comfortably on my hip. But gentle reader, I warn you never to carry a sick goose through the house without first wrapping it securely in a towel. Given the state of my shower I wouldn't have thought there could be anything left in her digestive tract. This was a grave error. We were almost at the front door when Rosalind delivered one final, high velocity reminder of her visit directly onto the CD player and rack.

As I write, Rosalind is plump and strong and almost ready to rejoin her family. But I'm rethinking a career as a goose farmer. There's too much drama, and I miss the fragrance of jasmine.

Three Dog Night

Two dogs are two dogs, but three dogs is a pack.

One canine or two will focus on their human as the Alpha Mega Plus Top Dog. Bringing another dog into the equation shifts the energy. Behaviours change. Hierarchies are reassessed. They all watch each other jealously to make sure that no one is getting more than their fair share of the human's attention. This means that until things shake down, there are dogs underfoot all the time. The newest one is usually the most emotional and needy, which makes the others cross.

I always forget this, somehow, when there's a dog-shaped vacancy in the household I'm tempted to fill. We all have to adjust to make space for the newcomer.

Hamish joined the family in December and Kalypso and Daisy, two females, were delighted to see him. They'd never had an opportunity to hang out with a male dog which had not been rendered uninteresting by surgery. But Hamish was so weak, recovering from a near-fatal case of mange and related infections, that he hardly acknowledged them at first. Daisy, a shocking flirt, tried all her wiles to attract his attention. She licked his face, tickled his ears and made indecent forays under his tail. Hamish, like any good Scot, was appalled by this forwardness and ignored her.

In fact, he ignored everyone but me. I fed him and painted his burning skin with potions and he wouldn't let me out of his sight. For several weeks he hardly noticed that there were any other canines in the household; he was too sick to be a dog among dogs. Then one day he made a half-hearted response to Kalypso's invitation to play. It seemed to do him good. The more he interacted with the other dogs the more energy he had. Eventually he started following them as they raced barking to meet visitors at the gate.

Some kind of agreement was quickly struck about what dog would sleep on which Persian carpet. (Don't ask me why I brought carpets to Bali. I was on another planet at the time.) Daisy, being black, prefers the darkest rug in the hall where she is essentially invisible and can trip me up at night. Kalypso likes the one with the white background, so that her long dark hair will show up in strong contrast. Hamish has chosen the dark red and blue one on which his newly acquired but already shedding white coat is highly visible. Wayan Manis chases them around with the little vacuum cleaner, muttering affectionately.

Now Hamish keeps up with Daisy and Kalypso as they dash around the garden chasing chickens and scaring off imaginary intruders. One of the reasons my garden doesn't look like a picture out of a tropical garden book is the effect of many dog-stopping fences and gates necessary to keep them away from the cliff. Daisy, bred to hunt, squeezes through a hole the diameter of a beer bottle after some hapless creature. As she goes baying off through the jungle, Hamish and Kalypso bark encouragingly from the garden while kicking up the grass in excitement. Hamish has developed the ability to leap a two meter high fence like a deer. No one pays any attention to me when I order them to stop.

Like people, when dogs live together they figure out how to get along, when to push a point and when to let it go. Dogs also like to be the boss and will constantly, subtly test one another and their Human to see if they can grab the top spot. They will sleep on each other's beds and sneak food out of one another's bowls. Dogs don't usually eat peanuts, but Daisy hangs around under the parrot's cage and picks up the unshelled nuts he drops. Kalypso, a much fussier eater, never showed any interest in peanuts until Hamish arrived. Suddenly she too would carefully pick up a peanut between her teeth, carry it to her favourite carpet and daintily deconstruct it over a period of several minutes. I finally figured out she didn't really want a peanut, she just didn't want Hamish to get any. (Now they all beg for peanuts.) Hamish accepts this as typical Alpha Dog behavior, then sneaks off to see if he can trump her by getting away with sleeping on my bed.

I thought it was only Bali dogs that liked to roost high up off the ground on tables, chairs and even garden walls. But Daisy has developed a passion for sleeping on the ironing board. Not only was this out of bounds for hygienic reasons, but it's a dangerously long way for a miniature dachshund to jump. We pulled the chair away from it at night so she couldn't make the leap. But Hamish soon decided that the ironing board would make an excellent perch and is easily able to achieve the height in a single bound. The day we found a small, dry dog dropping on the ironing board marking it as Daisy's indisputable territory was the day we started locking the pantry door. What are the chances of having two dogs that want to sleep on the ironing board?

Hamish had never seen a parrot and was so timid when he first arrived he was terrified to eat within several metres of Rama's cage. Then I caught him sitting directly under the cage, staring fixedly at the featherless cockatoo. Rama hung from one leg, swinging in a circle a few inches above Hamish's head, staring back. There was a certain bizarre resemblance between the two bald creatures, both with white tufts growing out haphazardly here and there. They seemed to be asking each other, "What the hell happened to you?"

Now an hour might go by without Hamish anxiously seeking me out. I often find him napping with Kalypso, his head on her paw. At night when Daisy barks in the garden, they both leap up. Hamish casts an apologetic glance at me, then disappears into the dark with his pack.

A Car With Character

For years I'd driven an elderly green jeep-like car, unprepossessingly boxy in appearance and not very comfortable. It was very difficult to get into the back seat and practically impossible to get out again. The air conditioner didn't work. It leaked in heavy rain. The petrol gauge was unreliable. Over the years it had some spectacular breakdowns, stranding me on volcano rims, in isolated rice fields and beside deserted roads in the dark. But I forgave it, because help was always nearby and the old car wasn't expensive to fix. And it forgave me when I drove it into deep, camouflaged holes or forgot to fill up its leaky radiator. We had a relationship.

These little cars are all over Bali. Economical to run, they have a high wheel base that navigates potholes well and a short turning radius that allows one to change one's mind between heartbeats. Marginally amphibious, they can be driven through floods up to half a metre deep. (Of course, the brakes don't work very well after that.) Once I was driving along and the car began to lose power. I kept gearing down but finally it ground to a halt. I got out and saw that smoke was issuing from the rear wheels; evidently something very dramatic had happened to the axle. In the west this would have meant a heart-stoppingly large bill at the mechanic. This particular repair cost about $10.

They are very easy to break into which is excellent if, like me, you are constantly locking yourself out of the car (but less so if you've left the car for two minutes to take a photo with all your worldly goods inside). I once managed to lock myself out in a pouring rainstorm and called Wayan Manis to come and rescue me. A few minutes later she roared up on her motorcycle, Niagara Falls rain cape flying behind her. To my astonishment she walked over to the car door and instantly opened it with her motorcycle key. After all, she observed logically, they were both Suzukis. I stopped leaving anything valuable in the car after that.

My first year in Bali, I didn't understand the importance of the Offerings to Metal Objects Day. I hardly spoke any Indonesian and had no idea what Wayan was trying to explain to me one afternoon before she went home. I nodded agreeably to everything she said (don't try this at home, it can get you into a lot of trouble) and went out to meet a friend for dinner. Quite soon my hand phone rang.

"Ibu, where is the car?" demanded Wayan in very slow Indonesian. "At Indus, with me."There followed a long explanation I didn't get, concluding with, "The car should be here, I need to make offerings."

"Can't you come and do it here?" I suggested.

There was a disapproving silence. Then, "When are you coming home?"

My chicken curry had just been served, and I admitted through its savoury fumes that it wouldn't be for at least an hour. Wayan made a thoughtful noise and rang off.

Wayan never gets cross with me, but she always gets her way. When I drove guiltily home quite a bit later, I found that she had laid out a series of complicated offerings on a tray in the house. Under each was a numbered scrap of paper with written instructions about where it should go and in what order. A few minutes later and only slightly the worse for a couple of glasses of wine, I was out in the parking lot in the pitch dark in sarong and sash with a flashlight between my teeth, a pocket dictionary in one hand and offering number one in the other. With some difficulty I deciphered the notes, praying earnestly for an accident-free future as I placed various little trays of flowers and incense on top of and inside the car and attached them to the mirror, the front fender and the door handle. The next day Wayan happily informed me that I had done it perfectly. Ever since then I've left this important job to the experts, but I still occasionally arrive home late to find a tray with an offering, a stick of incense and a note, 'For the car'. I now perform this task with panache.

On the subject of offerings, whoever designs cars for the Balinese market should include a wider shelf below the wind shield. It is not quite large enough to accommodate the round offering tray that's periodically required to ensure safe journeys. When driving up a steep hill, it's not uncommon to be blessed with a lapful of blossoms, fragrant pandan leaves and a slice of banana.

The old green car has hauled some strange cargoes including dogs, geese, ducks, baby pigs and parrots. Of these, only the ducks proved to be socially unreliable but fortunately they had been bedded down with newspaper. Sundry children, a washing machine and several jungles of potted and purloined plants have been ferried around the island over the years. The car carried up to four slender Balinese ladies in the back on the way to distant gamelan performances, or two large Australians on the way to the pub.

My car gets around more than I do. Friends borrow it to run errands. My staff take it on high holidays to visit distant relatives. It can be hard to explain to visitors that no, I can't pick them up this evening because my car has to go back to its village for a ceremony. When the car ran out of gas near the Campuan bridge one night I left it there and walked home. Even before my staff arrived the next morning, I'd had two phone calls and a knock at the gate from Balinese acquaintances who wanted to know why my car had spent the night in Campuan. Life in a small town is indeed a goldfish bowl. But that's reassuring, in its way.

Then one day as the next monsoon season was about to begin, I decided to upgrade to a car that didn't leak. I told my staff that I was willing to pay a little more rental for a newer, better car, then went out for lunch. On my return a few hours later, there was a red Katana in my parking space. I assumed Nyoman had taken my car out on an errand and someone else had parked there, but no. He had arranged with the owner to immediately trade in the old green car for a much newer model with air conditioning, power steering and a petrol gauge that really works, for just a few more dollars a month.

We keep going out to admire it. We go on little joyrides. Wayan Manis is talking about taking driving lessons. This car has character too; it likes to get flat tires in remote areas. A new relationship is just beginning.

Monsoon

Having grown up in Vancouver, I thought I knew a thing or two about rain. Those long gray winters of endless cold downpours are the main reason I fled my homeland in the first place.

But when it comes to rain, a monsoon is in a class of its own. As I sit on the porch watching solid ropes of water pour out of the sky, I often wish I had my father's rain gauge. There's a certain element of oneupmanship in this kind of volume.

After almost two decades in the tropics I'm getting to be able to read a monsoon sky. Sometimes the clouds just pile up until they can no longer hold their cargo, the humidity spikes and then the rain comes down. Sometimes there will be a low, ominous roar from the north that makes you look around uneasily. Then the squall smashes across the garden in a wild rush of wind and water. When it passes there is often a large banana plant lying gracefully across the pond, or a papaya tree will have succumbed to gravity beside the path. The puddles seep into the thirsty earth in minutes.

The river in front of the house is at least thirty metres straight down, running in a deep, narrow fissure. So when we can hear it roar we know there must be an awesome amount of water moving.

Wayan Manis recounts being marooned across the river from her house when she was young. She had crossed it to gather some herbs in the rice fields and a storm to the north had swollen the stream almost to the top of its banks. She'd spent a wet and lonely night in a hut in the rice fields, listening to the raging water. The Balinese have a healthy respect for rivers at this time of year. Flash floods are a constant hazard in the rainy season.

In the past, the Balinese had an ingenious technique for managing water. But building roads, shops and houses on rice fields and across natural waterways and irrigation canals changes drainage patterns. Huge amounts of water with nowhere to go follow the path of least resistance, which is often a road. In heavy rain, the hill roads around Ubud become rushing brown rivers up to half a meter deep. The sensible part of me knows this is dangerous, the other part wants to join the excited children who are surfing the torrent and screaming with delight.

I watch the shop girls along Jalan Hanoman push garbage into the little slots that lead to the drain under the sidewalk. The slots were made very small to discourage this practice, so sometimes they really have to work at it. Under the sidewalks the garbage piles up until a heavy rain comes. Then, of course, the drains back up and the road floods dramatically. Urgent men pull up parts of the sidewalk to claw out hundreds of plastic bags, bottles and clots of old offerings. The flood blasts more garbage across the road. Then the rain stops, the sun comes out and the water miraculously disappears. Within minutes, the shop girls are pushing the exposed garbage back into the drains....

Wayan and I battle the mud, flies, leaks and other monsoon peripherals remembering the long hot days when we prayed for rain. But we don't really mind, because a whole new cast of characters comes on stage at this time of year.

In the rains, the garden abounds in creatures. It seems to be a particularly romantic time for toads. One often finds a large, unlovely specimen with her little husband on her back, presumably in a passionate embrace. A day later, they are still at it. Sometimes there are three of them. Could there be something about toad sex we are missing?

Small, delicate tree frogs begin to venture into the house. They lurk in the shower, in unworn shoes and find their way into open drawers. When disturbed they can leap like giants, big eyes goggling.

Most amazing are the huge black and yellow spiders. Usually there are one or two in the garden but when the rains come there can be a dozen, each with her own large golden web. She tiptoes across this like a dancer to welcome each hapless insect that makes an ill-judged landing. Often there are several tiny orange spiders on the web as well. Wayan likes to think these are her children and that they are all living happily ever after. She refuses to believe that the small spiders are actually males, and that the brave one who finally succeeds in mating with the matriarch will also be her dinner.

The pumpkin vines rampage across the garden, surging ahead at about a metre a day. Maddeningly, the female and male flowers seldom open on the same day. In the rain there are few pollinators so we undertake this delicate task ourselves with mixed success. Among this jungle of juicy leaves we'll be lucky to harvest a couple of pumpkins. The tomatoes and lemons are spoiling before they're picked, but we're gorging on mangoes and durians instead.

And so it rains... and rains. There's no point complaining. Send a thought to the many places in the world where it never rains at all, then go out and dance in the puddles.

On Tonight's Menu...

End of day. Dusk emerges like a stealthy lover to embrace the garden. It's a magical time—a transition between waking and sleeping, reality and dreams. The colour of the light shifts to lavender, deepens, begins to fade. For a few minutes everything becomes very still as the creatures of the day prepare for sleep and the creatures of the night wake up... and realize they are hungry.

Down by the bamboo grove I put the pigs to bed. They accepted a piece of bread as I rubbed their hairy heads. Grumbling a little, they flopped down in the cool dust, dainty feet crossed and ears already twitching with dreams of breakfast. Their link in the food chain is the Bali Buddha Café and leftover bagels. In the next paddock, the geese honked loudly as they led their babies into the shelter. Their warning was heeded; down on the undercliff, the pythons and civet cats that might have fancied a gosling for supper made other plans.

Life is all about food, really. Around me, countless creatures were positioning themselves in the food chain tonight and putting each other on the menu. We are all something else's lunch.

A mosquito hovered too close to the web of a St Johns' Cross spider. The silvery web vibrated in the last of the light as the insect struggled to escape, and the landlady strolled out from behind the heavy white zigzag X in the centre of the web to survey her next meal. A few side orders were neatly bundled nearby. She wouldn't go hungry tonight.

It was dark now. As I neared the house a snake slid across the path ahead of me, more sensed than seen. She was on her way to the pond and its smorgasbord of frog spawn, dragonfly larvae and other interesting snacks. Frogs rarely last more than a night or two here and tadpoles seldom attain full froghood. But this critical information somehow never gets passed on to the rest of the tribe. Unlovely toads continue to make their way to the pond, have raucous sex among the lilies and produce strings of gleaming black eggs. A few days later the eggs are gone and the frogs too, their voices absent from the night symphony until the next rain brings another foolish lover and the fruitless cycle repeats itself.

Bats flickered in the darkness, too fast to see. There were at least three species in the garden, all with different high calls and squeals. Some eat their weight in mosquitoes each night. A few months ago others pollinated the flowers on my durian tree, and two dozen spiky fruits were ripening there. Another species gorges on a ripening papaya, weakening the stem so the heavy fruit crashes to the grass. It explodes open and the insects soon find it. Then predators find the insects. And so it goes.

I went to bar the front gate for the night. On the wall near my hand was a scorpion about five centimetres long, holding an insect between its crablike claws. It seemed wrong to kill it just as it was tucking into dinner. I spared its life, and a few weeks later when I was in the bamboo grove, its cousin stung my foot. The pain was unbelievably intense. Without hesitation Wayan crushed the creature with a stick. It must have a special niche in the food chain, though— nothing would eat its carcass. Two days later, when I could walk again, I buried it under a lemon tree.

The house lizards nudged their way across the walls hunting the small insects that sheltered between the bricks. A huge tokay lumbered out from behind a picture, his prehistoric skin an unlikely turquoise with red spots. When a large beetle landed nearby, the tokay's eyes gleamed with anticipation. He froze and the ungainly body tensed. The lizard struck like lightning and half the beetle disappeared into his wide mouth. He sat there for a bit as if considering the situation, while the long antenna of the luckless insect waved beside his face. Another few gulps engulfed it, and the tokay retired behind the picture to digest his meal.

The dogs seemed to be the only animals that did not kill strictly to eat. Their hunting instinct is hardwired into them; when they're in chase mode they hear and see nothing but their prey. We've lost count of the number of Pak Mangku's chickens that have met an untimely end in my garden and I'm afraid there have been a few cats as well. Two of the dogs are excellent ratters. One night I opened a low drawer to find a fat rodent sitting there. We were both too astonished to move for a moment; in that split second of hesitation as it leapt for freedom, Daisy snapped its neck. She kills for sport, not for hunger. It joined the scorpion under the lemon tree.

On the grass, a wasp had stung a spider and dragged its paralysed body to a quiet corner. She will lay her eggs inside the spider and when they hatch, they'll consume its still-living flesh until they're ready to hunt for themselves. An unpleasant position in the food chain.

A clumsy rhinoceros beetle at the end of its life span bumbled into the kitchen wall during the night. When I found it in the morning the ants had already eaten it clean, nothing but its crisp exoskeleton remaining. It seemed like a very tidy solution. I thought nothing would eat the bitter ants until I saw the pigs licking them off the wall of their paddock one day.

The garden hummed with life as I prepared for bed. Frogs, bats, lizards and less noisy creatures were checking out the night's menu. I gave thanks for my privileged position at the top of the food chain and drifted into sleep as the ongoing drama unfolded around me. It was, after all, a matter of life and lunch.

Bali's Secret Recipes

The Balinese have an arcane pharmacopoeia of their own which probably pre-dates the Hindu culture here. There is a long tradition of medicinal plants, but I am also learning that some of the creatures of the garden play a healing role. Sometimes Wayan will share these gems with me and I make hurried notes on little pieces of paper which immediately disappear. Months later I find a scrap tucked into a book with 'dragonfly soup' or 'roast spiders' scrawled on it. Or sometimes my friends borrow the books and return these memos with eyebrows raised very, very high.

The spider recipe came about one day when Wayan was dusting and came across a large web in the corner of the ceiling. Perhaps to disguise the fact that the feather duster had not visited this location for a few days, she began to chat. Because my Indonesian was still not fluent, sometimes she had to repeat a new concept several times before I comprehended it, and it was a few minutes before I understood that the subject under discussion was bed-wetting. It seems the Balinese have long known that a certain kind of house spider can cure this inconvenient habit. I was a bit slow to make the connection and she had to explain it word by word. The child must eat the spider, or preferably several of them, thus guaranteeing dry sheets for several weeks.

My first thought was that this was because the poor child probably became a chronic insomniac following this prescription, but Wayan assured me the kids enjoyed the snack. You didn't just put the spiders straight into your mouth, of course. The hapless arachnids were carefully roasted at the edge of the fire until their legs fell off, at which time they were considered done to a turn. And it was the brown house spider in particular, mind, not just any old spider.

I asked about the big black garden spiders with the yellow knees, whose huge golden webs seemed to span every clearing in the rainy season. These, it seemed, were particularly succulent. Once again they were roasted till the legs fell off, then the tough skin was split to reach the payload. "Lots of meat and eggs inside," Wayan recalled dreamily. Only a neophyte would fry these creatures quickly, because the fragile meat would vapourize and only the skin remain.

Some treats were gender-specific. Python meat, for example, was only eaten by men, and only the brave ones at that. Balinese believe that creatures that live near the river impart special energy, so they relish the snakes, porcupines, musang and other animals they catch in the ravines. It's getting rarer to find wildlife now, and because the Balinese catch and eat everything they see, the situation is unlikely to improve. The snake meat is usually boiled, then mixed with bumbu, a traditional mixture of garlic, shallots and chilies. "They say that python meat tastes like chicken, but I never dared to taste it," she confided. No other snakes are eaten here.

Frogs are a popular treat. Once plentiful at rice harvest time, they were usually barbecued. Toads are avoided. The capture of a prehistoric monitor lizard is reason for a party, with five or six men feasting on it. Wayan makes the bumbu, but declines to taste the main course.

And the choice remedy for a strong heart is almost never attempted by women, either. Once again it took several tries before I understood the story. "Baby rats, no hair, still red colour," Wayan explained carefully. "You must swallow them whole, alive, with arak." One hopes that the arak anesthetizes the poor creatures on the way down. This remedy was also popular in Java. I don't know what it does for the heart, but certainly must help keep the rat population down.

I was able to match this with a tale from the Philippines, where men consume duck eggs in which the embryo is almost ready to hatch. The bravest bite the heads off and wash the delicacy down with beer. Sometimes it seems we are not so very far from the cave after all.

Entering the culinary world, Wayan shared with me the recipe for Dragonfly Pepes (roasted in banana leaves). She makes a mean tuna pepes and the recipes are similar. First catch your dragonflies—hundreds of them. They are particularly abundant around Nyepi. As a child she would be sent out to the fields with a long stick rubbed with jackfruit. The dragonflies landed on the stick, attracted to the gummy juice, and were unable to fly away. Wayan recounts that on a good day you can fill a big plastic bag with dragonflies in this fashion in just a couple of hours.

Then comes the tedious business of removing the wings, roasting the dragonflies at the edge of the fire—not too hot—and then removing the tough skin. The meat is mixed with chilies pounded with garlic and shallots and just a little grated coconut. Then it is shaped into fingers, wrapped in banana leaves and grilled in the usual fashion.
She swears it is absolutely delicious.

Magic in my House

On my first journey to Bali in 1969, I bought a kris.

In retrospect it was an odd thing for a teenage girl to buy. I can't remember any details about its purchase. Perhaps I was enchanted by the carved ebony scabbard or the sinuous blade of beaten iron. Anyway, the kris was stored in a box in the basement of my parent's house in Canada as I traveled the world. For decades I never gave it a thought.

Then, 35 years later as I lay sleeping in my house in Ubud, I dreamed about the kris. I woke with the strong feeling that I should bring it back to Bali. On my next visit to Canada I opened the box in the basement and there was the kris, right on top. It felt warm in my hands.

I told Wayan and Nyoman this story on my return, and they nodded wisely as they admired the wooden scabbard. "I will ask Ibu Sarijan about it," Wayan said. Ibu was a mystic who could talk to spirits and was wise in the way of healing herbs. Wayan had grown up with her, and now Ibu was visiting their compound from her home in Java.

The next morning Wayan arrived in high excitement. Ibu had connected with the kris. Its spiritual home was Tampak Siring. Now Ibu wanted to see the kris itself. She arrived in mid-morning, a slender older woman with a strong face. She sat at the table and picked up the kris. Wayan and Nyoman watched, spellbound.

Closing her eyes, Ibu held the scabbard reverently against her forehead. Sitting beside her, the hair on my arms stood straight up as she called in the spirit of the blade. The next few minutes were profoundly magical. Ibu told me the name of the kris, and taught me the ritual to invoke its energy. She showed me how to anoint it with scented oil and ask it to bless my activities. The air around us seemed to vibrate subtly.

Then I asked where the kris should be kept. Ibu picked it up carefully with both hands and carrying it in front of her, entered the house. She paused for a moment, then made straight for my bedroom. In Balinese, she instructed Nyoman that it should be attached to the post of my old Chinese bed. Here it would protect me while I slept and ensure that no evil would approach me. She laid it on my pillow and went off to have a cup of tea. (Later I found her and Nyoman comparing leopard whiskers, which they kept in little plastic pouches in their wallets.)

I was astonished at the potency of the kris, awakened after many years in a foreign land. A friend told me that although the scabbard looked new, the blade itself—the sacred part—had probably been taken from an older weapon.

Traditionally the Balinese kris was a powerful object of ritual magic, charged with the secrets of metal smithing. Only a member of the Pande clan can make a kris. When forging a particularly powerful kris, the smith must observe a complex list of rituals and prohibitions. During its creation he must make offerings to it and to his furnace, working on it only on auspicious days. A special ceremony brings the kris to life when it's finished, and it is always treated with great respect. A kris is never held with its point down and never sharpened.

Members of the Pande caste are viewed as powerful magicians who understand the mysterious melding of fire and metal. Since the 13th century, when the kris first appeared as part of a temple decoration in east Java, these skilled metal smiths have passed the secret techniques of forging the kris blade from generation to generation.

Iron itself is too soft for this use, and the highly skilled Pandes knew how to alloy it with exact amounts of carbon and nickel to make steel. Melted together in a crucible, these elements are poured into an ingot which can be worked on an anvil.

The kris blade, which can be curved or straight, is created during a very labour-intensive process. The smith hammers the metal into ribbons, heats it red-hot, then folds the ribbons back on each other and hammers them together in a wavy design called pamor. Day after day the skill and energy of the smith is focused on the nascent blade. When at last it is finished, the pattern of the blade is enhanced with a mixture of antimony and lemon juice.

A kris has different kinds of power depending on the number of curves in its blade, the design of the pamor and the proportions of its blade, particularly in relationship to its owner's hand. A complicated system of numerology establishes the character of the kris, and whether it will be beneficial or harmful to its owner.

A powerful ritual object, the kris is used in trance dances and other ceremonies. Some have the ability to move from place to place of their own volition, and others can cause madness. A kris is said to rattle in its scabbard to warn its owner when danger is near.

It is accepted by my staff and by Ibu that my kris made the decision to come back to Bali, informed me during a dream and is now in its chosen place. "It is happy now," says Wayan. My house in Bali seems even more complete with its powerful yet benign presence.

Amorous Amphibians

Part of Bali's charm for me are the little surprises that punctuate the days. Being greeted by name by the tiny school children outside my gate. Fragrant offerings on my computer. The constant parade of birds, bugs, butterflies and reptiles through my garden.

So I was intrigued to return from shopping one day to find a large plastic supermarket bag hanging on the pantry doorknob, pulsing slightly and emitting strange noises. Upon examination, it proved to contain about two kilograms of copulating toads. I went looking for Wayan Manis hoping for an explanation and found her in the laundry.

"Wayan, there is a bag of toads in the kitchen," I announced. "Yes, Ibu," she agreed, hanging up the towels to dry.

Apparently the topic did not merit discussion. I went back to have another look. They were still at it, hunched in unlovely pairs on top of one another and glaring at me from indignant little black eyes.

It transpired that a friend of mine with a large garden had found the nocturnal cacophony disturbing. She'd asked her gardener to collect all the toads he could find and prepare them for transmigration. Nyoman happened to come along just then on an errand and was entrusted with the cargo of amphibians. He was instructed to release them in some convenient waterway, but he had brought them home instead. "They eat a lot of mosquitoes," he pointed out.

I quite like frog noises in the night and we have a lot of mosquitoes. When I suggested that we keep them, Nyoman happily distributed them around the garden and ponds. But the toads immediately disappeared and the nights were even more quiet than usual. Apart from discovering one grumpy newcomer inside a shoe and another in the shower, they all seemed to have vanished. I called Don, Ubud's authority on reptiles, amphibians, birds and bugs. Where had two kilograms of toads gone?

It seems the Bufo melanosticus or the Asian Spiny Toad is a shy creature, preferring to spend daylight hours in burrows or under piles of leaves. At night they roam to hunt.Tracking movements in the dark, they snap up anything that moves, as long as the size is manageable. Toads have been observed to swallow scorpions and centipedes even while the desperate prey is in the act of stinging them. Baby mice, reptiles and snakes, worms, spiders and all kinds of garden pests are devoured by these eating machines, which spit out only the hairy, poisonous caterpillars.

The toad is not a pretty animal. These ones are a mustardy greenish brown colour, depending on their mood, and liberally peppered with black. They are lumpish and have little spines on their thick skins. Another unattractive feature is the powerful toxin they exude from glands in the neck and the back legs which is reputed to be as unpleasant as that of a green pit viper. This effective defense mechanism causes predators to drop the toad instantly and retreat, foaming at the mouth. Unsurprisingly, they have no natural enemies except the Javanese spitting cobra.

Sometimes I encounter a toad while gardening, and it's always amazing to witness how invisible quite a large toad can be while sitting on a pile of mulch just a few inches away. A couple of times I've inadvertently trod on one in the dark. As my toes curl around the flaccid shape a signal races to my brain wondering, "What the hell is that???"

I'm sure the toad feels the same. We part company a split second later with great mutual relief. I remember one specimen in the highlands of Malaysia many years ago that was so large I thought it was an oversized lawn ornament... until a single giant leap took it into the jungle five metres away.

At the end of the rainy season when the temperature and barometric pressure are just right, Bufo melanosticus begins to get that gleam in his eye. This is when the males crank up the volume on the love songs, filling the night with loud croaks and honks. Romantically inclined females are irresistibly drawn to the music, hopping through the wet grass toward the torrid affair that awaits them.

Beauty is indeed in the eye of the beholder. They pair up with shameless haste on a first-come, first-served basis, with the male atop the much larger female. The males develop a thickened thumb at breeding time and use this to massage the female and stimulate her to spawn. Sometimes this can take several days.

We still have a lot to learn from the animal world.

A few days later, strings of black eggs can be seen suspended between pond plants and a little while afterward they hatch into tadpoles. This is party time for the fish, snakes and birds that consume them in huge numbers. It's a wonder any survive to serenade me through the next rainy season.

Why were the captured toads having an unseasonal orgy in a Delta shopping bag? According to Don, when a large number of toads are gathered together the excitement triggers the appropriate hormones and mass breeding takes place, barometric pressure notwithstanding. And they were probably that interesting mustard colour because they were too hot, he added accusingly as if it was all my fault.

Toads play a critical role in Bali's food chain, helping to control many pests in the rice fields. The pesticides used in the rice and vegetable fields kill off the toad's natural prey. In conditions when there are not enough insects the females don't develop eggs, so the toad populations are declining in Bali and elsewhere.

It's been a couple of weeks now since we released the toads in the garden. It seems that tonight the temperature and barometric pressure are perfect for toad love. The darkness is raucous with a mounting chorus of amorous amphibians. In my little corner of Bali at least, the show will go on.

Balance of Nature

They say you can't teach an old dog new tricks; or, if you happen to have a Bali dog and a dachshund, any tricks at all. Willful and headstrong, neither will even acknowledge me when they are in hunting mode. Prey may range in size from a housefly to a metre-long monitor lizard and everything in between. Even my intervention with loud cries and a stout bamboo pole hardly distracts them when they are dismembering a hapless chicken.

I've tried to explain that it would be nice if we could all live here together in harmony. After all, the creatures of the garden and the undercliff have been on this land for hundreds of generations. I imposed a house on their territory and will be inhabiting it for a mere two or three decades, so the least I can do is put them under my protection for the duration of my stewardship.

This sounds fine in theory but Kalypso and Daisy are not strong on strategic planning. They live in the moment, and their hunting instincts transcend any pretence that they listen to a word I utter. When they see something move, they go roaring after and, if at all possible, tear it to pieces.

Often this is a chicken, almost invariably belonging to the priest next door who also happens to be my landlord. I once asked my staff whether white chickens were more stupid than those of other colours, since they seemed to be the only ones the dogs were catching. It was explained to me discreetly that white chickens were gifts to the priest, and that the carnage in my garden represented a substantial percentage of his flock. We all maintain the polite fiction that his chickens do not fly into my garden and that my dogs don't murder them. "If they come in here, it's their own fault," Wayan Manis points out with ruthless logic. When I suggested that we pay for the carnage, she shakes her head. "Then he would have to be angry," she explains in a convoluted bit of cultural logic.

But I still keep thinking that the lion could lie down with the lamb if the concept of interspecies harmony could be explained clearly enough. Recently a young white chicken was seen browsing through the mulch in the vegetable garden; beside me, Daisy's muzzle started to quiver uncontrollably. I picked her up and carried her close to the interloper and began to explain in a stern voice that this chicken was under my protection and was not to be harmed under any circumstances. After a few minutes of this I put her down and held onto her collar, but she made no move toward the oblivious bird. Instead she turned her head away as if to say, "Chicken? What chicken?" and when I released her she trotted off to the house without a backward glance.

I felt pretty pleased about the rapid results of this technique, and every hour or so I would go find her in the garden and reinforce the lesson. Then I went to water the vegetables later that afternoon and there was an untidy pile of blood-stained white feathers beside the beans. "Daisy!" I roared. She emerged casually from under a nearby fern with a white feather stuck to her chin. Daisy believes she is in perfect balance with nature; nature provides chickens, and she kills them.

When it comes to finding balance with nature in my compound, snakes are a frequent challenge. When Wayan and Nyoman started working with me all snakes were immediately chopped to pieces, no discussion. Over the years they've become not only more tolerant but more interested, looking up different species in the reference book and examining captured specimens from a safe distance. Nyoman has become adept at persuading green pit vipers into empty aqua bottles for later redistribution.

Both of them are somehow convinced that snakes only manifest in the compound when I'm away. "They're afraid of Ibu," I once heard Wayan explain to someone. Perhaps coincidently, most snake dramas do seem to happen when I'm out of Bali. The latest took place when I was in Canada and my house sitter was spending a few days at the beach. Wayan Manis was tidying the daybed on the patio where I frequently nap, and found a snake curled up asleep under one of the cushions. Wayan, who really dislikes snakes despite all my rationalizations, launched herself off the patio and through a hedge of heliconia with a loud scream. The brown snake declined to wake up or move on, remaining in a sleepy knot until Nyoman coaxed it into jar. They told me later that they had never seen such a snake before and decided it must be magical. Don the snake expert came over and identified it as a Javanese spitting cobra.

Later that day Nyoman discovered a nest of green pit viper eggs, and tenderly transferred them to the undercliff. (Even I thought this was going a bit far.) Then the morning after my return the dogs cornered a snake in the pantry. It was before dawn and I couldn't see the markings very clearly, but it seemed to me to be the harmless little snake from the pond. But Wayan decided that this was altogether too many snakes and went off to consult her favourite balian. On his advice she made an unusual offering from white rice shaped like a sinuous snake. I gave it two eyes from chips of red chili so it could find its way back to the river, and we placed it on the ground with the appropriate ritual. As soon as we were finished, the dogs ate it.

I have to admit that I do check under the pillows on the day bed now before I retire for my nap. But as we're all seeking balance with nature in our own ways I like to think that she shrugs, and smiles, and keeps our encounters to a minimum.

Upacara

It all began with the snake.

The dogs woke me in the very small hours with furious barking. Usually this means a particularly large lizard is taunting them from the kitchen wall, but this sounded different somehow. I muttered my way out of bed and opened the door to the patio. A few feet away, Daisy was locked in mortal combat with a green pit viper.

A dachshund is bred to kill everything that moves, and the green pit viper is said to pack a deadly venomous punch. It was not a good combination. They had already managed to bite one another. Even half-asleep I realized that we couldn't have a wounded viper wandering around, and sadly dispatched it with a stick. The next few hours were desperate as I dosed the little dog the best I could and waited for the rest of the world to wake up and help me.

Knowledgeable friends rallied round and Daisy was well enough to chase a chicken less than 36 hours later. I thought this was the end of the tale, but my staff looked unhappy. Then the next day the glass door of my oven exploded into a thousand shards as I walked past the stove. Wayan and Nyoman began muttering darkly. The next day they asked if they could bring a balian around to visit.

He was a pleasant chap, carrying a staff intricately carved and painted as a serpent. He encouraged me to pick it up, and it seemed to vibrate in my hands with a life of its own. Then he went off for a stroll around the garden, watched closely by Wayan and Nyoman. On his return, he announced that a special upacara (ceremony) was necessary to placate the spirits of the river and the nearby temple. ("I knew it!" Wayan declared. She had always suspected that the correct ceremonies hadn't been performed when the house was built.)

Whipping out pen and paper, my staff questioned him closely about the offerings. Large numbers of chickens, coconuts and ducks were mentioned. It was to be a major ceremony, with effects lasting for 15 years, necessitating many offerings, a pedanda (high priest) and a gamelan. My queries about how much all this was going to cost were met with shrugs and rolling eyes. No one seemed to know. But I had helped find jobs for all of Wayan and Nyoman's siblings, and now both families rallied round to make the hundreds of offerings that would be needed for the ceremony.

As event manager, Wayan juggled endless lists and human resources within a radius of about 30 kilometres for the next few weeks. Oddly shaped bundles began to pile up in the pantry. There was much discussion about the price of ducks, which had doubled now that the bird flu scare had dried up the supply from Java. Nyoman built several tall bamboo alters in the garden, and constructed a new wall around the temple. A large table was balanced over the fish pond and covered with woven mats. Invitations were sent out to Balinese and international friends, and my best lace kebaya was hung ready. The anticipation in the air was evocative of children waiting for Christmas.

Just a few days before the ceremony, Nyoman's very old greatgrandmother Dadong decided that her time on earth was up. Neighbours and family gathered around the old lady, who was lying in state in the compound when my staff got home from work. Wayan was distraught. Not only was she very fond of Dadong, but a death in the family meant that our ceremony would have to be postponed for a month. The offerings were nearly finished, the padanda had been booked and the many complex details already arranged. Wayan made her way briskly through the crowd and took Dadong's cold hands in hers. "Not yet, Dadong!" she pleaded. "Don't die until after the ceremony. Wait until Wednesday!" A little while later, Dadong sat up and demanded a cup of tea. She is still with us today.

I woke early on the morning of the upacara and opened the door to a radiant garden. Behind the temple I thought I saw a tall man in ceremonial dress, waiting with a smile for the ceremony to begin. But when I looked harder there was nothing but shadows; it must have been a trick of the morning light. I walked through the garden in the sun, confirming my stewardship of this land and my intention to live harmoniously with all the creatures I shared it with. The light shimmered around me and I knew that my intention had been acknowledged. My private little ceremony was quickly over, but the main event was about to begin.

The offerings began to arrive just after six. Nyoman's small pickup truck was piled high with baskets of offerings and recently deceased fowl. His female relatives and I carried it all through the gate on our heads, and I left them arguing about how it should be arranged while I went to bathe and change. Twice the truck returned with more offerings. The alters were piled high now, and much of the grass was hidden under hundreds of painstakingly constructed trays, baskets and freestanding offerings. Wayan Manis roared up on her motorbike and hustled me off to the temple up the road to pray. We were the only supplicants. Pak Mangku's wife did the honours, pausing in her prayers to sprinkle liquid on the ground from an array of soft drink bottles topped with ornate garuda-head stoppers. "Arak," whispered Wayan.

By the time we'd prayed at two more temples on the street, my garden was full of excited Balinese and the first trickle of foreign guests. A small gamelan was set up on the grass. The pedanda arrived half an hour early, escorted by five young men. She was a striking woman of middle age, and when she donned her regalia a mantle of energy seemed to rise up around her. She seated herself on the table over the pond and tolled her bell, summoning the spirits.

The gamelan crashed into action and several of the women began to chant. The ritual that followed was complex and powerful. The bell clanged in hypnotic rhythm and smoke swirled up from the incense along with the prayers. Burning bamboo exploded and a trail of white feathers was strewn around the alter as the pedanda expertly flipped flowers over the piles of offerings. The ceremony took over two hours. After the blessing, we tucked into boxes of fragrant Balinese food as the women circled the alter with torches, staffs and holy water. Then the young men escorted the pedanda home, the guests left and the old women began to dismantle the offerings. I lay down for a dream-filled nap. The moment I woke in late afternoon, Wayan instructed me to bathe again before Pak Mangku's wife returned for the final prayer at dusk. The long day ended in yet another gentle shower of holy water.

When I opened the door next morning, shafts of sunlight speared through the jungle and across the garden to warm my feet. The light seemed to shimmer a little near the alter, and my eye caught the graceful curve of a small green snake. He looked at me for a moment, then disappeared through the grass down toward the river.

Rat Race

Rats are Bali's great levelers. No matter how humble or luxurious your abode, the ubiquitous Rattus rattus will soon invite herself over to have a look around. If the accommodations suit, she'll bring along a few of her close personal friends and a boyfriend or two. Then they will settle in and establish a dynasty.

I grew up in a house where pet rats, mice and hamsters were part of the family and often to be found on a shoulder or tucked into a pocket. So I lack the instinctive revulsion of many of my friends while holding that every wild rodent may have its place in the world, but that place is not in my house.

Rats are smart, tough opportunists. Probably originating in Asia, they moved to Europe along with the Romans and the Crusaders. Host for the fleas that caused the bubonic plague pandemics of the Middle Ages, rats also carry leptospirosis and other unpleasant diseases. They are incredibly adaptable and said to be, along with cockroaches, the only creatures that survived nuclear testing on the Bikini atoll.

Adventurous rats rode ships, trains and trucks around the world to set up new colonies, and their descendents can now be found on every continent. Individuals have a territory of about a hundred square meters and can produce up to 40 young during their lifespan. An adult rat weighs in at about 200 grams; once skinned and gutted, it would hardly be worth the effort to cook. But some creatures find it a tasty treat. Including an owl, python, cat or tokay in the household will help keep the rat population manageable.

My last home was in the rice fields and the rats were well entrenched. They galloped around the ceiling at night, danced in the carving of my old Madura bed and ate the insulation off my speaker wire. (Eventually they consumed enough insulation to cause a house fire, but that's another story.) There is no smell quite like that of a deceased rodent, and they always secrete themselves in some inconvenient corner or up in the rafters to die. An increasingly unpleasant aroma alerted me one day that something was amiss, and by the time Wayan arrived I had tracked it down. Together we moved a big chest to find a decomposed, rat-shaped puddle on the floor. Probably an overdose of insulation.

My dogs are both enthusiastic ratters. But Rattus rattus is a climber, scaling high walls in a flash and leaving the howling rat pack earthbound. Daisy finds this particularly infuriating; after all, she was bred through countless generations to kill rodents. When she does manage to flush one, she dispatches it most efficiently. But when they taunt her from roof beams or the top of the refrigerator, she's been known to leap two feet into the air in indignation.

The refrigerator is a point of constant interest. Rats have often sheltered behind it in the past and both dogs are obsessed with the idea that the big green box conceals their favourite prey. Daisy wedges herself behind it, making dangerous noises and sometimes pulling the plug out of the wall. Kalypso digs away patiently at the tile in front of it, determined to tunnel her way underneath. Even when we pull the fridge out from the wall to demonstrate that no rodent is lurking behind it, they both continue the hunt day and night. And just as I tell them they are totally bonkers, a fat rat emerges from under the fridge, scampers over my foot and leads a frenzied race into the pantry. He shelters behind my suitcases, which the dogs burrow behind in an orgy of excitement. Luggage skids across the room as Daisy flips it aside, and soon the hapless rodent is cornered and executed. Both dogs sniff the corpse briefly and wander off, leaving me to bury it in the garden. One down, dozens to go.

Patricia once recounted to me how she'd seen Kalypso fumble twice during the hunt and allow a rat to escape. I'm not sure how this was communicated to Kalypso at the time, but it was evidently a sore point. The next day she flushed a rat in the kitchen right in front of me and broke its neck. I congratulated her and buried it under the tomatoes. She dug it up again and laid it my feet, something she had never done before. I buried it twice more and each time she unearthed it. Finally I understood she wasn't going to let that rat rest in peace until my critical houseguest had witnessed her triumph. When Patricia woke up and was informed of the situation she made a big fuss of Kalypso's hunting skills, after which the rat (rather the worse for wear) was finally allowed the dignity of a permanent burial.

Not even Bali's luxury villas and five-star hotels are exempt from the ingenious rat, especially those with the open-air ambience that many tourists love. In one fine establishment that shall be nameless, a guest removed his dentures for the night and placed them on his bedside table. The next morning they were gone, and one can only imagine the enhancement of the already toothy rodent that scored this prize. An expensive hearing aid went missing in similar circumstances and many is the bar of soap that bears unmistakable tooth marks in the morning, no matter how exclusive the bathroom. (Perhaps the fashion for colonics has crossed species.)

One of my favourite restaurants in Ubud is an open-plan building that overlooks the Campuan ridge. I always take visitors there because of the glorious view and tasty food. The restaurant's temple on the balcony is kept well stocked with offerings, and robust specimens of Rattus rattus can often be seen enjoying this buffet. The visitor will squeak with alarm, "Oh my god, a rat!" I peer earnestly at the temple and enquire, "Was it dark brown, with a long bare tail? It was? How amazing! That was the Bali Highland Hamster; it's very rare, we hardly ever see them." The enchanted guest then spends the rest of the meal trying to catch another glimpse of the endangered creature and take its picture.

Rats were around long before we were and will probably survive us as a species. So we might as well be philosophical about sharing our space, while investing in a dachshund or two and perhaps a backup owl.

Respect

When I moved to Bali I confidently expected that I'd be able to grow my own vegetables. After all, there was plenty of sunshine and the soil was fertile. I would have help hauling the compost. What could go wrong?

Nine years later my daily harvest averages one chili, two tomatoes and a moth-eaten kale leaf. On good days I might get a lemon or a couple of beans as well. Growing food in the tropics is not easy. It's either too hot, too wet, too dry or the bugs eat everything. The soil needs constant nourishment, watering and protection from sun and wind. A whole generation of carefully nurtured seedlings can be wiped out overnight by a browsing insect or a heavy rainstorm. Chickens scratch up the pumpkin plants. Grasshoppers turn the chard into lace. Imported vegetable seeds germinate, take one look at the thermometer and wilt into compost.

It's heartbreaking enough when you're just a hobby gardener. Imagine trying to grow vegetables and grain to feed your family, or for desperately needed cash. I now know that the people who grow our food have the most important job on earth. No occupation deserves more respect than farming; we could not survive without the men and women who enable us to unthinkingly choose, buy, cook and eat fresh food every day.

Food... we can't live without it, yet we take it as much for granted as the air we breathe. Most of us have no idea where it comes from, how it's grown, when it was harvested or how it gets to our nearest store.

Research shows that the most wholesome foods are those that are grown locally and in season. So it makes sense to support local growers every chance we get.

There is no large-scale industrialized farming here. Bali's farmers still grow food in family plots, by hand. An increasing number of small independent growers are producing organic fruit, rice, vegetables and herbs. It benefits us all to seek them out and buy from them. Often you find these resources by word of mouth. My staff mentioned that they had a relationship with a farmer in Klungkung who had always grown Bali rice without chemicals; now I get fresh red rice delivered after each harvest. Gede has mulberry trees on his land in the mountains and is happy to plant whatever cool-weather crops his clients want. Oded coordinates a cooperative of organic growers in Ubud. Ben coordinates groups of farmers in Bedugul. There are cells springing up everywhere.

I used to pick up a red capsicum at the supermarket and huff, "Six thousand rupiah!" Now I regard it with wonder and think, "Only six thousand rupiah..." Because now I know how hard it is to grow, how many months it takes to ripen, how it needs just the right amount of sunlight, how the plant will rot in the ground if it rains too much and how much compost it needs. Then it is picked, trucked to Ubud using expensive petrol and the supermarket adds its profit margin. I wonder how much the farmer gets for all that labour. We unthinkingly slice it onto our salad with never a thought that someone had taken five or six months to grow it... and all the other food in our refrigerators.

A friend brought me a bag of birdseed from South Africa, and I scattered it around the garden. Forgetting about it until one hot Sunday morning a few months later, I saw that several millet plants had taken root, grown and had gone to seed. I remembered my trip to Rajasthan and decided to make a chapatti. In the West, this would involve going to the store, buying a bag of millet flour, taking it home, adding some water, and cooking the chapatti in a pan on the stove. When you're doing it from scratch you have to carefully gather all the tiny seeds, figure out how to get the husk off, pulverize the seeds in a mortar and pestle and then cook the chapatti over a wood fire. It took half the day to make one, and even then I cheated at the end and cooked it on the stove. As I ate it, I thought about the women in Rajasthan who had shared their simple meals with me. I realized that they spent the whole of their day cultivating millet, harvesting it, threshing it, grinding it, carrying water for miles in a pot on their heads to mix it with and then searching out a few dry sticks to cook it over. And then doing it all over again, day after day. Feeding the husband, feeding the children, eating last.

We live very privileged lives. Not only do we not have to raise our own food, we don't even have to think about where it comes from.

After that I thought I should get closer to the indigenous rice I eat here in Bali. Twice now I've taken part in planting heritage Balinese rice at a demonstration farm just outside of Ubud. There's an elemental pleasure in stepping through the cool, sucking mud, poking little holes in it with your finger and tenderly planting a single blade of rice. In a chemical-free padi there are tiny spiders walking on the water, tadpoles, frogs and other creatures to entertain you. But even so, a couple of hours felt like enough. Wading to the edge of the field and washing my legs in the irrigation channel, I was tired from bending for so long. I was glad my shift was over. But for millions of rice farmers around the world, the planting, weeding and reaping never ends.

Realistically, none of us will ever grow significant amounts of the food we consume. But let's send a blast of gratitude to the farmers of the world, and season every meal with awareness of the human hands that toiled to produce it for us.

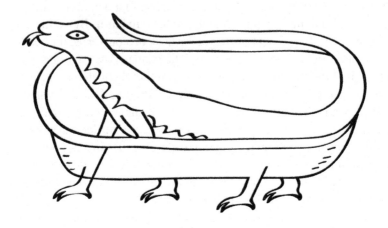

Dragons in the Bath

"Has Ibu seen the animal in the bathroom?" Wayan Manis asked.

It was an interesting question. 'Binatang', the word we used for animal, could refer to anything from a scorpion to an elephant. But because I was in the next room and hadn't heard anything dramatic, I was confident the creature would be benign. Wayan's vocalizations tend to escalate upon encountering large reptiles or rodents.

I grabbed my camera and went to the bathroom, where she had cornered a beetle of enormous proportions, nicely marked in yellow. I photographed it for posterity, released it into the garden and went back to work.

Half an hour later there was another wildlife call, this one much more agitated. "Iboooooooo!!" called Wayan from a far corner of the garden. "Ibu! Naga!" Reaching for my camera once again, I was halfway across the yard before I remembered that 'naga' meant dragon.

The dogs, wildly excited, were racing back and forth along the fence line. It took us a few minutes to catch them and lock them up, but the dragon obligingly waited for my return.

It was a magnificent specimen of a water monitor lizard, well over a meter long. It must have climbed a tree near the fence and fallen into the yard and now couldn't find its way out. A perfect shade of camouflage grey, it sported a generous dusting of big yellow freckles. Anxiously it paced the base of the wire fence, its prehistoric body lumbering awkwardly.

I had never seen Wayan so excited. She telephoned Nyoman, who was helping a friend move house, and a few minutes later the whole moving team had arrived. None of them had ever seen such a big naga. Inevitably the discussion soon turned to how they could catch it, an option I firmly squashed. I didn't want the poor reptile to end up in a pot being rendered for medicine and besides, it would be dangerous to catch. I pointed out its carrion-eating teeth, long sharp claws and powerful tail. While this discussion was going on, the monitor finally grasped the concept of climbing a wire fence and crashed off down the undercliff.

As I related this adventure to Paolo, he told me how he had once made a visit to the loo in the dark reaches of the night. Seated sleepily on the throne, he suddenly realized that there was a monitor lizard in the bathtub, glaring at him balefully. It was still there in the morning, when an enterprising neighbour dropped a sarong over it and released it in the rice fields. "It was only a little one," he pointed out, leaving the mind to boggle at the implications of a large dragon in the bath.

Kathy told me how a monitor had somehow fallen through her roof. It was only discovered when it came strolling down the stairs and out the front door as she was having tea on the porch. Exactly the same thing happened to her a few years later. Yet another friend recalled that he had once woken in the middle of the night to find a large monitor in bed with him.

The musang is another animal that haunts the undercliff and sometimes wanders into my garden. This civet-like creature looks like a cross between a cat and a dog with a smooth dark coat and long delicate muzzle. Its tail is as long as its body and its powerful short legs end in large, padded feet. I've had the opportunity to observe this creature closely because my dogs have killed two in the garden. Sadly I buried them under the trees.

But my sympathy for this species disappeared the morning I found my small flock of ducks dead in their paddock. Wayan, Nyoman and Pak Mangku joined me at the post mortem. The ducks hadn't been eaten, only their heads had been bitten off. I was shocked at the senseless slaughter; surely only my own species killed needlessly. But the Balinese assured me that this was typical of the musang. Nyoman, who is frugal, decided that since the ducks had been freshly killed we might as well eat them. He butchered them carefully and Wayan cooked them with herbs and spices from the garden. The stew smelled heavenly, but none of us could bring ourselves to eat it. It ended up going to the dogs.

What else lurked in the river below my house? Nyoman drew me a picture of what was indisputably a porcupine. I thought this unlikely, but found it in the Indonesian dictionary. They are not particularly rare. The Balinese eat them, of course. A few months later the dogs flushed one in the garden.

Both Wayan and Nyoman have changed a lot in their attitude towards wildlife over the past few years. They roll their eyes less often these days when I suggest that we try to live in harmony with the creatures who share the garden. Despite their doubts they have to admit that, apart from one scorpion bite, none of us have come to any harm from the snakes, lizards and other animals that inhabit the jungle I'm planting around the house. Nyoman no longer automatically kills everything he encounters, but brings it for me to look at.

Wayan, too, has overcome much of her distrust of wildlife. She used to scream lustily at the sight of a snake, however small. One day I heard an unusual squeak in the front garden and looked out the window to see her frozen on the path with a big papaya in each hand. "What it is?" I asked. "Snake, Ibu," she replied casually. "But it was only a little one."

Fine Feathers

"What the hell is that?" visitors often exclaim in alarm when they first catch sight of Rama. Conditioned to expect a gleaming white bird with a yellow topknot when they see a Sulphur-Crested Cockatoo, Rama comes as a bit of a shock. He looks like a badly plucked chicken. A few random bits of fluff decorate his naked epidermis here and there, and broken shafts of bigger feathers protrude from the wings and tail. From time to time he manages to produce one or two crooked yellow plumes where his crest should be, but these quickly fall out. He's not a prepossessing sight, but he has no idea of this. He thinks he's an eagle.

Rama has Parrot Beak and Feather Disease, a virus that decimates certain members of the parrot family both in the wild and in captivity. He was one of several captive-bred birds lent to me by the breeder, who had tried every mainstream remedy to beat the disease and asked me to experiment with alternative therapies. Nothing seemed to work. Two years later he was the last bird standing, the others having succumbed to the disease or to snake bite. Rama's wife died four years ago, so I brought him up to the house where he would have some company. His home is a parrot-proof cage near the kitchen door, well positioned to greet visitors and score snacks. He spends his day in or on top of the cage, or hanging off it by one foot while screaming deliriously at passers-by.

Parrots are busy birds; there is nothing sadder to see than a spotless parrot cage. Each day is spent diligently pulling to pieces everything within reach. At least twice daily we clear the ground under his cage of corn cobs, eviscerated mango pits, banana peels, apple skins, peanut shells and old offerings reduced to microscopic components. His sturdy black beak, capable of nipping off a finger, requires constant exercise. An old wooden doorstop, a baby teether and a set of keys are permanently attached to the cage, and daily offerings of hibiscus twigs, weeds, empty cardboard boxes and junk mail are enthusiastically welcomed. In fact, Rama is a useful security device, completely destroying old documents as efficiently as any shredding machine. Every once in a while he will undertake a drastic housecleaning, dragging everything moveable to the door of his cage and flinging it to the ground below with loud cries.

He has developed his own language over the past few years and practices often during the day, muttering darkly to himself when alone. At dawn he can be heard intoning, "Big bird big bird what a big bird." Once when the dogs were barking, I thought I heard a puppy barking along with them. I rushed outside to find Daisy and Kalypso tormenting a toad, with Rama barking away enthusiastically from the top of his cage. He's been known to croon, 'Perfect bird," to himself and will sometimes scream, "I love you!" with a dramatic lift of his ragged crest feather.

Apart from his appearance, Rama is in fact a healthy young bird with a voracious appetite and plenty of energy. He practices a distinctive form of Bird Yoga, stretching his wings and legs alternately, standing on one leg, extending one wing at a time behind his head and executing dramatic stretches from the top of his cage. He prides himself on being able to stretch much further than visitors believe possible, leaning out at daring angles from the cage to pull a lock of hair or nibble an earring. He seems to enjoy the startled shrieks that invariably follow.

Of course, having no feathers, he has never been able to fly. Sometimes when swinging from one toenail off the side of his cage, he will become over-excited and lose his grip. Unable to break his fall, he lands hard on the pebbles below. He picks up his rotund self and staggers around in confusion for a while until he gets his bearings, then sets off determinedly for some distant corner of the garden. Once we found him three metres up a bamboo trellis, where he had pulled himself up by his beak. We have to keep one ear open all day in order to rescue him when such a misadventure occurs (characterized by a soft thump and a muffled squawk), because Daisy takes far too much interest in these perambulations. She doesn't seem to be sure whether Rama is in fact a bird or not, lacking as he does the usual accessories. But anything that moves will trigger her killer instinct, so we maintain a constant state of vigilance.

For a while he was falling off his cage almost every day, and I finally figured out that he enjoyed being rescued and comforted so much that he was doing it on purpose. Now we've built bamboo climbing bars on top of his cage to extend his territory a little, and often stop by for a bit of social interaction during the day.

If you can overlook the wrinkled bare blue skin and broken feather shafts, Rama is quite a character. There can be nothing softer on earth to stroke than the neck of a bald cockatoo. The feet are black and scaly and amazingly reptilian. His intelligent obsidian eyes miss nothing. He enjoys having his beak stroked and ducks his head for a scratch, then extends his right foot politely to take a proffered peanut.

Every afternoon a pair of wild pigeons drops around to scavenge through the flotsam and jetsam of his day, finding a peanut he has missed or a succulent leaf flung away in a temper. He regards them with casual interest, seemingly unaware that they are cousins. As they fly off into the jungle he continues to tear up an old magazine, supremely confident that it takes more than fine feathers to make a fine bird.

The Battle of the Compost

I dreamed of having a garden for decades. Living in city apartments or landless row houses, I steeped myself in gardening lore and collected a long shelf of books. When at last I built my house in Bali with plenty of land, I just assumed that a knowledgeable gardener who shared my interest would come with it.

Big mistake.

Who on earth started the fallacy that any twit could be a gardener? Gardening takes attention and skill and quite a lot of learning. But in Bali the gardener is rarely respected or educated to do his job. Most of them would much rather be doing something else.

Wayan Manis' husband Nyoman came to work for me seven years ago as a handyman and gardener. He can build almost anything, carves complex motifs into all the wooden doors on rainy days, fixes everything that breaks and drives me to Denpasar when required. But his concept of gardening is to wander around the yard with a sharp implement hacking away at anything that sticks out. He absently treads on tender young plants and stares straight at a tomato seedling wilting for lack of water without seeing it.

Nyoman is exceptionally industrious, but he thinks gardening is a mindless task for which no skills are required. My definition includes thoughtful pruning, mulching, soil maintenance and producing lots and lots of compost. Nyoman makes it clear in his quiet way that these are bizarre and unnecessary practices.

Several years ago I asked him to find me a big, clean oil drum. In this I started a heaving witch's brew of cow manure, legume leaves, living soil, water and sugar. Stirred daily, soto tahi (manure soup) produces a fertilizer so potent that it needs to be diluted before application. (It's also a handy place to dispose of dead rats, snails and the remains of Pak Mangku's chickens when they wander into my yard to be murdered by Daisy.) Because this liquid compost is a living organism, it requires stirring daily to break the thick crust on top and introduce oxygen. I constantly remind Nyoman to do this and he constantly assures me that he does, but it's easy to tell when he doesn't because the crust is unbroken and the whole organism eventually dies. This is a man who keeps the music to dozens of gamelan tunes in his head and can play every musical instrument in Bali, but he cannot remember to stir the soto tahi. So I do it.

Now that I had a source of chemical-free fertilizer, I acquired a backpack sprayer. I showed Nyoman how to strain and dilute the soto tahi, pump up the pressure in the sprayer and spray the fruit trees and vegetables. He has never done this. On Sundays I do it myself, much to the astonishment of the neighbours.

According to Nyoman, the plants will grow whether you pamper them or not. He thinks I fertilize everything too much. He believes that pruning offends the fruit trees. He thinks mulching looks untidy. When transplanting bananas, he cuts off all the roots and of course the plants die. He shrugs this off; "They didn't want to live". I suggested leaving the roots on next time and, because it was a direct order, he did. The bananas throve. Nyoman declines to discuss this.

He still doesn't understand my obsession with compost. The Battle of the Compost has been going on for years now. I draw pictures, conduct demonstrations and provide information sheets in

Indonesian. He has attended several permaculture and composting workshops. We have visited various gardens to view their successful compost facilities. I have a big garden which is constantly being trimmed, yet I never have the piles of rich, light compost I crave.

I've lost count of the times I've wandered around the yard with a seedling on one hand and a pot in the other. When I ask Nyoman for some compost, he looks as if I was requesting a bucket of enriched uranium. This often happens when he's standing beside the big, three-bin covered composter he built after I took him to see how a real compost production centre should look. The bins are full but they are stone cold inside; a compost heap should be toasty. This complete absence of bacterial activity is almost impossible to achieve in this climate. I don't know how he does it. We live in the tropics, where biomass degrades so fast you have to hustle over your lunch salad before it turns to compost on the plate.

The only exception to Nyoman's complete lack of interest in green things is grass. He was slow to warm to the concept of surrounding my house with it; he preferred the concrete and packed earth of the Balinese compound which was easy to sweep. He muttered darkly about snakes. But as the years went by he was won over as he saw how the grass kept the garden cool and eliminated mud in the rainy season. His own compound is now grassed in. When I want a new section of my garden planted in grass, suddenly he's Mr. horticulture. He selects every plantlet with care, beds them in damp soil, covers them tenderly from the sun and never forgets to water them twice a day until the new turf is established. Meanwhile, everything else in the garden in perishing of neglect.

Nyoman thinks he's a good gardener because he keeps the grass cut and the paths swept. This man will spend all day under the hot sun picking up cow pies for me in the fields of Singakerta, he just doesn't want to know what I do with them afterwards. Even when I show him how twenty centimetres of rice straw will keep soil moist and healthy in the dry season, he won't do it unless I ask. He's happy to humour me by delivering sacks of fragrant straw, but I spread the mulch myself.

Janet, who shares my passion for the garden, agrees that we have to wait for the gardeners to go home so we can do the real work ourselves on their days off. We are puzzled by this. It's not how we thought it would be.

Gardeners are born, not made. My attempts to make a gardener of Nyoman continue to end in disappointment for me and bafflement for him. Yet we soldier on because we're fond of each other and I keep thinking he'll wake up one morning with a burning desire to graft fruit trees. Meanwhile, please excuse me. I have to check the compost.

And Then There Were

Two

I've always fancied keeping a few hens. I have a fantasy that my chickens will have long, peaceful lives and produce big brown eggs without any dramas. All my friends and relations who have ever kept chickens assure me that this is indeed a fantasy. Chickens, they tell me, are stupid, vicious, suicidal and sickly. Every predator within a five-kilometre radius will move heaven and earth to devour them.

But I have always had to learn things the hard way.

I decided on a small project, just three of four laying hens in a roomy chicken run with a coop for sleeping. Because it's true that every predator from homo sapiens on down enjoys a chicken dinner and my land is on the edge of a ravine, I knew the pythons, water monitors, civets, feral cats and Daisy would all be deeply interested in my new project. So before I left for a trip I designed a secure henhouse in meticulous detail. It was framed in bamboo, and stood off the ground with a slatted wire floor. The walls were woven bamboo, and it had a sloping roof to shed the rain. All the gaps were covered in fine wire to exclude snakes. It featured an attached plywood egg box with a hinged lid and a front door, and I could close the predator-proof chicken run with a string from outside. My staff was bewildered with these refinements. Bali chickens are seldom fed and just run around all day, roost in the trees at night and lay their eggs any old where. "Like a chicken hotel," marveled Wayan at my drawing.

I returned to Bali after dark a few weeks later and early the next morning strolled around the garden. I was surprised to find seven kampong chickens in a disused aviary. So I went to look at my new chicken house. Inside a half-fenced corner stood a massive structure framed in two-by-fours, with wire walls. It did have a nice little ladder up to the front door, but in no other way resembled my carefully designed chicken coop.

I gently pointed out the gaping holes and wondered aloud how we were going to enclose the chicken run to keep predators out and chickens in. After some consideration, Nyoman decided that he would weave a net from strong plastic string for the roof of the run, and use chicken wire for the walls. After four days of weaving the net and another four of fitting on the net roof and securing the walls and bamboo door, the place was finally ready for its new residents. Friends and neighbours came to admire it and the kids hung over the school wall to gape. No one had ever seen such a fuss being made for a few Bali chickens before. Sadly, the flock had already dwindled dramatically. After considerable in-house research, I have to report that the Balinese chicken is the stupidest animal ever created. Unable to decide in which direction to run from an oncoming car, it will invariably launch itself under the wheels at the last moment when it's too late to avoid it. When chased by a dog, it forgets it can fly and allows itself to be cornered and rendered into a small pile of feathers.

My staff had bought eight hens. One had disappeared before I returned; then there were seven. Three had made a run for it at feeding time; two had been instantly dispatched by Daisy and the other flew off down the edge of the cliff, never to be seen again. Then there were four.

The remaining hens were shut up in their new coop and locked into the new chicken run overnight. I woke early next morning and went to check them. Three chickens wandered around outside the enclosure, demonstrating that they could fly the coop and pass through the labouriously-made net without the slightest difficulty. The fourth lay disemboweled by the gate. Daisy lurked nearby, studiously avoiding my eye.

Then there were three.

We hustled them back into the run, but it was pathetically clear that they could leave it at will. By dusk, they had all escaped. Two of them were teetering dangerously atop a small tree near the kitchen and falling into my vegetable garden with startled squawks when they lost their footing. (Chickens seek the highest place they can reach to roost at night, it seems to be their sole survival instinct). The next day, they too had disappeared. Then there were none. Wayan and Nyoman lurked around the garden with the old fishing net and set traps, to no avail. On the third chickenless day, a hen spontaneously returned to the old aviary where they had first been kept and I managed to shut the door on her. Then there was one. Later that day I saw that the other two had broken into the chicken run and were scratching contentedly in the rice straw as if they had been their all their lives. Then there were three.

I finally smartened up and had Nyoman clip their wings; now they were unable to reach the larger holes in the woven net to escape. Soon after that I caught Wayan looking at the chickens in a thoughtful kind of way. It was the eve of Saraswati Day and I suddenly remembered the lavish offerings that appeared on my bookshelves at this time, topped with a succulent roast chicken. The next day I discreetly busied myself at the other end of the garden until I heard loud chicken noises which ended abruptly.

Then there were two.

But I'm already looking for the local equivalent of nice, motherly Rhode Island reds, because I now doubt I'll ever see an egg from this lot. And Daisy still lingers hopefully by the garden gate.

Zapped

It usually begins with a quiet rasping in the woven bamboo ceiling, just enough to send Daisy into high alert. A moment later the hysterical barking begins and I storm into the kitchen to find out what's cooking. Daisy is poised in the middle of the narrow room, her long muzzle quivering with frustration as she gazes at her prey.

The rat sits high on the roof beam, polishing her whiskers in a leisurely fashion. She knows she's invincible. She knows I don't have the heart to set a glue trap and that I won't put out poison in case other creatures sample it. She knows the dogs have no chance of catching her as long as she stays tantalizingly out of reach. She knows she has the run of the kitchen after dark, and that she and all her friends and relations that live in the roof are onto a good thing. She glances down at us mockingly from her bright black eyes.

What she doesn't know is that I now have a secret weapon, and that she is target for tonight.

A year ago, Patricia pointed out quite unnecessarily that I had rats. I couldn't help but be aware of this already. Between the dogs and the evidence of my own eyes it was clear that there were a lot more creatures living under my roof than I had indented for. It's part of the indoor/ outdoor exotic tropical lifestyle; if you don't seal yourself into an airconditioned room (and sometimes even if you do), quite a lot of Bali's wildlife wants to take up residence along with you. And the options for de-ratting your home are messy (glue traps), cruel (snap traps) or ineffective (shaking your fist and uttering hollow threats). But Patricia was not about to give up.

One day she delivered a stylish blue plastic box slightly smaller than a shoebox, designed in the United states by people who really knew their rodents. They also know the soft-hearted householder who can't bear to see suffering, even by creatures that are spoiling the fruit and driving the dogs to distraction. The RatZapper is actually a little electrocution chamber. The batteries go in the top, the bait goes into the back of the box, and the rat goes in the open end in search of a peanut which happens to be sitting on a metal plate... New users are advised to let the trap sit around for a day or two without turning it on; let the rats have a free lunch and get used to this novel piece of furniture. Then bait it again, switch it on and turn out the lights...

Why, I thought, would a smart animal like a rat fall for a pathetic trick like this? But I left the blue box on the kitchen shelf with a few peanuts scattered inside and sure enough, the bait was gone the next day. So I baited it again and turned it on. The following morning the light at the top was blinking busily; we had already caught our first rat.

I peered into the box a little apprehensively, but the late rodent had indeed gone swiftly into that good night. I tipped it onto a piece of newspaper and sure enough, there wasn't a mark on it. No blood, no wounds, no sign of stress. Just a puzzled glint in those still-bright little black eyes as if to say, "What the hell was that?"

Surely, you'd think, there would be some kind of energetic signature that something fairly unpleasant had taken place in the little blue box— some scent or other clue that these peanuts came with a towering price tag. But no. The next day there was another catch. A few day's pause and then another and another. One was so large that, even dead, I hesitated to handle it. It weighed in at 135 grams—well over a quarter of a pound to the undecimilized among us. A quarter pounder. Think about it. Suddenly, that bakso rumour began to make sense.

What was the rat population in my roof thinking about all this? Rats are social animals. Surely they were noticing that Uncle Bob hadn't returned from his last foray to the kitchen... and hadn't it been awhile since anyone saw Mavis? Sometimes there would be quite long pauses between catches, and I imagined emergency meetings in the rafters. What was happening down there? Where was everyone disappearing? Should scouts be sent? Perhaps the rat population ought to be considering emigration? I'd catch a couple of young males two days running, then nothing for a week. I often wished Rama could report on the nocturnal activities of the kitchen which was his domain. But his vocabulary remained limited to "Big Bird! Hi! I love you!" and some garbled phrase that might in fact be, "My god, this place is crawling with rats at night! You should do something!"

Rodent activity is pretty much nocturnal, unless some foraging rat has lost track of time in the fruit basket and finds itself still in the kitchen when morning comes and the humans arrive. This happened just yesterday. I'd checked both RatZappers and found them empty. (Yes, I have a back-up; the worst thing about this gadget is that people are constantly borrowing it.) Time passed, we got on with our day, then suddenly Wayan and Rama shrieked in unison. A rat had ambled onto the top of the refrigerator, caught sight of Wayan, panicked and decided to take cover... in the handy little blue box. ZAP!

We are delighted with this technology, and only wonder why Indonesia, which has enough rats, plenty of plastic and access to abundant batteries, has not come up with a local equivalent. Please get on the job, LIPI. Meanwhile, I'm off to bait the Zapper again. Aunt Bertha is target for tonight.

Postcard from the Edge

Somehow, there's been a shift in the energy of my little town this year of 2010. Ubud has become an international destination. There are several new real estate agencies with big signs. A Major Motion Picture was filmed here. Whole subaks are gradually disappearing as villas (some requiring pile-drivers) rise up where verdant rice fields used to be. Dusty, funky little craft shops all over town have morphed into boutiques with plate glass windows selling knock-off designer hand bags. The traffic is terrible. There's a tinsel Christmas tree in the batik shop across from the Post Office. Last week, I saw a man wearing a tie.

And what's wrong with all that? you might ask.

I don't mean to sound grumpy. It's true that I harbour some Luddite genes from another incarnation, but I am trying very hard to keep up. Things change. The world has found Ubud. But many of us who moved here 30, 20 or even 10 years ago are coping with culture shock.

Ubud was The Edge then, one of several Edges in Southeast Asia that included Chiang Mai, Kathmandu and Hanoi. Most foreigners who chose to live in places like this 20 years ago were seeking the essence of the country and its culture. We lived very simply. Going without the comforts was a small price to pay for the constant, electric excitement. Everything was strange and exotic and intoxicating. Every day was an adventure, a circus of smells and sights and tastes. It was the end of an era, before cultures were homogenized by globalization. We knew it wasn't going to last forever, authentic Asia, and we inhaled it deeply. We didn't travel with laptops or cell phones. There was no email; occasionally we could send a fax (remember those?) to our families. English books and western food were rare, medical care was terrible or absent. Travel was inconvenient and uncomfortable. In the days before mass tourism, our journeys were on overloaded buses and trains or in the backs of rickety trucks.

These days young people look at us -we are in our 50s and 60s now -and ask incredulously, "Why on earth would you DO that?" We can't explain why we did it, or how wonderful it was. And that world is almost gone now. Progress pushes back The Edge. Access to better nutrition, education and medical care come hand in hand with rampant consumerism, waste management issues and espresso. So I'm learning to savour the paradoxes as Ubud moves from The Edge to the mainstream.

Take electricity. Several of my western friends raised their kids here 20 years ago without any. Wayan Manis recently upgraded the electricity in her family compound to 1200 watts and many Balinese live with 450 watts. Most of them don't have refrigerators because they cook fresh food every day. They only use electricity for a water pump, lights (they use five watt light bulbs) and the TV. My house is generously wired for 2,000 watts, which I never come close to using.

But an interior designer friend tells me that new villas in the south of Bali are now routinely wired for 55,000 watts. All those air conditioners, garden lights and water features gobble a lot of juice, it seems. So what with electricity demand from all the new hotels and villas along with constant in-migration to Denpasar from Java and other islands, it's no wonder the lights are going out.

First it was random, then it was Tuesdays. For months we knew that Saturday night would be dark in Ubud. We became quite used to it. PLN (that national electricity supplier) kindly allowed us to cook an early dinner before pulling the plug just before dark. I had a bright rechargeable light that let me read for four hours, so the blackout was an excellent excuse to curl up with a good book. Most of our little restaurants in Ubud didn't have generators, so Saturday nights were dark and quiet. Cruising up Jalan Ubud Raya on my electric scooter, I saw people gathered companionably around the street vendors, faces glowing in the reflected light of kerosene lamps. They were not much inconvenienced by a few hours of darkness. Neither was Wayan Manis or her family. They lit coconut oil lamps, practiced gamelan and flute, made offerings and chatted. "This is what we did before television," she explained.

Ubud's duality was perfectly demonstrated for me some time ago on a trip to the Post Office. After months of renovations, Ubud's Post Office now rejoices in air conditioning, lots of orange paint and uniformed young ladies with computers. It's all very modern and efficient. Outside on the wall of the entrance is a new international public telephone, so up-to-date that it even accepts credit cards. On the shelf of this icon of modern telecommunications technology roosted a black hen with iridescent tail feathers. When I approached for a closer look, she lifted her wings threateningly at me; she was sitting on an egg. Two days later she was still there.

Sometimes we Old Asia Hands talk about starting a New Edge, somewhere up in the mountains where no one has ever seen the Golden Arches. Pack up the wagon trains with our wood-burning bread ovens, yoga mats and solar rechargers. Forge a new sustainable community in Pupuan or Catur. Or maybe we're getting a bit old for pioneering now. I've become soft and contradictory in the past few years. I grumble about development, and then go into town to meet a friend over iced coffee and pastries.

But now I've drawn my line in the sand. When they start chasing chickens off the public phones in Ubud, I'm out of here.

Animal Days

I'm a very slow learner. Despite continuing misadventures with Indian Runner Ducks, geese and Bali chickens, I still have a burning desire to keep fowl. I imagine fresh, organic eggs for breakfast. Tiny baby birds crouching under the outspread wings of their proud mama. Papa bird standing by to protect his little flock. Contented cheeps and chirps from the garden.

It is never like this in real life, however.

The goose got egg-bound, then had to be nursed through hypothermia in my bathroom. My first lot of ducks couldn't figure out how to breed, then trampled the ducklings that did manage to hatch. The second lot all had their faces bitten off by a civet in a single night. The chickens declined to be penned and dispersed through the jungle to be consumed by pythons or, if they were injudicious enough to return, by Daisy. But the blood of my farming grandparents would not be stilled. Last December, after a lengthy search, I acquired three Muscovy ducks, locally known as keririk.

These are big, heavy birds, low-slung and sensible. The red warts on their faces add a bit of character. Muscovies are calmer than the runner ducks of the rice fields and their blue eyes have a glimmer almost of intelligence. They make no sound except for a gentle hiss, need little water and grow to an interesting size; drakes can reach six kilograms. When I was researching Muscovies on the internet, the first few listings were about the breed, and the remainder were recipes for Muscovy Duck with Peppercorn Sauce and the like. "Are you going to eat them?" people asked as they came to view the odd-looking creatures. "Of course not," I replied indignantly. "This is breeding stock. We will eat the children."

The children were a long time coming. It took Diego, the unpracticed drake, several months to figure out how to do the deed. Jemima and Eleanor were patient with him as he treaded their heads, wings and shoulders before finally getting it right. The girls sat on the nest together and five fluffy yellow chicks hatched the day I left for Canada. A week later they all died of exposure in a cold rainstorm, according to my staff. (You'd think ducks would tolerate water better, but it seems newly emerged chicks aren't issued with raincoats right away.) By the time I returned the ducks were sitting on a new lot of eggs, which eventually hatched into six fluffy ducklings.

I bought a special watering device so they wouldn't drown and soon they began picking up millet and finely chopped greens from the ground. A few days later two of the tiny birds managed to scale the high walls of their parent's feeding bowl and fall in. One had drowned and the other, its wee head just above the waterline, was far gone with hypothermia. I dried it off as best I could, wrapped it in a warmed cloth and tucked it into my cleavage (I reckoned this to be the warmest place in the house). A couple of hours later it was kicking and cheeping, so I returned it to its family. Then there were five. The next day all the chicks figured out that they could escape through the wire mesh of their pen, and were all over the garden before I realized what had happened. I caught four; but the other was hanging limply from Daisy's guilty muzzle. We reinforced the pen. Wednesday morning I arrived with breakfast to find that one of the chicks had expired in a corner.

That did it. Having lost half the menu—I mean, flock—I decided to bring the chicks up to the house where I could keep a close eye on them. Nyoman made a big bamboo box and rigged a five watt light bulb to hang in one end. We lined the incubator with warm straw and soon the survivors were snugly nested under the lamp, sampling a tempting menu of worms and greens.

Walking out to the main road to buy some chick starter at the bird shop, I took a short cut through the temple. Tucked up close against a wall were two mangy little puppies that had been dumped there. It seemed to be a day for rescuing baby animals; I sat on the steps and called the Bali Animal Welfare Association (BAWA) ambulance. It was out on a call, so Wayan Doblet came in a car. The pups had growled at me and wouldn't let me approach, but the moment they saw Doblet they began to wag their tails. He picked them up gently. "Kintamani!" he pointed out gleefully. "And both males!" There wouldn't be any problem finding good homes for them, once they'd been treated for mange, vaccinated and brought back to condition.

Later that night I drove home, parked my car and stepped out to find that someone had left five tiny kittens in my parking space. As luck would have it, I happened to have an incubator to warm them in while I called BAWA for the second time that day. The ducklings gathered around the newcomers to have a look before I tucked the kittens into a box of warm straw and went out to meet the ambulance that came to pick them up. It turned out that they were too young to suck properly, so we had to look for a wet nurse. Ubud is the kind of place where you can call around to find out if anyone has a lactating cat. No one seems to find this odd.

Here is where the story gets very dark. Wednesday, too, was the day a man picked up a knife and slashed my friend Lucy's dog to ribbons. Poor Mentari managed to get home, where friends staunched the blood and called the BAWA ambulance. It must have been a hideous job sewing her back together again—the stitching runs from under the front legs, twice across the belly and under the back legs. She'll survive— terribly scarred—but justice will not be done. The man who did this to Mentari was a neighbour and was seen to attack her; however, Indonesia has no effective laws to protect animals. He will not be punished. Words cannot express the anger I feel about this.

I'm just one of a growing number of people who blesses BAWA for its 24-hour animal ambulance and clinic, its education programs in local schools, its neutering and adoption programs and other activities. I know of eight creatures which passed through the BAWA vets' gentle hands that Wednesday—there are many, many more every day. Donations are urgently needed to help them continue the work. Visit the website at www.bawabali.com to see how you can help. Call the animal ambulance if you see an animal in distress at 0361 981490.

Vision Quest

It's a chilly morning in August as I head northeast out of Ubud to the village of Kendaren. The John Fawcett Foundation (JFF) team has just arrived at the bale banjar and spends the next half hour sweeping, setting up chairs, hanging eye charts and laying out eye glasses, medicines and equipment. Villagers begin to mill around outside, huddled in jackets. The JFF team gathers into a circle and prays silently together that the day will go well and that they will be helpful to the people who come to the clinic. Then they go to their posts, the villagers begin to register and wait for their vision tests.

A few days ago, a JFF team came to Kendaren to talk to the head of the village and the local health office, and hand out flyers advertising the free eye clinic. About 500 people will be screened at today's clinic. Many will be issued with eye glasses, some will be given medication for minor eye ailments and a few will be slated for cataract surgery.

The team swings smoothly into the familiar routine. Today, most team members are nurses who have received extensive training in eye problems. Three village elders sit in a row and obediently cover their left eyes while a pair of nurses coaches each one through a session of reading the eye charts taped to the wall. If an abnormality is detected, the patients receive a detailed eye screening after the basic vision test. Those needing glasses have their prescription written on their card. At another table they're issued with a new pair along with a quick reading test to ensure that the prescription is correct. I watch each face light up in pleasure and astonishment as the words on the test sheet come into crisp focus and the person is able to read easily again. The dispensing technician smiles. The villager smiles. I smile. There's a lot of smiling going on.

There are fewer smiles in another corner, where the more serious cases are seen. When the vision is very poor, the patients are sent to a table where they're tested for glaucoma and cataracts. If the cataracts are deemed operable, there is further screening for diabetes and blood pressure and the person's phone number is taken. Very soon -usually the same day, sometimes the next day -a mobile surgery clinic will arrive and Australian-trained ophthalmologists will perform cataract surgery using the latest surgical techniques, often operating on 10 patients in one visit.

Since my mother lost an eye to cancer in 1968 I've been very sensitive about sight loss. My father is legally blind and can no longer use the computer, read or watch television, so my parents now have one 93 year old eye between them. The JFF Sight Restoration and Blindness Prevention Program is very close to my heart.

For over 22 years John Fawcett and the JFF have been providing free eye screening and cataract surgery, restoring sight to tens of thousands of poor people around Indonesia. The 28-member team includes nurses, doctors, technicians and administrators working with outside surgeons who volunteer their time. Staff turnover is very low.

The key components of the program include field screening for impaired vision, treatment of minor eye ailments, distribution of eye glasses, cataract surgery in villages for adults and in co-operating hospitals for children, and providing artificial eyes.

Indonesia has one of the highest incidences of blindness in the world. It's conservatively estimated that 1.5 percent of Indonesia's population (over 3.6 million people) is visually impaired with between two and three million of these people affected by cataracts. Cataract blindness is reversible through a safe, simple 20-minute operation using micro-surgery to remove the defective lens and replace it with a high quality inter-ocular lens.

"People are blind because they are poor and remain poor because they are blind," says John Fawcett, the Founder of JFF. "Usually it takes two family members to care for a cataract-blind relative, which removes three people from participating fully in the informal economy. So cataract blindness is as much an economic as a social problem." Restoring the sight of a person blind from cataracts ultimately returns three people to the informal economy, conservatively estimated by the World Bank to add about US$ 252 to annual household income. (That might be lunch money to some readers, but it's a significant sum to a poor rice farmer.) Restoring sight to all the cataract-blind in Indonesia would result in an annual net return to the national economy of about US$ 750 million. Currently, Indonesia has one of the lowest cataract surgery rates in Asia.

Ironically, Indonesia's poorest cataract patients receive some of the highest quality surgery and care in the country. In a wonderful example of technology transfer, the professional staff of the JFF team continues to upgrade its skills through training from leading Australian specialists traveling to Bali and visits to Perth by Indonesian doctors to study at the Eye Institute. Dr Wayan Gede Dharyata, JFF's Consulting Ophthalmologist, has generously supported the program for over 20 years by offering his excellent surgical skills, training new surgeons and assisting with strategic planning.

Since 1991 the Foundation has screened over three quarters of a million people for eye problems, performed more than 36,000 cataract operations and distributed over 300,000 pairs of eye glasses.

In 2012 the JFF screened and treated 54,632 eye patients, provided 2,146 free cataract operations on adults and 20 for children (children with cataracts require a general anesthetic in a hospital setting), distributed 31,387 pairs of eyeglasses, screened 3,024 school children and fitted 35 prosthetic eyes. Last year the JFF also served over 20,000 people on Lombok, undertook a mission on the island of Sumbawa and maintained a mobile eye clinic on Kalimantan. One of the mobile clinics is built to fit inside a Hercules C-130 aircraft of the Indonesian Air Force. This cooperation has enabled the JFF to offer screening and cataract surgery mobile clinics in more remote locations throughout the country.

The money to fund all this good work comes exclusively from donations -most of them individual -and there are never enough. The JFF has five mobile clinics, but due to funding constraints they have never all been operational at the same time. In 2012 two mobile clinics served Bali and one each served Lombok and Kalimantan. Keeping all five clinics on the road full time would allow the JFF to reach thousands more people a year. It takes AUD$ 13,000 to keep a bus on the road for a month.

It's surprisingly affordable to sponsor a mobile eye clinic mission in Bali. For just AUD$ 2,000 the mobile clinic will visit the village of the donor's choice and screen up to 500 people. This includes all costs including all screening procedures, staff time, eye glasses and medicines and cataract surgery and post-operative care for up to 10 adult cataract patients. Half a day is spent screening children at the local elementary school where poor performers are often found to need eye glasses.

The sun has burned through the chill and the day is heating up. We make our way to the village of Saba to the south, where the cataract operations began at 0830 this morning. The mobile clinic is parked on a small patch of ground between the local elementary school and the temple. Nearby are the ubiquitous boxes of nasi bungkus without which no community gathering in Bali is complete, and sitting in the shade of the van is a short row of elders already prepped for surgery. The operation will be brief and painless. They will go home to rest with the eye bandaged and tomorrow they'll return early in the morning.

The bandage will gently be removed, and they will see.

To sponsor a Mobile Eye Health Care Clinic, please contact jff@balieye.org

Lions and Tigers and Bears

It was a fragrant summer afternoon in my sister's herb garden on the mountainside. Towering cedar trees speared the vast Canadian sky as bald eagles wheeled overhead and bees drowsed among the clover. I was gathering lavender and thyme in the sun, rewarding myself with succulent strawberries from plants that grew not in tidy rows but randomly in the overgrown borders. Silence echoed around the forest clearing, punctuated by the heady perfume of herbs. The lavender lay in the flat basket like a painting. It was all quite idyllic. As I plunged my arms deep into the plants after another strawberry I was grateful that there would be no centipede, scorpion or pit viper lurking there. But there are larger creatures in these northern woods.

Bears.

Robin's nearest neighbour had come by the day before and they casually chatted about the bear and three cubs that were wandering the dense undergrowth and wild berry bushes which marked the perimeter of their properties. I squeaked in alarm. Our young cousin had been killed by a bear in the interior of British Columbia many years ago and I've never really felt comfortable in the woods ever since. Oh all right, let's be blunt; I'm a neurotic coward about bears.

The hardened mountain folk eyed me patronizingly. I was told that bears are nothing to worry about. Just clap your hands or call "Boo!" and they'll amble off, I was advised. "Hum," suggested Robin helpfully, with the relaxed attitude of someone who has been encountering ursine interlopers in the basil patch lo these many years. Then, equally casually, the stories started about bears drawn onto porches by the scent of barbequing meat. Bears tearing open the trunks of cars to reach a freshly caught salmon. Bears trashing kitchens. The bear that ripped the siding from a house down the road while a lone woman with small children cowered within. "Didn't they dart that one and translocate it?" "Nope, had to shoot it."

By this time the rustle of the cat prowling the undergrowth had me on high alert. A pine cone dropped from a tall tree nearby and I jumped like a rabbit. Robin and the neighbour kindly explained the difference between a Normal Bear, a Hungry Bear and a Bad Bear. Normal Bears are shy and would really rather have nothing to do with you. A Hungry Bear is a bold bear. and a Bad Bear kills little girls and gives her relatives nightmares. Later, Robin sent me back to the forest garden for more lavender. I eyed the ripe berries by the path with alarm; perfect bear bait. That evening some friends came for supper and sent their two small children to pick the berries, out of sight. I was the only one who was uncomfortable with this. These are people who routinely factor large, predatory mammals into their day, weigh the odds and get on with it.

Then there are the cougars (mountain lions), known for their lightning-swift attacks on pets, farm animals and the occasional passerby. A local explains that if one or two people think they might have seen a cougar, you don't really pay much attention. But if three people mention that they may have sighted one about the same time, it's probably a good idea to bring the dog in at night and confine the chickens like dangerous criminals.

One autumn, Robin made a deal with rampageous bears not to eat the apples from a certain tree. They trashed all the other trees in the orchard, tearing off the limbs and stripping them of fruit, but left her favourite tree alone. I have no difficulty believing this. I've negotiated similar deals with wildlife on my land in Bali; in fact, I have a renewable contract with the snakes in my garden not to come near the house. My brother-in-law tells of a Bear Whisperer on Vancouver Island, who can talk bears down from trees and lead them deep into the forest, safely away from civilization. These are Normal Bears, of course. There's not much you can say to a Bad Bear. "Boo" isn't going to cut much ice. Hungry Bears usually have their own agenda, too.

I realize now that the reptiles in my garden are other people's bears. One woman from Singapore refused to leave the security of my patio lest she encounter a deadly cobra or vicious tokay on the lawn. Another would not visit me at all because I kept ducks, and she felt I was irresponsibly dicing with death by courting Bird Flu. "You can't live in fear," I say. "They're more afraid of you than you are of them," I say. But just look at me in the forest. Scared bearless. Unbearably nervous. Way out of my comfort zone.

I was sitting on my porch in Bali with a friend newly arrived from Canada recently. It was late at night; the full moon illuminated the garden and the night-blooming jasmine poured its intoxicating perfume into the velvet air. Frogs celebrated in the pond. A warm breeze teased among the leaves. It was a glorious tropical night and all she could think about was snakes. We had to go inside. With sinister Bad Bears still lurking in my mind, I was more sympathetic about this than I used to be.

I factor the possibility of encountering snakes and lizards into my day and get on with it. But the thought of sharing a forest with a perfectly innocent bear minding its own business is way too scary.

Comfort zones. Go figure.